Only the Real Thing

Only the Real Thing

Aston Villa and The Coca Cola Cup 1993–1996

Ivan McDouall

pitch

First published by Pitch Publishing, 2025

Pitch Publishing
9 Donnington Park,
85 Birdham Road,
Chichester, West Sussex,
PO20 7AJ
www.pitchpublishing.co.uk
info@pitchpublishing.co.uk

A CIP catalogue record is available for this book from the British Library.

ISBN 978 1 80150 940 4

Typesetting and origination by Pitch Publishing

MIX
Paper | Supporting responsible forestry
FSC® C010615

Printed and bound on FSC® certified paper in line with our continuing commitment to ethical business practices, sustainability and the environment.

Printed and bound in India by Thomson Press India Ltd.

Contents

For Mum and Dad – thank you
for everything, all the time.

And for Arlo. Forever by your
side, at Villa Park and beyond.

Prologue: The Choice

AS ASTON Villa's 2023/24 season evolved, and it became clear that early progress under Unai Emery was becoming a longer-term, sustained entity, Villa podcasts, social feeds and phone-ins debated a seemingly key issue or 'choice' – whether the club should have been more focussed on achieving Champions League qualification or trying to win the Europa Conference League. It says a lot about a well-engrained wariness among the Villa public that there is a perception that the season would distil down to that choice. The idea of 'a choice' also gives lie to the progress – and crucially consistency – made and found under Emery. A simplified version of 'the choice' is around financial sustainability and long-term solidity that Champions League participation can bring versus the short-term glory of the trophy win. Personally, I could appreciate both sides; my high points as a Villa fan remain the 1994 and 1996 League Cup wins.

This choice – imagined or real – is nothing new and has reared its head multiple times in Villa's modern history. That is a history within which those twin League Cup wins remain Villa's last major trophies.

The 2008/09 season was Martin O'Neill's third as Villa manager since replacing the much-maligned David O'Leary, and the club had seen steady progress under the Northern Irishman. A sixth-placed finish in the previous term meant Villa would compete in Europe for the first time in six seasons, albeit through the circuitous route of the now defunct Intertoto Cup. The close-season had seen, as was always the case under O'Neill, several comings and goings with Brad Friedel, James Milner and others added to the core of Ashley Young, John Carew, Gareth Barry et al. It was a strong and balanced squad, blessed with experience and excitement. Accordingly, the season got off to a rip-roaring start with a 4-2 win against Manchester City and a Gabby Agbonlahor hat-trick, and September was populated with good home wins against Tottenham Hotspur, West Bromwich Albion and Sunderland (all, bizarrely, 2-1).

Alongside the strong league start, the first European adventure under O'Neill was well under way. It had all begun in July against Odense Boldklub, with a 3-2 aggregate win ensuring Villa jointly won the Intertoto and then entered UEFA Cup qualifying proper. It all had a sense of going through the motions, but goals from Martin Laursen, John Carew and Ashley Young gave a sense of some key figures for the upcoming season. Next up was a trip to Iceland where Hafnarfjarðar were dispatched 4-1 in the national stadium, Young and Laursen at it again, supplemented by Gabby and Barry. A routine draw back in B6 ensured that Villa found themselves in the first round proper. October led Villa to Litex Lovech, in Bulgaria, where again a strong first leg ensured progress, although again fans were treated to a weakened team in a drawn home leg, Marlon Harewood with the goal. The detail of this campaign will have been lost for many but considering what came later it's remarkable to note the geography and frequency of matches that Villa put themselves through. There was clearly, it appeared, a desire to progress in Europe.

And so we come to Ajax. In an act of symmetry in March 2024 Villa also played a two-legged affair with genuine European royalty, albeit rooted in the past. Things were a little different back in 2008 as UEFA fiddled constantly with their formats, meaning that although the defeat of Lovech saw Villa enter a 'group stage', it was a group where teams would only play one another once. Villa and Ajax were joined by Slavia Prague, MSK Žilina and Hamburg. The first group game, against Ajax at Villa Park, remains an iconic B6 night, a 2-1 win vindicating the elongated European campaign that had led them to this point. The Ajax team that Villa faced in 2024 was no longer dominated by household names, but the 2008 vintage certainly was – Thomas Vermaelen, Jan Vertonghen, Luis Suárez and Klaas-Jan Huntelaar would all be players at the forefront of world football for the next few years. Duly, Ajax started well that night but had little to show for their incisive passing and movement. When Martin Laursen powered in Ashley Young's corner in the eighth minute, it was wholly against the run of play, not that it mattered to those inside the stadium as wild scenes ensued. Vermaelen equalised, but Young was provider again for Gareth Barry to slot in what would be the winner. From that point Villa built control but couldn't extend the advantage, although a top performance from Brad Friedel ensured that they didn't regret that. As O'Neill reminded everyone afterwards, yes, Ajax had some talented players but Villa 'also had excellent players, and that should not be forgotten'.

The Ajax victory was followed up by a John Carew-initiated win in Prague, although Villa then contrived to lose at home to MSK. In a sign of things to come, the team fielded at home against MSK was radically departed from the line-up that had beaten Ajax. Isaiah Osbourne, Moustapha Salifou and Nathan Delfouneso all featured, alongside Brad Guzan in goal and Zat Knight in the centre of defence. In essence it worked out as Villa qualified for the last 32 anyway that evening due to other results. It meant Hamburg was a dead rubber and another weakened side lost 3-1. However, the fact Villa ended up third in the group meant they faced a group winner in the next round, and crucially, the opportunity for momentum in Europe seemed to have been lost. Many first choices didn't even travel to Germany, coupled with the fact that most of them hadn't played against MSK either. There seemed to be a shift in O'Neill's thinking and focus, meaning that what happened in the last 32 probably shouldn't have been as much of a surprise as it seemed at the time.

In the Premier League, a strong end to 2008 and an unbeaten January 2009 had catapulted Villa into the top four and fans began dreaming that O'Neill could break the glass ceiling of Champions League qualification. Villa sat comfortably in the Champions League places when attention turned back to UEFA Cup business in February 2009, and a two-legged tie against CSKA Moscow. In the first leg, at home, O'Neill played what was probably his strongest side – with the exception of Guzan in goal – with some injuries (including to Martin Laursen) forcing his hand. A 1-1 draw wasn't a disaster but clearly Villa had hoped that they could secure the tie at home, so only having a single Carew goal to show for some overall dominance was disappointing.

Now we come back to the concept of the 'choice'. It is important to consider some of the circumstances that were impacting O'Neill. The first leg against CSKA was sandwiched between losses to Everton and Chelsea, ending Villa's unbeaten league run that had stretched back to November. There were clearly alarm bells ringing as to how the club could sustain a Champions League challenge, precipitated by these dual defeats. It seems that here O'Neill made his choice – to prioritise Champions League qualification above all else.

The side fielded in the second leg at CSKA resembled those that lost to MSK and Hamburg earlier on in the UEFA Cup journey, albeit built on a relatively senior defensive line. Barry Bannan, Marc Albrighton and Craig Gardner all started, as did Salifou and Delfouneso. Villa's second string battled well but were always at risk of falling behind. Once they did there was no way back, eventually losing 2-0 and crashing out of the very competition that they had worked so hard to get – and stay – in over the season. O'Neill was, as ever, honest about the choices made about team selection and told the BBC, 'It's not a decision that was taken lightly. I am disappointed that we were beaten but I will have to wait to see what the rest of the season brings to see if that disappointment is worsened.'

One can only assume that the disappointment did worsen. A 2-2 draw at home to Stoke City off the back of CSKA was hardly immediate vindication for the 'choice' but that afternoon at Villa Park was halcyon compared to the four defeats that followed against teams around them – Manchester City, Spurs, Liverpool and Manchester United. Ultimately Villa wouldn't win again in the Premier League until May, an unconvincing home victory against Hull City. A season that promised so much ended exactly where the previous one had done – in sixth place.

It's easy in hindsight to fixate on and scorn O'Neill's choice. His missteps at the helm were few and far between, and who knows whether results in either the UEFA Cup or Premier League would have been any different if a full-strength side played in Moscow. However, the season, retrospectively, does hinge on that moment and opens the debate about choice and prioritisation that persists for many clubs in modern football.

If we return to today's vintage, the 'choice' seems largely a debate for fans. There was some early rotation in Europe from Emery, although I suspect that was tempered after a defeat in Warsaw. The team selection for the first leg in Amsterdam did suggest 'one eye' being firmly on the pivotal league meeting with Spurs on Mothering Sunday. John McGinn, Leon Bailey and the first-choice full-backs all started on the bench – albeit you can only really argue that Tim Iroegbunam was not a first-team regular among their replacements. Wholesale it was not.

Potentially, was the 'choice' made elsewhere? Arguably Villa's two most insipid showings in 2023/24 had come in the domestic cups, where defeats to Everton and Chelsea quickly put an end to their participation. Perhaps, with a longer campaign in Europe in the planning, these were not deemed a priority?

Aston Villa's season ended with a highly commendable, and much celebrated fourth-placed finish in the Premier League. The Europa Conference League campaign ended at the semi-final stage with a horrendous capitulation to Olympiakos of Greece. The question of the 'choice' remained unanswered – but what was clear was that even after a season of huge highs and demonstrable progress, Aston Villa's last major trophy remained the 1996 League Cup.

Introduction: Three Decades On

AS A callow 14-year-old in March 1996, if someone had told me that, as it stands, it was going to be the last time I would see Aston Villa lift a major trophy I'd have thought they were insane. The trips to Wembley in 1994 and 1996, both ending in success, had begun to create a veneer of expectation among a certain generation of Villa fans. We were too young to have witnessed the domestic and European success of 1981 and 1982 but are old enough now to be taking our own children to Villa Park. We have seen some further Wembley appearances and some false dawns in the Premier League but have equally seen relegation and rebuilding on varying scales of success. True – as the prologue alludes to – we have just witnessed a season of serious but unprecedented highs, but we are still without a trophy win since those mid-90s days.

Maybe this is modern football? The unchecked riches of Champions League qualification are seen as a benchmark for success. Still, though, a trophy win brings with it the outpouring of celebration that finishing fourth cannot. As if to prove the point, Aston Villa finished fourth on a Thursday night when Spurs failed to beat Manchester City. There was no collective outpouring of celebration that comes with winning a final and lifting a cup.

Over the course of 2024 I have attended a range of 30th anniversary events with players from the 1994 League Cup win. These have been hugely attended by people from my generation who experienced the time as teenagers, but also younger fans for whom the 1994 and 1996 wins remain iconic. It is clear that the history of winning a trophy remains important and central to fans' cultural identity within the club.

It was attending those events and hearing from the likes of Dean Saunders, Ray Houghton and Andy Townsend that prompted me to embark on this project. What follows aims to capture the glorious campaigns across 1993/94 and 1995/96 that resulted in the two League Cup (as sponsored by Coca-Cola) successes. The games, players, managers and iconic moments will all be present, but it is important to put the cup-winning campaigns in a context of the time – post Italia '90, the dawning of the BSkyB-endorsed Premier League, commercialism and internationalism. If the 1994 win and the associated campaign represented the early shoots of change in modern English football, those changes were largely ingrained by 1996. This can be seen through the managers and players – the 1994 triumph seems a wholly different time to the 1996 success.

The journey this book takes is also a personal journey and exploration of my own Aston Villa fandom. I came of age with the Premier League (for better and worse) and these years of 1993 to 1996 were so important in defining my view and experience of football in the intervening three decades.

I hope that for many reading this there is a shared sense of nostalgia for the period. A recognition of true Villa legends, some of whom are no longer with us. A reliving of iconic Villa 'moments' that will persist through the annals of time. But equally I hope that people see the League Cup successes within that wider football and societal context.

As a Champions League campaign waits for Aston Villa in 2024/25, we can feel secure in our club's ambition and sure footing. Qualification for the Champions League was largely enabled by a strong home record over Unai Emery's tenure, a record I was able to share sitting in the North Stand with my son Arlo. It was a season for the ages. And yet those heady days of March 1994 and 1996 remain a personal benchmark of 'success' that all the other factors only aspire to.

Chapter 1

1990–1992: New Beginnings

THE 1990 World Cup was bad for Aston Villa Football Club. Firstly, England's campaign of uneasy joy in Italy had catapulted the club's best player and principal asset – David Platt – to the forefront of the footballing world's attention. Platt took centre stage on 26 June 1990 in Bologna as England laboured to break down a Belgium side some decades away from their golden generation. His last-minute volley in the last 16, assisted by Paul Gascoigne's lofted free kick, remains an iconic England tournament moment and set a tone for the national team's (via hindsight's rose-tinted lens) progress to the semi-finals. Platt picked up where he left off against the Belgians by scoring against Cameroon in the quarter-final, although England's ultimate win was unconvincing. Platt did return to play for Villa in the 1990/91 season, scoring 24 goals across all competitions, but the die had seemingly been cast. His successes for England on Italian fields had piqued interest and it was no surprise that he left for Bari in the summer of 1991.

The bigger impact of Italia '90 on Villa was off the field. For all of Platt's importance, England's exit at the semi-final stage also prompted a change of management. Bobby Robson had been subjected to some scathing criticism over his tenure, much at odds with his later casting as a national hero. Italia '90 represented a natural end for Robson, who would go on to be much more appreciated in club management. The man who the Football Association anointed as his successor was the then Villa manager, Graham Taylor.

After finding his managerial feet at Lincoln City, Taylor had enjoyed a roller-coaster decade at Watford, in part alongside Elton John, before seeing a new challenge at Aston Villa in 1987. Villa had just been relegated but Taylor secured promotion back to the top flight at the first attempt and in the 1989/90 season he led the team to a shock second-placed finish behind Liverpool. Taylor had transformed the culture at Villa much as he had at Watford. He seemed to have the much-sought-after ability to help talented stars shine, but equally to initiate the best results from more limited players. Taylor was a hard-working man of high standards – from dress codes to training regimes. He wasn't universally popular at Villa – 1982 European Cup winner Gary Shaw, who passed away in the autumn of 2024, would have vouched for that – but his characteristics chimed with the FA, and he would take over England duties once the dust had settled on Italia '90.

Another character in the Italia '90 story, Dr Jozef Vengloš, would take the helm at Villa – the first non-British manager to lead a First Division side. Vengloš had coached Czechoslovakia to the quarter-finals at that summer's World Cup and was a vaunted tactician and man-manager. It's also likely that Villa chairman Doug

Ellis revelled in the fact that he was appointing a foreign manager and was the first to do it. Ellis was fond of telling Villa players he had invented the overhead kick; it seems likely this look abroad was another way of casting himself as a footballing pioneer.

Whatever the original intention from Ellis, he would have been dismayed at the 17th position Vengloš oversaw – a severe drop-off from the previous season's title challenge. This was despite the core of Taylor's team remaining, and Platt continuing to cast his reputation as the goalscoring midfielder *du jour*. In many ways Vengloš was a man before his time – at least where English football was concerned. Tony Daley – whose Villa career would span all these managers – speaks frequently about the changes to diet and health awareness that Vengloš brought in. Many players were not ready for this; many resented the changes, leading to disharmony. English football, moored adrift from Europe following the Heysel ban, seemed suspicious of outsiders. Vengloš came under huge scrutiny, especially when results didn't materialise, although he did oversee one of the great Villa Park nights when Inter Milan were vanquished 2-0 in the UEFA Cup. It's fascinating to think that later in the decade many of Vengloš's ideas were echoed and implemented by Arsène Wenger at Arsenal, which bears out the journey of this book. The way English football operated changed intrinsically between 1990 and 1996. Vengloš himself had predicted a 'great exchange of ideas, which can only be good for football' as he foresaw many other players and coaches more freely travelling and working across Europe. Turned out he was absolutely on the money.

Vengloš's last team selection – for a 2-2 draw against Chelsea in May 1991 – is instructive of the mixture of stability and upheaval that would characterise Aston Villa's playing staff as they approached the dual League Cup wins. Villa lined up as follows: Nigel Spink, Chris Price, Kevin Gage, Derek Mountfield, Kent Nielsen, Paul McGrath, David Platt, Gordon Cowans, Gary Penrice, Tony Cascarino, Dwight Yorke.

Gage, Mountfield, Platt and Cascarino never played for the club again, all departing in the summer of 1991 to pastures new. Price, Penrice and Nielsen were around the squad initially but were all moved on eventually after a handful of appearances late in 1991. They were followed by the Villa legend Gordon Cowans, a member of the European Cup-winning team, who joined Blackburn Rovers in November 1991.

The other three starters in Vengloš's final game would all have a more lasting influence on the club and the League Cup successes. Nigel Spink, like Cowans, was a member of the team that won the 1982 European Cup, and he would go on to play for Villa until January 1996. Spink was an unused substitute in the 1994 final and had departed before Villa beat Leeds in 1996 but despite his lack of impact in this story his legacy at the club is undimmed, making a magnificent 361 league appearances over 19 years. Spink was the oldest player in the team that drew with Chelsea, and the youngest was Dwight Yorke. Yorke would also go on to bridge both League Cup successes, from a valued squad member in 1994 to an integral starter in 1996. Last mention here is to Paul McGrath, another bona fide legend at the club, born out by fans wearing 'GOD 5' on their replica shirts to this day. McGrath would start both finals and in that sense is the key carry-over from the Taylor–Vengloš era. It's also worth mentioning that the substitutes against Chelsea – young full-backs Bryan Small and Neil Cox – would both endure into the 1994 final era, Cox coming on as a substitute in the final and Small (alongside Yorke) as a tracksuited squad member at Wembley.

With Vengloš having graciously handed in his cards, the question for Ellis as chairman was where to look next. It had been a strange half a decade for Villa that encompassed relegation, promotion and a second-placed top-flight finish alongside two dalliances near the bottom of the league. It felt like a pivotal moment for the club and the man given that responsibility was of course Ron Atkinson.

The appointment of Atkinson seemed a natural fit. Born in Liverpool (he tells a good joke about his pram being stolen) but schooled in youth football at Villa, he made his name as a manager in the Midlands. He was extrovert and ebullient but believed that self-confidence was rooted in an innate understanding of – and success in – the game. He also had a point to prove after, in his view, being cast aside by Manchester United despite, at that time, being the most successful Old Trafford manager since Sir Matt Busby. Although what unfolded under his successor Alex Ferguson would put him in the shade, two FA Cup wins and five successive top-four finishes was not to be sniffed at. Atkinson had begun to rebuild his reputation as Sheffield Wednesday manager, and indeed cemented his cup winner reputation by leading them to League Cup success in 1991. His departure from Wednesday was not well received by their fanbase, not that his new employer Doug Ellis cared, clearly viewing Atkinson as something of a kindred spirit and a key driver for the success he desperately wanted for Villa.

The watchword for Atkinson (and Ellis) was clearly going to be change – both in style and personnel. When Big Ron paraded his eight new signings in the summer of 1991 few could have imagined the significance many of them would have on the club, and the intertwined stories and tragedies each would bring to Villa and us as fans. Time also lends us a sadder and more introspective view on those featured here – it is incredibly hard to believe that half of the players brought in are no longer with us. 'Holte Enders in the Sky' indeed.

As football fans of a certain longevity or vintage, we draw associations with particular players and resonate with others more than some. No matter how long or short your Villa fandom is, however, what remains true is that all those players who don the claret and blue grab a place – however big or small – in our collective memory as supporters and as our own lives progress those memories grow but also diverge as players move on and careers develop.

When Les Sealey joined Villa, it was on the back of winning the Cup Winners' Cup with Manchester United, so it was no great surprise that he was the starting goalkeeper for the 1991/92 season. However, Nigel Spink replaced him midway through and Sealey never played for the club again. Indeed, the overriding memory of Sealey is playing against Villa in the 1994 Coca-Cola Cup Final after first-choice United keeper Peter Schmeichel was suspended. I vividly remember the front of the *Sports Argus* leading with the fact Schmeichel would miss the game after he was sent off in a league match – clearly perceiving it as a boon for Villa. Sealey was helpless on that glorious day at Wembley, but his presence underlines those strange connections and links football can throw up, further embellished by the fact the goalkeeper he replaced that day ultimately ended up at the Villa too. Sealey passed away in 2001, aged just 43, the first of this group to leave us.

The League Cup campaign of 1993/94 includes memories of many of these players – not least Shaun Teale and his diving headed goal (and iconic celebration) in the seminal Tranmere Rovers semi-final. Signed from Bournemouth, Teale formed a strong partnership with Paul McGrath through the Premier League runners-up campaign and then the League Cup win. Ultimately, he was replaced by another, younger defender also brought in by Atkinson in the summer of 1991. His tally of 147 appearances for Villa is certainly nothing to be sniffed at, and in another twist of the footballer's journey Teale left to join the very club against whom he scored that iconic goal – Tranmere. Teale was last seen 'modelling' Villa's 2019/20 third kit based on the legendary green, black, and red Müller away kit from 1994.

Paul Mortimer had already left the club long before the League Cup campaign of 1993/94, making just 12 appearances after failing to establish himself under Atkinson. Arguably The Valley and Charlton Athletic was his spiritual home with 199 of his 265 career appearances coming either side of his brief Villa spell. Incidentally, he is the only player signed by Atkinson that summer who I don't remember seeing play.

It's easy to forget that Kevin Richardson joined Villa having previously won league titles at Everton and Arsenal – along with the FA Cup and, like Sealey, the Cup Winners' Cup. He was ever-present in his first two seasons at Villa Park and became an integral part of Atkinson's dressing room and side – ultimately captaining the team. The abiding memory will be of him lifting the League Cup in 1994 – but we should remember he was also named man of the match that day, controlling midfield with a panache and industriousness we came to love. Somewhat bizarrely, I was a mascot at Wembley and will always remember Richardson's kindness in involving me. It felt a proud day for the club when he won his solitary England cap later that season against Greece. He followed Atkinson to Coventry in 1995 as he made way for another future League Cup winner and all-round cult hero, Ian Taylor, in Villa's midfield. Richardson remained involved in the game once his playing days were over, including a spell as assistant manager to his former Villa team-mate Steve Staunton at Darlington, and most recently coaching Newcastle's under-18 academy sides.

Steve Staunton was signed from Liverpool for what would turn out to be the first of two spells at Villa Park. In the first, beginning with his signing by Atkinson, he made 208 appearances and cemented the left-back spot over the Premier League runners-up campaign and then 1994 League Cup win. He was also on the bench when Villa beat Leeds at Wembley in 1996 and in his second spell he won the Intertoto Cup in 2001. His international career with the Republic of Ireland also reminds us of the pride we have with those connected to Villa and part of this shared history. In USA '94, along with McGrath and Andy Townsend, the Villa connection with Ireland gave life to a World Cup for which England failed to qualify. I will always be incredibly fond of the Irish white away kit worn over that campaign and 'Stan' was a big part of that. When he became Ireland manager, although I was a little fearful on his behalf, again those Villa links and memories served as a quasi-support and well wishing.

Of all the players signed by Atkinson in this period of change, Ugo Ehiogu is the one I saw most for Villa and arguably formed a lynchpin to my own developing support – as his career progressed, I could align that with my own fervour. When he died in 2017, I was genuinely shaken and sad, a knock to your own consciousness as those who you have built your own memories and ideas of, depart. My first memory of Ugo is at best hazy, and at worst made up, but centres on an under-21 game Villa played against Inter Milan. I'd somehow ended up in a box, watching this rangy centre-back called Ugochuku being shoved up front and scoring a couple of goals. I'd decided he was the best player on the pitch. The die was cast. Later memories are firmer – another player involved in the 1994 League Cup campaign although with a non-playing involvement in the final. When you are drawn to the images and videos of the non-playing, tracksuited players celebrating that final win you are reminded of the ebullience and freedom of youth displayed in the likes of Ugo and Dwight Yorke. It is only made sadder when aligned with his early death. I was aggrieved when he left for Middlesbrough but prefer to fondly remember his return to Villa Park in 2001 when he scored for England there against Spain. Incidentally, that would rank second in my list of Ugo goals at Villa Park – after the ultimately fruitless 90th-minute 'winner' against Trabzonspor in the 1994/95 UEFA Cup. A giant of a man sadly missed.

Yet another sadly departed player among Ron Atkinson's initial tranche of signings is, of course, Dalian Atkinson, unlawfully killed by police action in 2016. Dalian made just 85 appearances for Villa but among those are some truly iconic moments that will remain pivotal pieces of Villa history – just ask my 12-year-old son. *Match of the Day*'s goal of the season for 1992/93 was rightly his stunner against Wimbledon in the rain, umbrella and all. The partnership with Dean Saunders that developed was my first experience of what a strike pairing could do and was finely captured by the now departed *Heroes and Villains* fanzine as 'Deano and Dalian's Excellent Adventure' in the style of Bill and Ted. Again, the League Cup campaign is awash with fine and lasting memories of Dalian – of course the final and the joyful first goal, but let's not forget that crucial consolation at Prenton Park in the semi-final to make it 3-1 going back to Villa Park, and no less important the only goal away at Arsenal in the fourth round, resplendent in green and black. RIP Dalian, another of the Villa family dearly departed.

Finally, Atkinson brought in Cyrille Regis, whom he had famously managed down the road in West Bromwich. Perhaps best – and rightly – remembered for his exploits at other Midlands clubs, Regis made 52 appearances for

Villa, scoring 12 goals. His picture still hangs in the academy building at Villa Park, visible for all to see in the Family Fun Zone, an important reminder of a genuine Midlands footballer and stand-up bloke. Another 'Holte Ender in the Sky', Regis left this earth in 2018.

In line with the expectation of change, Ron Atkinson's debut season as manager was one of ups and downs. On the surface there was improvement – a seventh-placed finish, up from 17th under Venglоš. However, this glossed over an appalling run of form starting on New Year's Day 1992 which saw Villa win just once and score only an almost unbelievable two goals across 12 league games. Spring brought some solace with wins against Chelsea, Liverpool and Spurs, but there remained work to be done. The expectation of transition was well founded, the season being characterised by debuts for the eight news signings detailed in this chapter but also the likes of Dariusz Kubicki, Earl Barrett, Alan McLoughlin, Garry Parker, Steve Froggatt and Mark Bosnich. Many of these would prove to be important players for Atkinson, and in the case of Bosnich for a succession of Villa managers. Goalscoring duties were shared largely by Regis and Yorke – with the Trinidadian scoring 17 times across all competitions. As the season drew to a close, more change was to come both on and off the field. What was to unfold across the next two seasons under Atkinson would be unprecedented.

Chapter 2

Alive and Kicking

WHEN SKY launched into our living rooms in the summer of 1992 with their 'Whole New Ball Game', few could have imagined how the Premier League would mushroom into the ridiculous global behemoth as it exists today. But the initial promotional advert that Sky unleashed was essential in setting a tone that would be tweaked and expanded over the next 30 years.

It could not have been more different to what had come before. Soundtracked by Simple Minds' 'Alive and Kicking', the advert was a game-changer in terms of perceptions of professional football. As the sport tentatively, in the wake of Italia '90, moved away from the dark days of hooliganism and stadium disasters, for many a rebrand was needed.

New Order (with the 'help' of Keith Allen) had made the link between popular culture and football at the Italian World Cup. The coupling of 'World in Motion' with firstly England's success and the everyday appeal of Paul Gascoigne and his tears had begun to shift mindsets on English football. It was a dour World Cup but somehow

England emerged with credit – the defining game for me, for example, was the Cameroon quarter-final in which Gary Lineker's two penalties gave England a largely undeserved success. No matter; a die had been cast.

When you watch the Sky advert now it can seem dated and almost laughable but at the time it signalled to many a new dawn of regular live football in your living room. For many of my generation, whose interest had been fuelled by Gazza, Lineker and Pavarotti, this was an exciting prospect. It also tried to showcase footballers with a glamorous exoticism – David Seaman playing with his children in front of an ostentatious mansion or Anders Limpar waking up in a luxurious bedroom and then splashing water over his face like a male model. The aim was clear – this was football, but not as you have ever known it. And it was live on Sky Sports.

The advert featured a player from each side that would contest the inaugural Premier League, with the same players also featuring in the billboard promotion and other marketing. Villa's representative was of course Tony Daley. Although Daley was in essence, through this media campaign, the face of Villa in the new Premier League he was also a player who bridged the pre- and post-Premier League eras for the club. Many Villa fans would make no argument with the idea that Daley's best days were in the old First Division – and in many ways his story is one of the changing face of English football.

Born in Birmingham, Daley made his Villa debut in 1985 – at the age of just 17 and still an apprentice. It was during the following season that Daley really arrived in the team, making 26 appearances and scoring his first goals for the club. He went from strength to strength, a tricky and pacy winger who, while not prolific, scored some wonderful goals. As Villa finished second in 1990 Daley scored – for this writer – his best goal, against Luton Town at Villa Park. That goal was what Daley was all about – a player who made the old cliche about getting fans off their seat wholly true. I recall a club VHS called *The Pain and the Glory* which soundtracked Daley's best moments to Gabrielle's 'Dreams'. They can come true, and they often did at Daley's feet in those dog days of the old First Division.

International recognition followed – partly thanks to his former Villa manager Graham Taylor – and Daley made seven appearances for his country between 1991 and 1992, including the disaster at Euro '92 as England crashed out. He never played for England after that European Championship, which gives weight to an idea that his best football was behind him by the time the Premier League arrived that August.

It made sense that he was Villa's face in the Sky promotion as he probably was their most recognised player at that point. Paul McGrath was possibly an option, but Dwight Yorke was a long way off being a household name and Dean Saunders wouldn't join from Liverpool until a few weeks into the season.

But despite Daley's place in the Sky campaign there was a nagging sense that here was a player of the previous era, struggling to make the same mark in football's brave new dawn. There were of course moments of cult magic and lest we forget that Daley was heavily involved in a runners-up campaign in 1992/93 and the League Cup win in 1994, losing a boot on the Wembley pitch before collecting his sole career medal. Even that day, Daley, as was often the case, was overshadowed by those around him – it was of course his shot that cannoned off the post for Dalian Atkinson to win a penalty after Andrei Kanchelskis stopped his goal-bound shot with his hand. Dean Saunders stepped up to score his second of the game. By July 1994 Daley was gone – reunited with Graham Taylor at Wolves – but injuries plagued the winger, and he made only 21 appearances across four stop-start years.

There is no doubt Daley will be remembered as a Villa legend and he remains a welcome face at Villa Park, also offering comment on AVTV for under-21 games. But there is an irony that the man who was chosen as Villa's face of the Premier League never really set the new format on fire. Certainly not in the way he had prior to being seen 'Alive and Kicking' for Sky Sports.

Chapter 3

1992/93: A Whole New Ball Game

FLASH FORWARD 30 years and the global behemoth of the Premier League can seem it was ever so. The reality of 1992 and the Premier League's first season was that it remained slightly unclear how and what would be immediately different – with the possible exception of the expanded television coverage. Football certainly seemed more available but for the match-going public there were limited tangible differences. For Aston Villa, given the stop-start narrative of 1991/92, expectations were certainly not heightened just because of the new format. Villa's pre-season was one of predictable continuation of some highs and some lows of the previous campaign. Highlights included a free-flowing win away at Dynamo Dresden, but this was followed by disappointing trips to Peterborough (Villa's goal in a 1-1 draw scored by trialist Frank McAvennie) and Portsmouth where Villa were defeated by a single Pompey goal.

Once the season proper started, initial results did not point to any significant step forward. The season opener at Portman Road versus Ipswich stuttered into life eventually, but initial attention was focussed on the new refereeing outfits (a move to green from the traditional black) and the fact that the goalkeepers could no longer pick the ball up from a back-pass. Villa started with veteran Nigel Spink who seemed nonplussed with the rule change in essence, although seeds were sown in terms of a nagging doubt that Spink was lacking the ball-playing skills to cope longer-term with a new way of playing. The defence was made up of what would become Ron Atkinson's go-to back four – Earl Barrett, Paul McGrath, Shaun Teale and Steve Staunton. The summer had seen sporadic suggestions that Barrett was unhappy with the idea of playing at full-back – he had made his name as a centre-back with Oldham – but Atkinson seemed convinced his pace suited him to a wider remit. In midfield, Kevin Richardson anchored and captained the side alongside Garry Parker. Richardson's contributions would be consistent across the year, but Parker's were more fleeting. On the terraces, Villa fans could recognise his ability but there were regular lapses in terms of misplaced, often overly ambitious passes. From a forward-thinking point of view, Atkinson's approach seemed muddled. The newly acquired Ray Houghton started along with youngster Steve Froggatt but a front two of Tony Daley and Dalian Atkinson seemed ill-suited. Atkinson wasn't helped by the fact that Dwight Yorke was on international duty with Trinidad and Tobago and the previous season's joint top league goalscorer (with Yorke), Cyrille Regis, was only fit for the bench, in a beginning of physical decline that would characterise his season.

The sense of muddle up front characterised Villa's play with Froggatt often beating his man and sending crosses into dangerous areas only to be met by Ipswich defenders and nobody else. Gavin Johnson scored for the home side after 33 minutes and Villa huffed and puffed in search of an equaliser. It was only once Regis entered the fray that Villa seemed to have a better shape and approach – Daley and Froggatt provided more natural width and Regis was on hand to support Dalian Atkinson through the middle. On 83 minutes, it was Regis who squared to Dalian for the equaliser against one of his former clubs – and Aston Villa's first Premier League goal. Long before the days of teams like Manchester City and Liverpool accumulating eye watering 99-point seasons, the old adage was that away draws were satisfactory – if not good – results, so Villa left Suffolk relatively content with a first Villa Park game of the Premier League era to come.

Villa's next two games were at home and were almost a mirror image of one another, firstly against Leeds and then Southampton. Dalian Atkinson scored for the second and third consecutive matches, but Villa were beset by defensive frailty in conceding late goals, contriving to draw both 1-1. Both fixtures were nowhere close to the 'Whole New Ball Game' that Sky's marketeers had branded the new format – more closely aligned to a traditional sense of hard-fought, physical English football.

Ron Atkinson's team selections were consistent at the back and in midfield, but he still struggled to get the right mix up front. Dwight Yorke had returned from the Caribbean but was substituted early in both matches with minor knocks. The men who replaced him provided the assists for Atkinson – against Leeds, Cyrille Regis flicked on a corner for the goal and versus the Saints trialist Frank McAvennie headed across goal for Atkinson to volley home. Three games and three draws was not disastrous but equally it couldn't be described as a strong start. The two key characteristics of Villa's opening triple were a worrying tendency to concede late, but on a more positive note the pace that Atkinson, Daley and Froggatt brought to the table was clearly going to be a challenge for teams. That nagging doubt that an out-and-out striker was needed continued to dominate anyone connected to Villa's thoughts.

It would get worse before it got better. A Tuesday night sojourn to Goodison Park to face fellow unbeaten side Everton would underline the issues that had begun to be highlighted in those initial draws. The game was, again, characterised by high commitment over high quality, with Villa's main excitement coming from Earl Barrett's barrelling runs down the right, further backing up his manager's views on his 'natural' position, even if those views were not shared by the player himself. It was yet another late goal that would be Villa's undoing – this time from Maurice Johnston in the 88th minute of normal time. Steve Froggatt had hit the post not long before, and Villa's failure to score had again cost them dear. That sense a striker was needed wasn't going away. After four winless games Villa lay 16th in the embryonic Premier League table.

Going into another away game against Sheffield United, Ron Atkinson – publicly if not privately – dodged the striker issue, instead urging his midfield to step up and add goals to their solid all-round play. Garry Parker, Ray Houghton and Kevin Richardson had been ever-present in the side thus far, and while they were central to Atkinson's passing game that killer instinct in linking to the forwards seemed to be missing. Against the Blades, Parker did indeed step up – opening the scoring in the fourth minute with an exquisite drive from outside the penalty area. Any hope that an early goal might unleash Villa was frustratingly absent from fruition, with several chances missed to shut down Dave Bassett's men. A late goal arrived again, though with much relief it was for Villa, with Garry Parker adding a second long-range effort with four minutes to play. Those elusive (midfield) goals had come accompanied by a first Premier League clean sheet.

It was one step back, before another step forward over two consecutive home games. A dispiriting 3-1 reverse to Chelsea, when Villa took the lead through captain Richardson, was hard to swallow – although less than 20,000 made the effort to actually see it, possibly an indictment of the team's slow start. It was a future Villa League Cup hero, Andy Townsend, who ran the game, preying on a defence that seemed cut adrift as the match went on. It was telling that in the next game, against Crystal Palace, Ron Atkinson felt the need to speak to fans beforehand on the pitch, reassuring them that everyone was pulling together and the search for a striker was nearing a positive conclusion. As is so often the case, Palace presented a good opportunity for Atkinson's men to get back on track. The Londoners hadn't won all season and never looked a difficult proposition for Villa, who led 2-0 by half-time with first goals of the season for Dwight

Yorke and Steve Staunton – the former with an impetuous flick and the latter with a 30-yard blockbuster. When Ray Houghton rattled the bar in the 72nd minute, winger Steve Froggatt was on hand to score his first league goal for Villa and wrap up a well needed, but well deserved 3-0 win.

Villa's search for a striker was finally realised in time for the next game. Dean Saunders joined from Liverpool in a £2.3m deal that was exciting if a little surprising. Saunders had scored 23 goals for Liverpool in the previous season, and if Anfield didn't seem to appreciate the Welshman, then Villa certainly would. He immediately looked the part at Elland Road against a Leeds side Villa had played just weeks earlier. In front of the Sky TV cameras for the first time Villa looked comfortable and probing on the ball, with Saunders' movement alongside Dalian Atkinson causing Leeds issues from the off. It was that movement that led to the opener from Garry Parker who scored his third of the season, but again Atkinson's team couldn't hold on with former Villa man Steve Hodge equalising as the final whistle loomed. Sitting in mid-table, Villa headed back home, hoping that a corner had been turned with Saunders the catalyst.

And so it proved. In front of the biggest crowd of the Premier League season so far Villa vanquished Liverpool 4-2 on an afternoon when, suddenly, everything seemed to gel. The personnel were the same, but it seemed the one exception to the early season drag – Dean Saunders – had galvanised everything Ron Atkinson was hoping to do and achieve. Saunders scored twice, alongside a welcome return to goalscoring for Dalian Atkinson and another strike from Parker. Crucially, and in a foreshadowing of things to come, Parker's goal was a direct result of the developing relationship and interplay between Saunders and Atkinson. Everything pointed to not only goals from the duo but assists too. The season finally seemed to be under way as Villa could start looking up from seventh.

As September bled into October the 'Deano and Dalian' show would swing into full force. Saunders scored four and Atkinson two across two 3-2 away victories against Middlesbrough and Wimbledon. While Villa's new strike force were dominating the headlines it should be noted that Atkinson's team selection – and the consistency of that – was bearing fruit in engendering a togetherness and style of play. The goalkeeper and back four had been ever-present (Spink, Staunton, Barrett, McGrath and Teale) while the midfield axis of Richardson, Parker and Houghton seemed like they were made to play together, driving Villa forward but supporting the defence simultaneously. It was Dwight Yorke who would feel the key pain in this consistency, lacking chances to build on his personal success in 1991/92. Of the goals that Saunders and Atkinson shared over these two games, it was of course Atkinson's solo effort at Selhurst Park that would stand out and be remembered for decades to come. The jinking run and delicate chip over Hans Segers remains one of the iconic Villa moments, celebrated under the umbrella of a visiting supporter. The manager wryly commented that his namesake 'does it all the time in training, although I have tried to stop him'. Suddenly Villa sat fifth and the Holte End was beginning to dream that anything was possible.

Villa's first foray into the *Monday Night Football* broadcasts came in mid-October against Blackburn Rovers in a live Sky match that was billed as a clash between two expensive star strikers – Dean Saunders and Alan Shearer. The fireworks and Sky cheerleaders couldn't prompt any goals, however, and the game was characterised instead by a superlative display from Nigel Spink and his opposite number Bobby Mimms leading to a 0-0 stalemate. The point saw Blackburn stay in second with a Villa side that was now effectively picking itself stepping up to fourth.

An away trip to Oldham was next up, and conversely the team that picked itself had to be changed. Parker, Froggatt and Daley were all in the treatment room so Bryan Small was chosen at left-back with Steve Staunton playing higher up. The Irishman lacked the pace of those missing, but an abundance of drive and effort dovetailed well into Atkinson's way of playing. Trailing to the erstwhile former Villan Ian Olney, Saunders turned provider for his strike partner in the 82nd minute – Dalian Atkinson heading home his seventh goal of the season and ensuring his side's ninth game without defeat. The togetherness that was mentioned earlier and had been so keenly developed by the manager continued to bear fruit – as former Oldham player Earl Barrett commented in allusion to the Chelsea game earlier in the season that the sense Villa heads might drop after conceding 'was not happening now'.

A further two home wins and clean sheets followed. Queens Park Rangers were dispatched 2-0 with more goals from Atkinson and Saunders in another televised game which also saw the full debut of Chelmsley Wood youngster Dave Farrell on the wing. Villa fans were buoyed by a jump to third, the highest echelon that the team had reached since finishing as runners-up under Graham

Taylor in 1990. If the supporters were given a boost at that point, they were on cloud nine a week later as another Dalian goal subjected the visiting Manchester United to a 1-0 defeat. It was only Villa's second league win against United in 13 games, and newly anointed Manager of the Month Atkinson must have revelled in a defeat for his old side. Small started again at left-back, allowing Staunton to move forward in what was becoming a regular boon, and it was his assist that led to Atkinson converting what was the only goal.

Villa were rampant again in a goalless draw at Tottenham, thwarted only by a standout display from Norwegian goalkeeper Erik Thorstvedt. Consolidated in third, an aside from the game (and a reference that would re-emerge in the 1994 League Cup campaign) saw Shaun Teale go off injured late on, breaking a 70-match sequence of full appearances for the rugged central defender. Ron Atkinson described him that day as John Wayne, saying 'he has true grit'. Teale would be replaced in the next game, against surprise league leaders Norwich, by Ugo Ehiogu and the change in back-line make-up showed as the Canaries sprinted into a 2-0 lead. Goals from Ray Houghton and Garry Parker gave Villa hope, but Norwich conjured a winner that maintained top spot. Not that Atkinson was bereft, describing Ugo as better than Paul McGrath at the same age and alluding to the fact that Villa were able to maintain their style and vigour even in defeat. Veteran sports journalist David Miller, writing in *The Times*, described the game as 'the finest English league game I can recall in some years, played at breathtaking pace in broad sweeps back and forth across Villa Park's perfect surface'.

As 1992 entered its final month, Dalian Atkinson scored twice in a 2-1 away win at Sheffield Wednesday which meant a happy return for him and his former manager to their former stomping ground. The victory at Hillsborough saw Mark Bosnich make his first appearance of the season, and utility defender Neil Cox was also drafted in. Stubborn to the end, Atkinson started Earl Barrett in midfield with Steve Staunton playing alongside McGrath at centre-back. While the early season settled side is a thing of the past, the core had remained and the likes of Cox and Small deputised for absentees admirably, while Staunton's effortless ability to slot in – and have an impact – wherever needed made him a crucial cog in Atkinson's third-placed claret and blue machine.

Although the preferred back four was back in place for a home game against Nottingham Forest, change was necessitated elsewhere as Cyrille Regis came in for an unwell Dalian Atkinson. Roy Keane had put Forest into an early lead, but it was Regis who equalised after half an hour, delicately chipping an on-rushing Mark Crossley. If Regis's intervention was welcomed, the winner came from an unlikely source – he of two goals in his previous 139 league games, Paul McGrath. Villa found themselves in a lofty second place, a position that was consolidated a week later via a Garry Parker goal in a 1-1 draw against Manchester City, although modern-day VAR might have judged Dalian Atkinson to be offside and interfering in the build-up.

A local derby against Coventry City filled the traditional Boxing Day slot, at noon no less, and Villa were trounced 3-0. It was a genuine low point of the season, with expectation having been ratcheted up. Injuries remained an explanation if not an excuse with Daley, Froggatt, Atkinson and Yorke all ruled out, a fact that helps to explain Villa's record of one goal in the past three games. Dean Saunders was also on a five-match run of not scoring. Allied to lapses in the defensive solidarity that had been built, the result felt like a real dampener and one that made a response at home to Arsenal necessary. Fortunately, that was exactly what materialised with Saunders' penalty the difference in Villa's final foray of 1992. Froggatt and Yorke had returned in a game of firsts – the first penalty in a Villa match all season and the first time Ron Atkinson had won an evening kick-off since taking the helm of the club. Atkinson shrugged when asked what the difference was between the abject Boxing Day display and the dominance of Arsenal, replying, 'Well, this time we turned up.'

It's a sign of a successful season when 'records' start to change and fall, and Villa's opening Premier League game of 1993 saw them win at Anfield for the first time since 1977. Further goals for Parker and Saunders were enough for Villa despite falling behind to John Barnes. Parker's effort was a scorcher from outside the area again, and Saunders' third of the season against the club who sold him months earlier vindicated Ron Atkinson's tenacious chase of the striker. Parker and Saunders were on target yet again against Middlesbrough in a scintillating 5-1 win. Goals were also scored by the centre-back duo McGrath and Teale, and pleasingly Dwight Yorke whose stop-start season seemed close to being ignited. Atkinson described how his team had paralysed the opposition and it was a standout performance that put Villa top of the league and in the forefront of the minds of others as real challengers. It helped that the performance was, again, televised – Villa were unbeaten in the five games they had played in front of the Sky cameras.

It was more of the same (albeit off camera) against Sheffield United ten days later as another Saunders goal, accompanied by efforts from McGrath and Kevin Richardson, saw Villa ease to victory after a stale first half. Incidentally, Villa became the first English team to field two German players in a league game – the lesser-sighted Matthias Breitkreutz and Stefan Beinlich. Both would be gone by the end of 1994, and their involvement pointed more to ongoing injury issues. They would, however, be involved again as Villa slumped to defeat away at Southampton as January drew to a close.

There was a clearly renewed sense of vim and vigour as Ipswich were beaten 2-0 at Villa Park. Both goals were something else. Dwight Yorke's diving header finished a flowing move that exemplified Villa's slick style that had, largely, dominated the season. Dean Saunders' volley was equally special. Mark Bosnich started in goal against Ipswich and was chosen again in the next league game as Villa succumbed to a 1-0 loss to Crystal Palace. It was the beginning of a changing of the guard goalkeeper-wise as the long-serving Nigel Spink would find himself increasingly marginalised by the young Australian. Whoever was in goal, it seemed that Villa had lost the knack of pinning consecutive wins together at just the wrong time; the fact they remained in second place was some consolation.

Sometimes those wins need to be ground out, and as had become a theme all season, when Villa needed to pull something out of the hat they largely did. A solitary Ray Houghton effort was enough to edge out Chelsea in a scrappy game before unlikely scorers Earl Barrett and Neil Cox saw off Everton. The Everton game gives a marked impression of how the Premier League was beginning to change the landscape of English football – both goalkeepers were Australian, for example, and there were also a Tobagan and a Yugoslav on display. It was this development that would continue to evolve as the new format bedded in, making football almost unrecognisable. It was that Tobagan – Dwight Yorke – who ensured a third straight win with the only goal against Wimbledon in a game that saw Villa slash their entry prices in an effort to boost the attendance. You could stand on the Holte End for just £5 and season ticket holders could bring a guest for just a quid. Given that Villa's 2024/25 admission prices include, for some games, a £78 ticket in the Holte the gulf between the matchday experience is there for all to see. The Premier League would create a global product of huge revenues and infrastructure. The days of £5 entry would be gone soon enough.

Three wins were followed up by two draws – against Spurs and Manchester United. The United game represented in many people's eyes a title decider, with Villa sat in second but level on points with them at the top. Mark Bosnich, now clearly established as the first choice, was outstanding and Steve Staunton scored a wonderful curving drive in the second half. Back at Villa Park the now defunct Holte Suite was used to show the game live on Sky, such was its perceived importance, although many felt there was a missed opportunity given Villa had taken the lead and that a point in essence didn't change the overall picture. With just nine league matches to come, Villa would need to make the most of any opportunity that came their way if they were to overhaul the Old Trafford club.

A return home against Sheffield Wednesday gave that opportunity, after a draw in the Manchester derby. A superlative Dwight Yorke double ignited Villa Park as Villa went top of the league. Crucially they seemed to be regaining some of the consistency in terms of team selection and player availability just at the right time. It turned out that the elation of Wednesday was short-lived with Villa heading to East Anglia and another crucial clash with third-placed Norwich. Garry Parker missed a gilt-edged chance after rounding the keeper and Villa were ultimately punished in a 1-0 loss. They slipped back to second, and there was increasing focus on the fact that only nine goals had been scored in the previous 11 outings. Tellingly, it was a goal from an unexpected source, Paul McGrath, that got the side back on track against Nottingham Forest, although a 0-0 draw against Coventry at Villa Park was a real blow. On the same day Manchester United famously beat Sheffield Wednesday in the sixth minute of added-on time, a result that saw Alex Ferguson celebrating on the pitch and the birth of 'Fergie Time'.

A rare Tony Daley header overcame Arsenal at Highbury before Dean Saunders finally got back on the scoresheet at home to Manchester City. A ninth of the season for Garry Parker and one for Ray Houghton made sure that Villa were still absolutely in the title hunt, even if there was a growing sense that United would be unlikely to slip up. Not that City fans had given up hope, adorning the away end at Villa Park with a banner wishing Villa luck 'from the City of Manchester'.

They may have been less hopeful after Villa's next game – a 3-0 reverse to Blackburn Rovers. Ron Atkinson admitted that Villa 'had made it very difficult for themselves' although the harsher reality was that Manchester United needed just two points from their final two games to claim the title. If the Blackburn thrashing was bad, what followed seemed worse in impact if not in scoreline. The 1-0 loss to Oldham was by far Villa's worst performance at home with the team outrun and outgunned by a side at the other end of the table. Villa Park was packed but, on the pitch, there seemed some acceptance that the Blackburn loss had been the key one. The defeat handed the title to Manchester United and disappointment pervaded the fanbase. A final-day loss at QPR was inconsequential but telling, and gave Manchester United a lead at the top that belied the nip and tuck of the title race.

It had been an exceptional season from a strong team, managed with aplomb by Ron Atkinson. It's easy in hindsight to be sanguine about the second-placed finish – despite the frustration at the time and also within the context of Manchester United's dominance to come. Still, there were huge gains over the year that pointed to future success and sustainability after the yo-yoing fortunes of 1988 to 1992. The question would be whether Villa could persist as contenders beyond this first glorious Premier League season. As Shaun Teale wrote in his autobiography, 'The answer was a *no* in the League but a firm *yes* in the League Cup.' It wasn't the first time that England's newest trophy had offered Aston Villa Football Club solace and success.

Chapter 4

The Football League Cup

ASTON VILLA'S 1992/93 League Cup campaign – the first season the competition was sponsored by Coca-Cola – did not align with their success in the newly formed Premier League, although there were some highlights. The run began with a two-legged tie against Oxford United, a club that Ron Atkinson, Dean Saunders and Ray Houghton all had connections with. Atkinson fielded his strongest team, fresh from the league mauling of Liverpool, and that selection largely paid dividends. Second-half goals from centre-half pairing Paul McGrath and Shaun Teale seemed to have put Villa into a comfortable position going into the home leg, although a late Joey Beauchamp goal was probably not in Big Ron's script.

Perhaps because of that late goal, the Villa side in the second leg again was strong. Ugo Ehiogu replaced McGrath and Dwight Yorke came in for Steve Froggatt, but other than that it was as expected. Dalian Atkinson scored after just 11 minutes which seemed to send Villa into a slumber, comfortable and coasting at 3-1 on aggregate. An 88th-minute goal from Oxford's Nick Cusack may have initiated a momentary wobble of self-confidence but when captain Kevin Richardson rocketed one in from outside the area, the job was done. A 4-2 aggregate success was all well and good, although Atkinson was not amused, castigating his charges for 'not wanting to break a sweat'.

The reward for navigating past Oxford was a contest with Manchester United at Villa Park. It would be the first of two home games against United in the space of ten days. As we have seen, the league encounter was won 1-0 thanks to Dalian Atkinson and it was his footballing other half Dean Saunders who did the damage in the Coca-Cola Cup. Saunders' header from a Kevin Richardson cross was enough to secure a 1-0 win and progression. Atkinson joked afterwards that the result 'had never been in doubt' and although that was tongue in cheek, knocking out the holders gave a sense of real possibility of a decent run in the competition. Ipswich were next up, in a tie that Villa were marked down as clear favourites.

Drawn at home, Villa could feel confident, but the Ipswich contest came off the back of a stinging defeat by their East Anglian neighbours Norwich City. Such was the consistency of team selection at the time, it was a shock to see Dariusz Kubicki make what would be his solitary appearance of 1992/93. Kubicki aside, Villa were at full strength, and a back-and-forth game saw them lead 2-1 going into the final ten minutes through the usual combination of Atkinson and Saunders. Chris Kiwomya scored late on for Ipswich to force a replay, something neither team would have wanted, although the positive spin was now on Deano and Dalian's combined 20-goal season so far. As if to confirm the fact they would have preferred to not have a replay, Villa put on a ghastly display in what was a drab match overall. In the end, settled by another goal from Kiwomya, Villa could have few complaints. So, a League Cup campaign was over for another season, a disappointing footnote in terms of Villa's rich history in the competition.

The Football League Cup had originated in the 1960/61 season, its genealogy contested and debated over the years. There was some truth in a desire for Football League administrators to take advantage of newly floodlit stadia across the country and it remains to this day (bar the final) an exclusively night-time affair, but the new competition represented the dichotomy that football administrators faced – amid tumbling gate revenues whether an increase in volume of games would be counterproductive versus an ideal of competition and opportunity raising quality. *The Times* was in no doubt, predicting a 'dose of mediocrity', and there was concern that the new European Cup, in its early incarnation, was really where attention should be lying as opposed to a largely superfluous, additional midweek competition. That view was shared by some of England's richer clubs at the time – Manchester United and Everton among them – but Football League secretary Alan Hardaker knew he was representing a bigger cross-section of the football community and pushed ahead with the plans and secured a majority among member clubs.

While some teams tipped their nose at the new competition, Aston Villa were invested from that first season. Villa at the time were still historically a huge club and had won numerous honours, but the reality was that those were in the rear-view mirror. The last major trophy was the FA Cup in 1957 but the club had been relegated in 1959 from a top flight that they had last won as far back as 1910. For Villa and others, the League Cup represented a valid opportunity to retain or create some status and success. Joe Mercer's young Villa side were coping well back in the First Division and they kicked off their League Cup campaign in October 1960 against Huddersfield at Villa Park. Gerry Hitchens scored Villa's first goal in the competition as they enjoyed a 4-1 win, advancing to face Preston who were also beaten, after a replay, thanks to two more Hitchens goals over the two games. Replays were the order of the day, and two more were required to advance past Plymouth Argyle with more goals for Hitchens and a brace in the first match for 1957 FA Cup hero Peter McParland. Wrexham proved a simpler hurdle as yet another brace from Hitchens ensured a 3-0 win. Villa faced Burnley in a two-legged semi-final that ended 3-3 on aggregate and necessitated another replay. Hitchens scored again in a 2-1 win at Old Trafford to put Villa in the final.

For the time being, the final would also be two-legged but partly due to the number of replays Villa had contended with, alongside the new competitions developing in the football calendar, it would actually take place at the start of the 1961/62 season. In August 1961 Villa lost the first leg to Rotherham before winning the second at Villa Park 3-0 with goals from McParland, Alan O'Neill and Frank Burrows. If the fact that Villa's second game of the new season was a cup final wasn't odd enough, the fact that Gerry Hitchens – who had scored 11 goals across the cup campaign – was sold to Inter Milan in the summer of

1961, and therefore was gone before said final, made the situation even odder. Either way, Aston Villa were the inaugural winners of the Football League Cup.

Villa would finish runners-up twice before they could taste more League Cup glory. In 1963 they would lose out, ignominiously, to arch-rivals and second-city neighbours Birmingham City over a two-legged final. The League Cup had for a spell offered Villa some respite from a dour league season, but the 3-1 defeat to Blues (Bobby Thomson scored the goal) signalled a spiralling decline. They were relegated in 1967 to the Second Division and Tommy Docherty made good on his promise to get Villa out of that league, by contributing to taking them down further in 1970. The 1970/71 season thus began in the old Third Division, a situation it clearly became clear was not going to be as easy as some around the club thought it would in terms of getting out of. The League Cup offered solace again, however – 62,500 packed Villa Park to see goals from Andy Lochhead and Pat McMahon defeat Manchester United 3-2 on aggregate across a two-legged semi-final. However, lowly Villa couldn't contend with Tottenham Hotspur in the final, now moved to Wembley as a one-off game not under floodlights, with a Martin Chivers brace putting paid to another campaign.

The 1974/75 season saw an upturn for Villa across the competitions they competed in. Vic Crowe had overseen an escape from the third tier, but inertia had set in during their days in the Second Division. In June 1974 Ron Saunders replaced Crowe to kick-start an unprecedented and as yet unsurpassed era for the club. Saunders oversaw promotion back to the First Division at his first attempt across a swashbuckling season of 25 league wins and 79 goals. At the forefront of Villa's bombastic play was one Brian Little, who as the club's manager would have his own influence on League Cup success. But it was as a player that Little impressed across 1974 and 1975, scoring 20 league goals and wowing crowds with his trickery and fashionably free-flowing style. Little would have a key influence in a League Cup run, scoring a brace in a resounding 6-1 mauling of Hartlepool and also the deciding goal in the semi-final versus Chester City. The final itself, at Wembley against Norwich City, was not akin to much of Villa's entertaining season, ultimately being settled by a solitary Ray Graydon goal, following in after his penalty had been saved. Nonetheless, Villa had secured their second League Cup featuring a team of players who would go down in club history. Little was one, but Charlie Aitken (Villa's leading appearance-maker of all time), Chico Hamilton, Ian Ross, John Robson, Chris Nicholl and Frank Carrodus all featured at Wembley that March afternoon. Some would be back just two years later as Villa continued their League Cup love affair.

Consolidated back in the top flight, the 1976/77 season seemed ripe for a cup run. The League Cup campaign started at Villa Park, the visiting Manchester City put to the sword by two of 1975's heroes, Brian Little and Ray Graydon. Young Scotsman Andy Gray had joined from Dundee the previous season and, well on his way to becoming a quintessential cult hero at Villa Park, he scored a brace in the next round against Norwich, again at home. For the third round in succession Ron Saunders' men again found themselves at home, this time against Wrexham, who were beaten 5-1 in a swashbuckling performance for the ages. Brian Little, Frank Carrodus and Chris Nicholl all scored, along with Gray, as the Welsh team were hammered. To bear out the exuberance Villa were playing with these were their 30th goals in nine home games, on the way to a century of goals across the season. Yet another home tie, against Millwall, may have lacked the excitement of the previous round but Little and Nicholl ensured straightforward passage to the semi-final stage where Queens Park Rangers awaited. After a stalemate in the first leg, John Deehan rescued Villa in the second to force a replay. Step forward the effervescent Brian Little, whose hat-trick in a 3-0 procession at Highbury saw Villa swagger into their second League Cup Final in three years.

The 1977 League Cup Final between Villa and Everton has been described by *These Football Times* as 'the never ending final' for good reason. The first match, at Wembley, finished 0-0 to little fanfare (it wasn't televised, and league fixtures were going on simultaneously), prompting sportswriter Brian Glanville to describe it as 'dull and eventful as a seaside town in winter'. The replay was held at Sheffield Wednesday's ground, Hillsborough, as two weary sides again slugged it out on a swamp of a pitch. Everton contrived to score two goals – unfortunately for them one of them was at the wrong end as Roger Kenyon's own goal gave Villa the lead before ex-Birmingham City player Bob Latchford found himself unmarked to equalise. Latchford's goal was so late that legend has it the trophy had already been carried pitchside with claret and blue ribbons. The first game, for reasons unknown, didn't feature extra time and in the replay an additional half an hour still couldn't separate the two teams. It was the first English cup final to have still not been decided after a replay and there seemed to be some confusion as to what would happen next.

What did happen was a third replay, this time at Old Trafford – three games, in three cities, over a calendar month. As if that wasn't enough, Villa and Everton traded blows to take the second replay into extra time, meaning the tie had lasted for some 330 minutes. From a Villa point of view, the game was fittingly settled by Brian Little's tenth goal of the cup campaign, although Chris Nicholl's sledgehammer of a goal to equalise makes a compelling argument for being the standout moment. It was Nicholl who lifted the trophy for a team now containing the likes of Dennis Mortimer and Gordon Cowans, who would prove pivotal members of the 1982 European Cup win to come. Villa had won their third League Cup after a long campaign, epitomised by that final that never wanted to die. The next time they would mount a similar challenge would be in the 1993/94 season.

Chapter 5

1993/94: Transition

THE SUMMER of 1993 saw some inevitable comings and goings at Villa Park. The erstwhile Cyrille Regis departed to Wolverhampton Wanderers in August in search of more playing time, but in reality he was approaching a point where top-flight performance would be difficult, while squad players Mark Blake and Martin Carruthers left for Portsmouth and Stoke respectively. The incomings were more interesting. Andy Townsend arrived from Chelsea, in what seemed to be a key addition for Ron Atkinson, his all-action performances for his old side against Villa over 1992/93 showing his worth. Townsend was an experienced campaigner with over 300 career appearances, so the signing felt like one that was aimed at instant impact. Townsend's quality was not in doubt, but Atkinson had fielded such a settled side over the previous season that clearly something was about to give. Also on his way to Villa Park was Guy Whittingham on the back of a record-breaking season for Portsmouth, in which he scored 42 league goals (48 across all competitions) on the way to his team, with deep irony, missing out on promotion to the top flight by virtue of goals scored. Last but not least was a return – for a third spell – for Gordon Cowans.

Townsend, Whittingham and Cowans felt like Atkinson signings. The aim was clearly to consolidate and have an instant impact as opposed to some huge overhaul or rethink. Townsend would compete with Garry Parker and Kevin Richardson in the middle of the pitch, while Whittingham represented a new option to bolster the Dean Saunders–Dalian Atkinson partnership. The latter made complete sense given Big Ron's nagging doubt that the title had been lost at the end of 1993 due to a lack of goals in the run-in. Indeed, in terms of Townsend there was a perceived gap in depth in that position – although given Parker's injury issues and Richardson's captaincy and ever-present status it was clear what Ron's plans were. Cowans – to some surprise – would play 15 times in all competitions in this third spell, but by early 1994 he was gone again, this time to Derby County.

If changes to on-pitch personnel seemed about consolidation as opposed to revolution, off the pitch there was a growing sense that the sophomore Premier League season would see some, local at least, insurgency. This was most strikingly obvious in what Aston Villa would wear during games. Villa had worn Umbro kits from 1990 through to the end of 1993, joining the ranks of many teams and individual athletes to be adorned with the 'Double Diamond' logo of the UK company. For 1993/94 Villa unveiled a new kit manufacturer – Japanese company Asics. The switch felt different and seemed to mark a line in the sand in terms of the potential for global scope of the Premier League – even in the very simplistic move from an

English manufacturer to a Japanese one. On these small changes would be built the multi-national behemoth of the Premier League we experience today all around the world.

The same emerging trend can be seen in terms of front-of-shirt sponsorship. Villa had been sponsored by Mita or Mita Copiers since as far back as 1983, meaning the company had been the main sponsor in the old Second Division, through promotion and ultimately title challenges. While Mita was a global grand in a relative sense, the value of the sponsorship must have been in question given the longevity of the relationship, and with the growing expectation of exposure through televised football. Mita was replaced by German company Müller, in a move that was clearly aimed at building a profile in the UK and can be somewhat linked to Müller's huge UK presence today. From Villa's point of view, it represented a change and fresh approach – albeit also initiating team photo shoots of players eating Müller yogurts and the much missed 'Cornered' feature in the matchday programme where players had to name their 'favourite Müller yogurt'. The dual shirt transition – manufacturer and sponsor – was a clear signalling of the Premier League beginning to take hold, and for many Villa fans it gave 1993/94 a sense of newness that hadn't been immediately forthcoming in the previous campaign.

The last key visual change to what Villa would display on the pitch was the inception of squad numbers. No more would players wear 1-11; instead they would be assigned a squad number that would stay with them for the season. This number would, for the first time, be accompanied by the player's name on the back of the shirt. In one fell swoop, the market for replica shirts grew exponentially, with embryonic club 'superstores' now able to print shirts with a certain player's details and in turn boost their incomes. Publicly, the reasoning was more aligned to audiences being able to recognise players more easily, especially those watching on television. Something that in modern terms is so normalised felt revolutionary in 1993.

Aston Villa's first numbered squad for 1993/94 assembled as follows:

Goalkeepers
1 – Nigel Spink
13 – Mark Bosnich
30 – Michael Oakes

Defenders
2 – Earl Barrett
3 – Steve Staunton
4 – Shaun Teale
5 – Paul McGrath
16 – Ugo Ehiogu
17 – Neil Cox
23 – Bryan Small
24 – Dariusz Kubicki

Midfielders
6 – Kevin Richardson
7 – Ray Houghton
8 – Garry Parker
14 – Andy Townsend
15 – Gordon Cowans

19 – Stefan Beinlich
20 – Matthias Breitkreutz
21 – David Farrell

Forwards
9 – Dean Saunders
10 – Dalian Atkinson
11 – Tony Daley
12 – Steve Froggatt
18 – Dwight Yorke
22 – Guy Whittingham
25 – Graham Fenton

The numbering gave a sense of where Atkinson's head was at in terms of selection, if one works on the basis that 1-11 might be the starting XI. As it transpired that wasn't entirely the case – a growing phenomenon as the Premier League evolved, albeit not by the English national team, initially, at Euro 2024. In the opening game of 1993/94, against Queens Park Rangers, Villa did line up 1-7 and 9-11, the only exception being Garry Parker (8) missing out at the expense of Andy Townsend (14).

That match would also be the first in front of the newly expanded Witton Lane stand, now two-tiered and largely on a par with the other stands in terms of height. The development, in part due to Lord Justice Taylor's report on English stadia in the aftermath of the Hillsborough disaster, transformed Villa Park. While Taylor's report and recommendations were justly rooted in safety concerns for the match-going public, the coinciding of the report with the newly monetised Premier League allowed clubs – Villa among them – to begin to overhaul facilities that were outdated and prohibitive for some segments of society. The Premier League was about to change the match-attending experience, but also those experiencing it as, for example, families became a key market segment. Facilities were key to that drive, slowly dragging English football out of the dark days of hooliganism and perceived danger on the terraces.

Villa didn't disappoint in the shadow of the new stand, routing the visitors 4-1 in a bombastic showing that was facilitated front and centre by new signing Andy Townsend. Two goals for Dalian Atkinson and one for his strike partner Dean Saunders were added to by a piledriver from Steve Staunton to put the icing on the cake. Villa followed up with two draws – 0-0 at Sheffield Wednesday and 2-2 at Wimbledon, where Staunton scored again alongside a neat finish from captain Kevin Richardson. Brummie Lee Sharpe's two goals for Manchester United at Villa Park then put paid to an unbeaten start, although it was a high-quality game between two top sides, and a seemingly injury-free Dalian Atkinson scored again. Nevertheless, it felt like Villa needed a response and they edged past Tottenham Hotspur a week later thanks to Staunton's third goal of the campaign – this time from the penalty spot.

The Spurs game had given Villa fans a sense of change in approach from Ron Atkinson – perhaps a nod to the need to shore up a defence at a cost to some of the free-flowing football of the opening day. This argument would be backed up in a midweek win at Goodison Park, where a Guy Whittingham goal on his first start for the club was enough to see off Everton. Whittingham's slick finish, after a long through ball from Cowans, pointed to the prowess that had afforded the ex-soldier so many goals for Portsmouth. A 0-0 stalemate with Coventry was Villa's third clean sheet in a row, although there was frustration that they couldn't convert at least one chance, with special focus being directed at Dean Saunders, who hadn't scored since the thrashing of QPR.

As Villa turned their attentions to a UEFA Cup tie in Bratislava and another League Cup campaign, they could reflect on a solid start to the Premier League campaign. After the Coventry deadlock Villa sat in fifth, with three wins and one defeat, but perhaps more concerningly three draws. Draws wouldn't be an option in the League Cup in a campaign that would come to define Villa's season and late-20th-century history.

Chapter 6

The Coca-Cola Cup 1993/94: Early Stages and Foundations

BEFORE VILLA could commence an assault on the League Cup, Ron Atkinson's side began a UEFA Cup campaign, afforded to them by 1992/93's second-placed finish. A two-legged tie against Slovan Bratislava began away from home, a game that represented Villa's seventh continental run. The lack of European experience in Atkinson's team was exemplified by the fact that only Paul McGrath, Nigel Spink and Gordon Cowans had represented the club in Europe previously – and it was the latter two who stood out in a 0-0 draw. Cowans' vision and range of passing remained undimmed in Czechoslovakia, but it was Spink's performance between the posts that buoyed Villa's hopes in advance of a second leg at home. If Europe had shown signs of promise, a return to league action against Ipswich also saw a return to goalscoring form for Dean Saunders.

For the second round of the League Cup – sponsored by Coca-Cola for the second consecutive season – Villa had been drawn against second-city rivals Birmingham in an appetising start to the domestic cup campaign. Villa and Blues hadn't faced one another since the 1988/89 season, so fans on both halves of the city were keen to secure bragging rights. That campaign had actually seen three iterations of the local derby, won by a staggering 13-0 aggregate score by Villa. As with 1993, the first meeting was a two-legged second-round affair in the League Cup, with Villa winning 2-0 at St Andrew's thanks to goals from Andy Gray and Kevin Gage. This was followed up with an even more resounding win at Villa Park – a 5-0 castigation of the Blues, with Gage scoring two alongside strikes from Derek Mountfield, Tony Daley and Ian Olney. The third contest was in the Simod Cup (also known as the Full Members' Cup), a competition that had been devised to compensate for the fact that English teams had been banned from Europe in the wake of the Heysel Stadium disaster in May 1985. Villa won 6-0 at Villa Park in a one-off tie that heaped more misery on their close neighbours – another Mountfield goal was accompanied by an Alan McInally brace, and one each for David Platt, Bernie Gallagher and Allan Evans. The passage of time since those last meetings inevitably raised expectations for the Coca-Cola Cup clash, although Villa's dominance at the end of the 1980s was tempered by the fact that (in symmetry with Europe) only Gordon Cowans and Nigel Spink had played in a Birmingham derby previously.

The first leg took place at St Andrew's on Tuesday, 21 September 1993. Police instruction had limited full attendance but there was a fervour around the ground that only such a local derby can prompt. Villa, in sponsorless claret and blue shirts (Müller would only be confirmed later that month) and black shorts, lined up as follows: Nigel Spink, Earl Barrett, Shaun Teale, Paul McGrath, Steve Staunton, Kevin Richardson, Gordon Cowans, Andy Townsend, Dean Saunders, Dalian Atkinson, Guy Whittingham. The substitutes were Mark Bosnich, Ray Houghton and Garry Parker.

The game lacked the caginess that can sometimes characterise a two-legged tie, with both teams openly attacking and creating chances. The chief thorn in Villa's side was Paul Peschisolido, whose pace and general status as an irritant caused issues for Teale and McGrath – the latter was booked for an unceremonious curtailing of one thrusting run. Yet Villa started to dominate midfield where the dual engines of Townsend and Richardson bridged their transitions between defence and attack well, both hitting the woodwork with middle-distance efforts. Villa were dealt a blow, however, after half an hour, when Nigel Spink was forced from the field with an injury, to be replaced by young Australian stopper Mark Bosnich. Spink was no stranger to the sliding doors moments of goalkeeping replacements, having taken over from Jimmy Rimmer in the early stages of the 1982 European Cup Final before putting on a career-defining performance in a landmark win. While the second round of the Coca-Cola Cup was no European Cup Final, Bosnich would never look back from this point, not least in terms of the League Cup.

On 36 minutes Dalian Atkinson, admirably if ineffectually tracking back, upended Andy Saville for a stonewall penalty. Up stepped John Frain to the spot, but he was thwarted by a solid save from Bosnich – beginning a theme that would define the League Cup campaign.

It was the type of headline-grabbing that would come to define Bosnich at Villa, with no challenge too big for the not always quietly confident Australian. The save sucked the air out of the Blues and the game began to stall as the second half became a battle of wills. As full time drew close, left-back Steve Staunton heaved a hopeful curving ball forward that seemed to deceive Chris Whyte in the middle of Birmingham's defence. Captain Kevin Richardson glided in unnoticed to meet the ball and guide it past goalkeeper Kevin Miller – 1-0 to Villa at 'half-time' in the tie.

Before the second leg Villa would play three times – and three times those displays would betray some of the issues the side and Ron Atkinson faced. Despite dominating, a point was saved at Oldham Athletic thanks to Dean Saunders before a nervy second leg against Slovan Bratislava at Villa Park. A sense of relief prevailed after a late Slovan goal burst the bubble of comfort that had been set up by goals from Andy Townsend and Dalian Atkinson. A heavy-legged Villa side then contrived to lose by two goals to Newcastle at Villa Park in a performance that Big Ron described as an 'absolute disgrace'. Villa remained seventh in the league and still in Europe but there was a nagging sense of inconsistency around Villa Park, while goalscoring, which might not have been described as a drought but certainly wasn't a torrent, remained a talking point. Atkinson had persisted with a front three of his namesake Dalian, Dean Saunders and Guy Whittingham with stuttering effect. All three were similar in their approach – lots of forward movement but none of the three was impactful when trying to drop deeper and link to midfield. Equally the lack of width, through the absence of the likes of Steve Froggatt, Tony Daley and Dwight Yorke, meant Villa often seemed narrow and easily neutralised.

It was perhaps with that in mind that the side was tweaked for the return leg against Birmingham on Wednesday, 6 October 1993 and Villa lined up as follows: Mark Bosnich, Neil Cox, Shaun Teale, Paul McGrath, Steve Staunton, Kevin Richardson, Gordon Cowans, Andy Townsend, Dean Saunders, Dalian Atkinson, Tony Daley. The substitutes were Nigel Spink, Ray Houghton and Guy Whittingham.

The 1-0 lead from the first leg seemed to put Villa in a position of stick or twist, with the Blues offering some early endeavour to try and get back into the tie. Mark Bosnich made some smart saves, including one at the feet of forward Carl Shutt to settle the nerves, but Villa struggled to create. The game turned on a flashpoint involving Paul Tait and Kevin Richardson. Richardson hacked down Tait as he looked to progress down the Villa right, a tackle that would result in a booking, but it was Tait's reaction that was more problematic. The young midfielder squared up to Richardson, moving his head in the skipper's direction. Richardson, raising his hands in mock innocence, was then pushed in the chest by Tait, 'forcing' him over the advertising hoardings and into a vacant seat in the Trinity Road stand. Looking back, there was some humour to be seen in the proceedings, although referee Gerald Ashby (from down the M5 in Worcester) immediately sent Tait off.

Inevitably, Birmingham began to be undermined by being a man light, but it took Villa until the 82nd minute to capitalise on that advantage. The previously felled Richardson released Dean Saunders from in his own half – Blues manager Terry Cooper and the St Andrew's fanbase might still debate whether he was onside – who raced clear and slid home the winner. Villa had, uncomfortably, progressed 2-0 on aggregate, Saunders' goal giving a gloss to the outcome that hadn't always seemed inevitable. Ultimately the job was done, and Villa had progressed – while Birmingham kept up their unenviable record of never having scored in any of their six Villa Park cup ties (five against Villa, and one versus West Bromwich Albion in the 1968 FA Cup semi-final).

Leading up to the next round of the Coca-Cola Cup, Villa would remain inconsistent in Europe and the Premier League. A 0-0 draw at West Ham is best remembered for the two sides of Mark Bosnich – flying one-handed saves alongside slips when trying to dribble out of his own area – and a throwback display from Tony Daley, who by this stage had found himself on the transfer list amid a rumoured switch to Italian side Udinese. Both men's Villa stories would have much more to run. In the UEFA Cup Villa were drawn against Deportivo La Coruña, at the time flying high in the Spanish top flight. It was that man Bosnich again who grabbed the headlines with a wonderful penalty save from Brazilian striker Bebeto in the third minute – underlining the sense that Bosnich was never one to be overawed, this was his European debut. A Dean Saunders goal was cancelled out by the Spaniards, with Villa relatively happy with a draw to take back to Villa Park. An unconvincing win against Chelsea in the league, secured by an early Dalian Atkinson goal and featuring Andy Townsend at left-back, rounded out another unreliable spell, as a trip to the north-east awaited in the third round of the Coca-Cola Cup.

Villa faced Sunderland at Roker Park on Tuesday, 26 October with a team impacted by Dean Saunders being stricken with chickenpox and utility player Neil Cox asking for a transfer away from the club. Neither would be involved as Villa lined up as follows: Mark Bosnich, Earl Barrett, Shaun Teale, Paul McGrath, Bryan Small, Kevin Richardson, Garry Parker, Andy Townsend, Guy Whittingham, Dalian Atkinson, Tony Daley. The substitutes were Nigel Spink, Ray Houghton and Ugo Ehiogu.

On the face of it, a 4-1 away win might have suggested an ebullient Villa easing into the next round. Scorelines can be deceptive, however, and this was no walk in the park. Sunderland started like a runaway train, exuding constant pressure and threat, but hadn't bargained for Mark Bosnich. A sensational display from the goalkeeper, who his manager would later describe as a 'trapeze artist', was all that stood between Villa and a battering – a fact born out by the memories of the surviving team members at the events remembering the 30th anniversary of this campaign all confirming the result was owed to their stopper. That said, the waves of forward press from the home team did leave them vulnerable to Villa counter-attacks, and it was from two of those that somehow the away side found themselves 2-0 ahead at the break. Firstly, Kevin Richardson played through Dalian Atkinson to score after a powerful run before Richardson himself scored from a Tony Daley assist. The half-time status quo was unfathomable; the home crowd lulled into a disbelieving quiet.

Bosnich was finally beaten as the second half began, although the early verve with which his goal was peppered did not persist, especially once substitute Ray Houghton shinned in a third. Dalian Atkinson added his seventh of the season, and Villa's fourth of the game, in the last minute to seal possibly the least likely 4-1 away win ever seen. Similar to the result against Birmingham in the previous round, however, the watchword remained progress; progress in terms of being in the next round, as opposed to progress in style and vigour, but progress nonetheless.

It would be a full month before Villa's next tie in the League Cup, so attention again switched to Europe and consolidating a position in the upper echelons of the Premier League. The UEFA Cup campaign came to a hugely disappointing end in the second leg against Deportivo, beaten by a single goal at Villa Park, in a performance that Ron Atkinson told his team they should be 'ashamed of'. In a more positive sense, agony in Europe was sandwiched between three consecutive league wins against Swindon, Arsenal and Sheffield United. The first and third of those were against sides already seemingly doomed to relegation with Dalian Atkinson and Guy Whittingham ensuring victories by the odd goal. The Arsenal result was impressive but undeserved – a late Whittingham goal squaring things up before an even later Andy Townsend winner. Arsenal manager George Graham agreed with his opposite number that a 'mugging' had taken place. Not that Atkinson would have been complaining as his

Villa side sat in second place, although what followed was increasingly emblematic of his tenure and the struggle for real consistency in terms of a title challenge. Successive defeats at home to Southampton and away at Liverpool pushed Villa down to fifth. The Liverpool reverse was actually Villa's best performance in some time, displaying a conviction and style that seemed to have been lost some time in 1992/93. The fact the result went the wrong way was a frustration and again emblematic of the manager's difficulty in calling a consistent tune. The next round of the League Cup would offer some comfort, again.

On Tuesday, 30 November Villa returned to the scene of their recent 'crime' to face Arsenal at Highbury in the Coca-Cola Cup fourth round. Despite being a second game in 48 hours, Atkinson only made one change from the Liverpool defeat as Villa lined up as follows: Mark Bosnich, Neil Cox, Shaun Teale, Paul McGrath, Earl Barrett, Kevin Richardson, Garry Parker, Ray Houghton, Andy Townsend, Dean Saunders, Dalian Atkinson. The substitutes were Nigel Spink, Tony Daley and Guy Whittingham.

Ron Atkinson's selection masked how the team would line up on the pitch, with usual centre-back Shaun Teale employed in an unfamiliar left-back role. The intention behind that shift was to deploy Earl Barrett in the middle, with specific focus on neutralising the pace and pressing of Arsenal's striker supreme Ian Wright. As discussed, Barrett had burst on to the scene as a centre-back at Joe Royle's Oldham, so the transition made some sense, and ultimately would bear significant fruit. The midfield four of Richardson, Townsend,

Parker and Houghton also tweaked Villa's style – a focus on industry and passing as opposed to width, with Tony Daley on the bench. Again, Atkinson's adjustments would bear fruit.

It was an important fixture for Atkinson, who had seen his side knocked out of Europe and was facing the harsh reality that even before the turn of the year Manchester United looked untouchable in the league. There was a real sense for both sides that the domestic cups represented a genuine opportunity for success, and indeed had become a priority in the circumstances. Arsenal were a sterling cup outfit, having won the League Cup and FA Cup in 1993 and were on a run of 25 cup ties without defeat. Given that context, the fact that Dalian Atkinson opened the scoring as early as five minutes in, brushing off Nigel Winterburn before slotting under David Seaman, was a start dreams were made of. Arsenal, it seemed, were having an off-night, failing to respond in the way many would have expected, and it was Villa who would go closer to scoring next when Saunders saw his goal-bound shot deflected off Seaman's heel and out for a corner. Ultimately Atkinson's game plan worked with Barrett excellent throughout against Wright, and even two disallowed Villa goals couldn't prompt an Arsenal fightback.

Villa's 1-0 win was enough to reach the last eight and expectation was growing that a real opportunity lay in their view. For all of Arsenal's cup prowess, Villa's win meant that they had knocked the League Cup holders out for two successive seasons, having defeated Manchester United at Villa Park the previous year. Added to that, Ron Atkinson's established reputation as a cup winner was not to be abated, with one-off games seeming to lend his tactical tweaks more prevalence.

The quarter-final would have to wait until January 1994 with a busy Premier League schedule ahead, alongside the third round of the FA Cup. As it would materialise, Villa only managed two wins in that period, lending the Coca-Cola Cup campaign weight even without playing a further game in it.

Chapter 7

A Shift in Focus

VILLA'S RETURN to league action following the League Cup success at Arsenal saw them stay in London to face Queens Park Rangers, with Ron Atkinson naming the same team. A Paul McGrath own goal in the early exchanges was not the gift the Irishman would have hoped for, but Villa responded well with fellow birthday boy Kevin Richardson's low strike levelling things up. Former Villan Gary Penrice put the home side 2-1 up, before Garry Parker levelled again. It was a reward for Parker's overall performance at Loftus Road, where he dominated midfield in a display that harked back to his standout 1992/93 campaign. It was Parker's first goal since April which underlines his marginalisation since the arrival of Andy Townsend, a trend that would only continue as the season wore on, despite his key intervention here. Villa really did enough to win, but just failed to convert chance after chance. Dean Saunders cut a frustrated figure, the statistic that he had only scored six times in 39 games since February 1993 beginning to weigh heavily. Not that his overall contribution was in question, but his industriousness was not seeing goalscoring fruition, a fact that to dog Ron Atkinson over significant parts of his Villa tenure, whichever striker the manager chose in his team.

Another 2-2 draw followed, this time at home against Sheffield Wednesday. Kevin Richardson was out, ending a streak of 128 consecutive appearances, with Shaun Teale taking over the captain's armband. Neil Cox's powerful header had equalised proceedings in the first half before Saunders had the opportunity to put some of his frustrations aside with a penalty soon after half-time. The Welshman powered the spot kick home, giving lie to an idea that he was somehow lacking confidence or self-belief in his goalscoring ability. Teale's own goal meant another draw – only two points accrued from the past 12. They'd also dropped five out of six at home, and a 1-0 loss to Wimbledon at Villa Park didn't salve the nerves of the 17,940 who bothered to turn up. A switch to five at the back for a visit to Old Trafford failed to work, Eric Cantona scoring twice in a 3-1 Manchester United win that demonstrated the contrasting trajectory the two sides had taken since slugging it out for the title earlier in the year. A much-needed win was to come at Norwich after Christmas, but home fans would again be disappointed on New Year's Day 1994 when an Alan Shearer goal led Blackburn to victory and saw Villa slip to eighth. Atkinson didn't mince his words, questioning the passion and belief of his side who would now need to approach two impending cup ties with renewed focus and vim.

If Atkinson and Villa could have picked opposition to get back on track it may well have been Exeter City, then playing in the third tier. As with many games in the early rounds of the FA Cup, however, it wasn't straightforward. The build-up had been dominated by unwanted attention on Paul McGrath, who had failed to arrive for the coach departure to Devon. McGrath's personal health and fitness issues have been well documented, but Atkinson was fuming and was forced to pair Teale and Earl Barrett in the middle of defence. Another emphatic Saunders penalty got Villa over the line, with the team vocalising the oft-used cliche of 'just being glad to be in the hat for the next round'.

The second chapter of a January cup double saw Villa face off with Tottenham Hotspur in the quarter-final of the Coca-Cola Cup on Wednesday, 12 January. With Paul McGrath 'forgiven' and back in the saddle, Villa lined up in a familiar way:

Mark Bosnich, Earl Barrett, Paul McGrath, Shaun Teale, Steve Staunton, Ray Houghton, Kevin Richardson, Garry Parker, Andy Townsend, Dean Saunders, Dalian Atkinson. The substitutes were Nigel Spink, Neil Cox and Tony Daley.

Over 5,500 Villa fans made the voyage to a wet and windy White Hart Lane with a real expectation that their team could reach the League Cup semi-finals for a then record ninth time. In contrast to recent outings, Ron Atkinson's side attacked the game with gusto and assurance, although that conviction was mirrored by the hosts. Mark Bosnich had to be at his trapeze-like best to thwart a Jason Dozzell effort and Darren Anderton struck the woodwork for Spurs. At the other end, home goalkeeper Erik Thorstvedt matched Bosnich with a stunning save from a Dean Saunders free kick which saw the sides go into half-time all square. Villa sprang into life in the second period, no one more than Dalian Atkinson, who had been a bystander in the first 45. Dispossessing Spurs midfielder Vinny Samways, the ever-enigmatic Atkinson coursed forward before sliding in Ray Houghton, whose cross-cum-shot opened the scoring. In line with the ebb and flow of the game thus far the lead was short-lived, and Darren Caskey soon equalised for Spurs, a deflection off Shaun Teale deceiving a despairing Bosnich.

Villa's winner came from an unlikely source – Earl Barrett scoring just his second goal in 92 appearances for the club. Garry Parker was on corner duties and his floated set piece from the left was met by the head of Barrett, the ball squirming under a despairing Thorstvedt. The goal seemed to quash Spurs' spirits and the home side failed to capture any of their earlier adventurous attacking play, Atkinson's first-choice defence seeing out the game impeccably, marshalled by the returning McGrath and his Irish colleague Steve Staunton. As the whistle blew on the quarter-final a sense that Villa had come back to life pervaded. That record ninth semi-final had been secured.

The Coca-Cola Cup run had given Villa much-needed relief in a season that had at times verged on if not disaster then certainly disappointment, especially given the context of a high-flying 1992/93 campaign. Equally, a lesson should be learned from that experience in paying due care and attention to the domestic cup campaigns, by proffering an opportunity for success and also as a check and balance to the slog of a league campaign. Moreover, Villa's run to the semi-final had been fraught with difficulty. The opening two-legged affair with neighbours Birmingham

City was never going to be easy given the local fervour and context, while the next three ties had all been played away from Villa Park. Although Villa had largely suffered in front of their own fans in the Premier League, playing away would always present a challenge in one-off games, although some would argue that the relieved pressure had aided and abetted Ron Atkinson's men. The Sunderland win against Spurs had been secured through a Mark Bosnich performance that beggared belief, but the Arsenal victory had been more of a domineering one. To follow that up with a tough quarter-final against Spurs was a credit to the manager and players. Atkinson seemed to have settled again on a consistent side that navigated the fine balance between cavalier and solidity and the place in the last four vindicated that.

Villa would face either Tranmere or Nottingham Forest in the semi-final and it was clear that the focus of the club had begun to shift toward potential cup success.

Chapter 8

A Semi-Final for the Ages

IF ASTON Villa's focus had shifted, their next league outing certainly didn't give that sense, and instead the team seemed buoyed by cup success. West Ham were the visitors to Villa Park in mid-January and were summarily dispatched in a type of performance that the home fans hadn't witnessed for a considerable time. A contributory factor was the return of winger Tony Daley (Garry Parker again was the odd man out, a further crystallisation of his season as a whole) who added width and verve to the side and came close to scoring in the first half. It was Kevin Richardson who did break the deadlock, hammering in a 30-yarder to the joyfully relieved strains of the Holte End. Martin Allen's equaliser set the pulses racing momentarily but in contrast to some home displays Villa's ambition remained undimmed, and a Dalian Atkinson brace put the Hammers to the sword. A controlled performance away at Chelsea only garnered a point, but two more home wins further galvanised Villa. Andy Townsend's epic swerving, instinctive effort secured a 1-0 win against Leeds, but it was an ebullient 5-0 thrashing of bottom side Swindon Town that had Atkinson and the Villa Park faithful purring. Dean Saunders' first hat-trick for the club, alongside one goal for Steve Froggatt (on his first sighting for four months) and another for Villa's leader Richardson dispatched Swindon comprehensively, and saw Villa elevate themselves to a healthier sixth in the league table. In the FA Cup a first goal of the season for Dwight Yorke had put paid to Grimsby Town in a game that saw the first red card of Ron Atkinson's spell as Villa supremo – Shaun Teale dispatched from the field after a contretemps with Grimsby's Steve Livingstone. League revitalisation and FA Cup progress would be firmly put in the shade, however, by an impending League Cup semi-final.

Villa would face First Division side Tranmere Rovers, who had started their campaign with convincing wins against Oxford and Grimsby, before taking on top-flight Oldham Athletic. The Premier League side were unceremoniously dispatched 3-0 to set up a quarter-final with Nottingham Forest. Forest had been strong favourites but a 1-1 draw in the East Midlands took the tie back to the Wirral and a rambunctious Prenton Park. Forest were sent packing 2-0 and Tranmere found themselves in the last four, a two-legged tie away from Wembley. Their campaign should have highlighted some considerations and concerns for Villa, especially given Tranmere's home turf energies and backing – but these were lessons that Ron Atkinson's side wouldn't learn quickly enough.

For the first leg, on Wednesday, 16 February, Atkinson was pressed into a change in defence which meant he deviated from his first-choice side, with Villa lining up as follows: Mark Bosnich, Neil Cox, Earl Barrett, Paul McGrath, Steve Staunton, Ray Houghton, Kevin Richardson, Tony Daley, Andy Townsend, Dean Saunders, Dalian Atkinson. The substitutes were Nigel Spink, Steve Froggatt and Ugo Ehiogu.

Despite the suspension of first-choice centre-back Shaun Teale, the line-up was as Atkinson would have largely desired. Neil Cox had deputised across the back line admirably all season so was ripe to cover at right-back, meaning Earl Barrett could partner Paul McGrath in the middle. As we know, Barrett had seen himself as a centre-half for much of his career and through injury, suspensions, unauthorised absences or tactical tweaks Ron Atkinson had become happy to use him there more frequently.

The country had been hit with inclement weather in the days leading up to the game, which had begun to put it into doubt. Villa were unable to train fully at Bodymoor Heath the day before the first leg as a blanket of snow had fallen, although that was transposed into heavy rain in the north-west. The pitch at Tranmere was heavy, a narrative that prompted many to assume Villa's passing game would be impacted severely – but lest we forget the hosts were also a passing team, driven precociously by Pat Nevin, so any impact would likely be shared. Unsurprisingly, it was Nevin who laid on Tranmere's opening goal after just five minutes, slotting in left-back Ian Nolan to smash in a cross-cum-shot that Mark Bosnich could merely flail at. It was a devastating blow for Villa so early on, especially as it further ignited an already rowdy home support who sensed a giant-killing. Not for the first time in Atkinson's tenure, there was a sense of dilemma, between protecting a scoreline for the second leg, or moving to level up the tie. Villa were caught in that quandary and after a further 20 minutes they found themselves consigned to a 2-0 deficit. Tranmere's sophomore effort had more than a slice of luck attached, as defender Mark Hughes shanked a volley goal-bound in the hope of someone getting on the end of it, only to see it nestle in Bosnich's net.

Villa's predicament was broken open in the second half as Atkinson clearly sensed the need to narrow the deficit facing his team before the return at Villa Park. Much huffing and puffing ensued, but Villa couldn't create anything of note or even gain a foothold in a game that their lower-division opponents were dominating in defence and midfield. With Dean Saunders, Dalian Atkinson and Tony Daley all anonymous, Villa were dealt a further blow when Steve Staunton, who had played despite an ongoing groin issue, was forced off with injury. In essence, his replacement Steve Froggatt could lend the aforementioned anonymous trio some support in attack, but the winger had only been on the pitch for four minutes when John Aldridge delivered the hammer blow to Villa's night. Despite clamours from the bench of an offside infringement, Aldridge was released on halfway and powered through on Bosnich's goal – his initial shot hit the post, but he emphatically beat the Australian goalkeeper to the rebound to put Tranmere 3-0 up, in dreamland and surely on their way to a showpiece Wembley final.

What happened next was arguably the pivotal moment in Aston Villa's 1993/94 season. At 3-0 the tie felt dead and buried, the home crowd revelling in a famous Tranmere victory, secure in the knowledge that with the second leg at Villa Park to come, momentum and confidence was firmly ensconced with their team. But all was not completely lost, as in injury time Kevin Richardson lofted a long free kick into the Tranmere penalty area. Tony Daley managed to head the ball across the goalmouth to an awaiting Dalian Atkinson, who contorted his frame to volley in the most valuable of away goals. There was no hiding from Villa's position as second best that night, but Dalian's late lifeline was just that; an ever so slight momentum shift that reminded everyone that, maybe after all, this tie was not quite over. Ron Atkinson mulled over scenarios in the aftermath, settling on an idea, 'If you were given a one-off chance to get to Wembley by beating Tranmere 2-0 after extra time, you would maybe fancy your chances.' Supporters were keen to believe and had celebrated the late goal with a vigour that demonstrated that (at least) *desire* to believe. Through the lens of time and hindsight, you can view Dalian Atkinson's goal as possibly his most important in a Villa shirt. The stage was set for a momentous afternoon at Villa Park in the second leg.

More ignominy was to follow, however, before Villa could go about righting the wrongs of Tranmere and Prenton Park. Hot on the heels of that defeat they crashed out of the FA Cup to another First Division side, Bolton Wanderers, all screened live on the BBC for maximum exposure. A poor game, lit up by a swerving free kick from Bolton defender Alan Stubbs, meant that Villa's season lay on a precarious cliff edge. The Boxing Day fixture against Manchester City, postponed due to a frozen Villa Park pitch, was played on the Tuesday after the Bolton defeat and saw heavy rotation by Ron Atkinson, including a debut for Graham Fenton. The youngster, originally from Tyneside, had been at Villa as a trainee since 1990 and had only recently been recalled from a profitable loan spell with West Bromwich Albion. Bigger moments were to come for Fenton, but he gave Villa some life against City, even if a stalemate ensued, with Fenton's senior colleague Dean Saunders putting an 82nd-minute penalty past the post. Villa lay marooned in sixth, neither here nor there in reality, and a week that saw two dispiriting cup defeats and an innocuous 0-0 home draw meant that more and more emphasis would be placed on the second leg with Tranmere, and what seemed to be Villa's only remaining salvation for an inconsistent and frustrating season.

The second leg of the semi-final was played on Sunday, 27 February at a cold, but bright, Villa Park. With Shaun Teale back from suspension, but with Steve Staunton's groin ruling him out, Villa took the field as follows: Mark Bosnich, Earl Barrett, Paul McGrath, Shaun Teale, Neil Cox, Ray Houghton, Kevin Richardson, Andy Townsend, Tony Daley, Dean Saunders, Dalian Atkinson. The substitutes were Nigel Spink, Graham Fenton and Ugo Ehiogu.

What was to unfold on that late February afternoon remains an iconic Villa Park moment, characterising the changing face of 'modern' football in ways that few games have since. Despite the first-leg embarrassment there was a slightly incongruous feeling of optimism around the ground, and among the fanbase. Tranmere were not to be underestimated for sure but remained a lower-division side who – surely – Villa could find the necessary swagger and resilience to get past and make a Wembley final for the first time since 1977. That optimism was perhaps conversely rooted in the nagging sense that defeat would mean a season that had promised so much petering out to nothing.

The first-leg result meant Villa had to seize the initiative and the home side attacked relentlessly for the opening quarter of an hour, though with no tangible reward. Indeed, they looked vulnerable themselves and were reliant on Mark Bosnich after just five minutes to thwart John Aldridge while lying on his back in the goalmouth. On 19 minutes Andy Townsend and Tony Daley combined adroitly on the left side, the Irishman eventually coursing towards the byline to drive a low cross into Tranmere's penalty area. Waiting in the box was Dean Saunders, who expertly judged the ball's movement to dart into the near-post area to gleefully nudge past goalkeeper Eric Nixon. It was the sort of poacher's goal that Saunders hadn't always taken over his Villa spell, but as he gleefully wheeled away none of that mattered – Villa were 1-0 up and had the foothold in the game they had needed, and the fans' optimism had clamboured for. Optimism transitioned to giddy expectation less than five minutes later when they went 2-0 up, levelling the aggregate score in the process. Captain Kevin Richardson drifted in a free kick from the right and Shaun Teale, surging into the penalty box, dived to head home. Teale's celebrations remain fixed in the consciousness of a generation of Villa fans – seated on the turf pumping his fists in unadulterated joy before being mobbed by his team-mates. That unadulterated joy was mirrored across Villa Park's iconic four stands.

Fans should perhaps have known better than to assume a serene procession to Wembley was in the offing. In their desire to get forward, Villa remained vulnerable to counter-attack, and in the 27th minute they were gravely undone. John Aldridge darted forward on the break and took the ball round the advancing Bosnich, who unceremoniously took down the Tranmere striker for an indisputable penalty. Of greater concern was whether Bosnich would be sent off for the offence, with referee Alan Gunn clearly considering that option. The fact that Paul McGrath and Neil Cox were covering was a mitigating factor as was the fact that Bosnich had forced the contact wider from his goal. Ultimately Bosnich remained on the field to face the penalty, in what would become a feted theme in the game. Aldridge converted to put his side 4-3 ahead on aggregate, simultaneously piercing the atmosphere and belief around Villa Park.

The near hour of play that followed lacked purpose, and the atmosphere had descended into a disconsolate state as the reality of another dashed Wembley dream came into sharp focus. With the clock on 88 minutes, Dalian Atkinson popped up in midfield to win the ball back for his team, his run forward then being curtailed by some desperate Tranmere defence. Villa tried to take the resulting free kick quickly, but Gunn pulled play back, possibly to their advantage as the teams reset for the dead ball. Daley picked it up on Villa's right and whipped in a sumptuous cross which Atkinson powerfully met to head Villa's third goal of the afternoon. As Kevin Keegan said in the original ITV commentary, the quality of Villa's crossing had been a key facet of their game and ultimately had led to all three goals. As in the first leg, Atkinson had come to Villa's rescue again, levelling up affairs at 4-4. With an acceptance of extra time looming, there remained time for one more potential twist as Tranmere won a free kick just outside Villa's penalty area. Liam O'Brien's effort was on target and there were plenty of Holte End hearts in mouths as it crashed against the post, Bosnich beaten. Earl Barrett hammered the ball out of play and the 90 minutes came to a close after the most breathless of denouements.

Extra time proved idle and unproductive as both teams were reluctant to attack with any real relish, save for giving themselves a problem at the opposite end of the field. The one exception to that was in the 33rd minute of the extra period when Dalian Atkinson threw caution to the wind and embarked on a mazy run, slaloming Tranmere defenders at will, reminiscent of his goal of the season at Wimbledon in 1992/93. Alas the striker couldn't find the target as Eric Nixon bravely smothered the ball at his feet, and the tie would be decided by a penalty shoot-out. It's worth pausing here to recall Villa's last penalty shoot-out, at Wimbledon in the FA Cup during the 1992/93 season. That night Villa's chosen takers were Garry Parker, Dean Saunders, Steve Staunton, Neil Cox, Dwight Yorke, Shaun Teale and Kevin Richardson. All would score with the exception of Cox and Richardson, the latter taking the final penalty and blasting it over the crossbar to give Wimbledon the win. Mark Bosnich was in goal that foggy night at Selhurst Park but couldn't get close to any of Wimbledon's efforts – their one miss coming when Dean

Holdsworth crashed his kick against Bosnich's right-hand post. A calendar year on it would be interesting to see what lessons had been learned in that defeat, from Ron Atkinson's point of view when choosing – or asking players – to step up but also from those players' points of view in terms of coping with the inevitable pressure that a shoot-out elicits.

Returning to Villa Park and Tranmere, first up for Villa was Dean Saunders, in front of the North Stand housing the Tranmere away following. Saunders made no mistake, calmly sending Nixon the wrong way, before Kenny Irons repeated the trick with Mark Bosnich – both penalties in the same corner. Up next for Villa was Shaun Teale, who had scored in the Wimbledon shoot-out the previous season, and some iconic commentary harking back to the aforementioned John Wayne reference – as commentator Alan Parry waxed, Teale loaded his gun and fired the bullet straight down the middle. Emphatically, Villa were 2-1 up. Tranmere substitute Tony Thomas's long run-up secured a leveller before Graham Fenton stepped up to give Villa a slight advantage again. Now up stepped Mark Bosnich, who athletically saved Ged Brannan's kick to his right, once again demonstrating his penalty-saving prowess as he had against John Frain in the early stages of this very Coca-Cola Cup campaign. As we often see with shoot-outs the kick after a miss is crucial in consolidating an advantage and Dalian Atkinson ensured his goalkeeper's efforts did not go to waste with a confident spot kick to put Villa 4-2 up.

Dave Higgins needed to score for Tranmere, and he duly did – shifting the ball into the roof of Bosnich's net.

Young defender Ugo Ehiogu had come on as a substitute for Ray Houghton for extra time and – to some raised eyebrows – it was Ugo who would take Villa's fifth and potentially match-winning kick. Ehiogu's powerful drive from the spot was in vain as it crashed back off the crossbar, the taker's hands on his head summing up a deflated Villa Park. For the second time in the match, John Aldridge deceived Bosnich to set things back to all square at 4-4. Into sudden death and the gauntlet was passed to Villa captain Kevin Richardson, who, of course had smashed his penalty over the bar in that Wimbledon FA Cup episode. With a horrible twist of fate Richardson did exactly the same here, with Eric Nixon redundant as the kick sailed over his bar and into the joyous Tranmere fans behind it.

The advantage had suddenly shifted back to the away side as Liam O'Brien was handed the opportunity to complete a marvellous Tranmere victory. What O'Brien hadn't fully bargained for was Mark Bosnich. The midfielder opted for the same side as Ged Brannan, whose kick Bosnich had saved. Again, the Australian guessed correctly and firmly pushed out the effort. As he leapt to his feet amid the clamouring home support, Bosnich slammed a finger to his chest – it was difficult to argue that it was, indeed, all down to him. The next man to take on the responsibility of a sudden-death penalty was Tony Daley. The wide man scraped the ball past Nixon to give Villa another tenuous advantage and presented Bosnich with the opportunity to once again step up to the plate as the game's key player and influencer. Inevitably he didn't disappoint, making his third save of the shoot-out, this time from Ian Nolan, to give Villa the win. As fans streamed on to the pitch and Bosnich was enveloped by his relieved and grateful peers, Alan Parry summed it up neatly, 'Bosnich the hero. Aston Villa go to Wembley.'

The semi-final could not have been more dramatic – imbued with the twists and turns of a classic match that would long live in the memory. Villa were in the final of the Coca-Cola Cup; a season in danger of drifting into obscurity had been rescued through the most extraordinary of finales, Mark Bosnich embodying the passion and drive of Ron Atkinson's team in their determination to offer themselves, the club and most importantly its supporters a long-awaited opportunity to secure some silverware. 'Wembley here we come' was the attitude.

Chapter 9

Coke Cans and Cadbury's

HAVING SNUCK past Tranmere in dramatic fashion, Villa would have to wait until the middle of the subsequent week to find out their opponents at Wembley. The other semi-final had seen two of Ron Atkinson's former clubs, Manchester United and Sheffield Wednesday, face off, with only the hardiest of Yorkshiremen predicting anything but a United win.

United had conquered all before them over the 1993/94 season – at the time of the League Cup semis they occupied the top spot in the Premier League, a position they would never relinquish, and were about to progress to an FA Cup quarter-final. United had won the first leg against Wednesday 1-0 thanks to a Ryan Giggs goal, but it was in the second leg – three days after Villa had confirmed their Wembley spot – that they really came alive and put the opposition to the sword. A 4-1 win at Hillsborough saw United in an attacking groove that had characterised their season. Two goals from Mark Hughes and one each for Brian McClair and Andrei Kanchelskis meant a 5-1 aggregate win and confirmed that the 1994

Coca-Cola Cup Final would be contested by Aston Villa and Manchester United.

It would be a full calendar month until the showpiece, so while there would be some administrative beginnings of booking coaches and getting measured for suits, Atkinson knew that it remained important to keep competitive in the Premier League. Villa were seventh, which was disappointing but not disastrous, and of their next five Premier League games four would be against teams below them in the table. There was also the issue of players wanting to secure a starting spot at Wembley – for those established starters it was about maintaining form and remaining injury-free, but Atkinson also indicated that there would be some rotation in advance of the final, giving some on the fringe an opportunity to impress and push for, at least, a squad place.

Three days after the Tranmere epic, Villa found themselves at White Hart Lane to play a struggling Spurs side. Villa were still missing Steve Staunton and were newly shorn of Andy Townsend and Ray Houghton after the pair picked up knocks in the semi-final. In came Garry Parker and Steve Froggatt and it was the former who had an almost instant impact, putting Villa ahead after just eight minutes. Almost unbelievably it was over to Mark Bosnich, who after his penalty shoot-out heroics saved two more in north London in an eventual 1-1 draw. The Australian had now saved eight penalties in all competitions across the season. A rare Tony Daley effort (the winger hadn't scored since the final day of 1992/93) saw off Coventry at the start of March and nudged Villa into fifth. Four points from a possible six after the wearying elation of reaching the Coca-Cola Cup Final was a solid return.

Unfortunately, worse was to come and Villa lost their next three games – miserably at home to Ipswich and Oldham and away at Leeds. It was as you were as they returned to seventh spot, and the unsettledness of results was mirrored in team selection and player availability as the final loomed large. Paul McGrath, Andy Townsend, Ray Houghton and Dalian Atkinson all missed a game over this losing spell, although Steve Staunton did make a timely return against Oldham. The boon of Staunton's return was not nearly enough to salve the frustrations of Villa fans who booed the team off against the Latics, an unusual farewell for the trip to Wembley. Not that Ron Atkinson had much sympathy. 'I don't blame them booing,' he said. 'I started it. The performance was an insult to themselves [the players], the fans and to professional football.' Some send-off for the team from their manager as they approached the club's biggest game in nearly two decades – a game that Manchester United were clear favourites for.

Atkinson's stance seemed to soften as he curated a meticulous build-up to the encounter with his old team at Wembley. Suits were fitted and made by Birmingham chain Ciro Citterio and there were several photocalls organised by the League Cup's sponsors Coca-Cola, which involved inflatable Coke cans and players wearing branded clothing adorned with the soft drink giant's logos.

In a masterstroke by Atkinson, he held training sessions at Cadbury's in Bournville, a collection of works and recreation grounds that Villa had a long history with.

There was some truth in Atkinson's belief that the turf at Cadbury's was similar to Wembley, and the players would clearly benefit from a change of scene – playing in a major final was different to other games and therefore required a different approach in the build-up. Similarities in turf aside, the historical links with Cadbury's and Bournville were a boon for the team. In 1896 legendary Villa officials George Ramsay and Fred Rinder were invited to inspect and give feedback on the chocolate company's new men's recreation ground, a sprawling 14-acre estate for cricket, hockey and football. Ramsey and Rinder were so supportive of the new venture that they sent an Aston Villa representative team to compete in the inaugural match on the Bournville site in October 1897 – just months after Villa had won the Football League and FA Cup double. That early link set a tone, but it was Atkinson's own memories of the build-up to Villa's 1957 FA Cup win that ultimately prompted the choice of Bournville for training. Villa were due to face Manchester United in that final, as they were in 1994, and the manager remembered as a young player that Villa trained at Cadbury's before making their own trip to Wembley. If it was good enough for them, it was good enough for us was Atkinson's commentary.

Historical alignment complete, Atkinson took his team to London several days before the final, taking players and their wives out for an Italian meal and a couple of beers (and potentially some karaoke from the boss) to lighten the mood, before taking up residence in Windsor and training at Bisham Abbey. They were entertained by comedian Stan Boardman (who would also travel with the side on the coach to Wembley) who further kept the mood light and relaxed, even quipping on club film footage that he might 'have a game if Paul McGrath didn't turn up'.

It was on the training pitches in Berkshire that Villa and their manager suffered a slight fitness scare, with Mark Bosnich punching Shaun Teale when coming for a cross, leaving the defender with a suspected broken nose. Not that that was likely to stop Teale, in the same way that recent surgery recovery was unlikely to persuade Steve Staunton to sit it out. In essence therefore, Atkinson had a fully fit squad to pick from and the team he chose was as follows: Mark Bosnich, Earl Barrett, Paul McGrath, Shaun Teale, Steve Staunton, Dalian Atkinson, Andy Townsend, Kevin Richardson, Graham Fenton, Tony Daley, Dean Saunders. The substitutes were Nigel Spink, Neil Cox and Ray Houghton.

The selection of Fenton was the surprising outlier. Although the young Geordie had been significantly involved since his loan spell at West Brom, playing him in the final was a huge call, and one that was rooted in Atkinson's tactical tweaks. As we have seen, earlier in the season Atkinson had utilised Earl Barrett at centre-back to counter specific Manchester United (and Arsenal) players and ways of playing, and this was born from a game between the sides that Atkinson had been on punditry duties for ITV at.

Arsenal played a five-man midfield that was aimed to subdue Eric Cantona while simultaneously countering the energy of Paul Ince and Roy Keane. Atkinson liked what he saw and believed that adding Fenton to the side would provide that energy and bite in the middle, in contrast to the more experienced Ray Houghton, who was ostensibly the man to miss out once the youngster was selected. It wasn't the only tactical endeavour that Atkinson wanted to put into practice, instructing Dean Saunders that he would start – and stay – in the middle of the pitch with Dalian Atkinson and Tony Daley offering pace from the flanks, both to attack with vigour but also to peg back the Manchester United full-backs Denis Irwin and Paul Parker. There were still only three substitutes allowed, which made things difficult for squad members who had been part of the campaign but ultimately wouldn't be involved at all in the final itself. The likes of Ugo Ehiogu, Garry Parker, Bryan Small and Steve Froggatt were well managed by Atkinson and were kept involved in the build-up and experience of the final even if they wouldn't play in it. Neil Cox was chosen as a substitute, ostensibly to offer cover for the recently returned Steve Staunton but, as Cox has regularly admitted since, he was often on the bench due to the fact he could also cover goalkeeping duties – which he did do once during his Villa career later this season, taking over after Nigel Spink was sent off against Southampton.

It was already common knowledge that Manchester United would be missing their inspirational goalkeeper (and future Aston Villa goalscorer) Peter Schmeichel and their side contained no surprises: Les Sealey, Paul Parker, Steve Bruce, Gary Pallister, Denis Irwin, Andrei Kanchelskis, Roy Keane, Paul Ince, Ryan Giggs, Eric Cantona, Mark Hughes. On the bench were Gary Walsh, Lee Sharpe and Brian McClair.

The scene was set and Atkinson, despite his anger only days before after the Oldham home loss, pithily dismissed the idea that United would not be faced with a significant challenge by his side. 'I'll tell you something,' he said, 'we're a better team than that "Legover" Warsaw lot they played in the Cup Winners' Cup.'

Chapter 10

The 1994 Coca-Cola Cup Final

WELSH REFEREE Keith Cooper led Aston Villa and Manchester United out in front of 77,231 fans on Sunday, 27 March. Immediately behind Cooper were the respective managers, Ron Atkinson and Alex Ferguson, a relationship that was characterised by some prickliness given that the Scotsman had replaced Atkinson at Old Trafford. Behind their managers lined up the teams, resplendent in newly en vogue walk-out jackets. As the teams arrived the atmosphere was palpable, prompting seasoned ITV commentator Brian Moore to suggest he had never known a louder and more vibrant final at Wembley. Legendary English footballer Nat Lofthouse was the guest of honour and as Kevin Richardson introduced his team to the 'Lion of Vienna', Villa fans belted out a deafening rendition of 'Holte Enders in the Sky' and 'Birmingham Are You Listening', songs that remain Villa Park staples to this day. To watch back the game now, you are struck by an old-fashioned-ness that would begin to wane as the Premier League bedded in. Summariser Kevin Keegan quipped that Paul McGrath could have played with

Lofthouse, despite Nat being 34 years McGrath's senior. Even more incongruous was Moore's pondering as to what language the guest of honour was speaking to Manchester United winger Andrei Kanchelskis, stumbling around his Ukrainian and Russian identity. It's salient to remember that in 1994 English football remained dominated by British players, and therefore the likes of Kanchelskis were still considered a novelty. That was born out by Villa fielding just one non-British player in the form of Australian goalkeeper Mark Bosnich, while Kanchelskis was one of just two in the United line-up, along with Eric Cantona. Things would soon begin to shift in that respect.

Designated the away side, United wore their green and yellow change strip, a nod to their own history of Newton Heath and railway workers, while Villa wore their now iconic claret and blue Asics shirt adorned with the Müller sponsor. It was Villa, through Graham Fenton and Dean Saunders, who kicked off and immediately they began to probe down United's flanks, Earl Barrett being thwarted before switching to his opposite full-back Steve Staunton, who played in Tony Daley down Villa's left side. Daley's mazy run and cross was cleared easily but the start signalled Villa's intentions not to merely be a bridesmaid to United's surge towards a domestic treble.

United responded and Shaun Teale was forced to clear before failing to cut out a Kanchelskis centre that Dalian Atkinson turned behind for a corner. With just two minutes gone Keegan decreed, prompted by the open start, that 'we have a classic on our hands'. Although Bosnich punched the resulting corner away, Villa then seemed to struggle to clear their lines but once they did the pace and guile of Dalian Atkinson and Fenton drove them forward. Already the selection of Fenton seemed like a stroke of genius from Ron Atkinson as the Manchester United defence were caught between two stools when the young forward dropped deep to collect the ball. A driving run from Paul Ince pointed to a change in tone and he slipped in Mark Hughes, Villa requiring Paul McGrath and Kevin Richardson to combine to block and take the ball away from Manchester United's Welsh striker. United grabbed the ascendency, the raw pace of Kanchelskis continually causing issues. Villa remained resolute, however, and they maintained their shape exceptionally, meaning the counter-attack was always an option for Atkinson's side. Mark Bosnich was certainly the busier goalkeeper in the early exchanges, but Atkinson would have been pleased that there was no genuine clear-cut opportunity. The first chance did come in the 14th minute when Ryan Giggs broke into the area, but Hughes was unable to convert close to Bosnich's goal. What followed – in front of the Jiffy Condoms advertising hoarding – was a spell of sustained United dominance, orchestrated by Eric Cantona.

For Villa, Dean Saunders seemed isolated in his unfamiliar lone striker role, being asked to hold the ball up against his natural instincts. At the other end Bosnich was called upon yet again to palm away a diving Roy Keane header. The Australian then clattered the same player, outside of his area, although the referee remained unmoved despite United's protestations that an offence had occurred, even suggesting Keane had dived. From that incident Villa seemed to gain a sense of renewal, a surging Dalian Atkinson forcing a corner. Staunton's first delivery was poor but an immediate second saw the Irish left-back swing in a dangerous kick right under Les Sealey's crossbar. A third successive Staunton corner, this time from Villa's left, saw Fenton lash in a strike from outside the area. The game ebbed and flowed, but it was clear that Kevin Richardson and Andy Townsend's industriousness in the midfield was beginning to reap rewards.

In the 26th minute, right as Kevin Keegan suggested that Villa were 'coming into it' a little more, they struck with conviction. A ball in from Townsend was neatly flicked on by Saunders to find Dalian Atkinson, who deftly touched it past the onrushing Sealey. Atkinson wheeled away in delight, tongue out, arms outstretched in what would be a defining image of a man whose life descended into difficulty before an early exit from this world. The goal felt seminal – going one up seemed essential if Villa were going to succeed, and it was Dalian again who had struck that crucial goal. His goalscoring could never have been described as prolific but it was hard to argue that when he did score, they were absolutely essential to Villa's cause – as demonstrated through the League Cup campaign, with the Arsenal winner and two timely goals against Tranmere now followed up with the opener at Wembley.

At 1-0, the goal buoyed Villa, who seemed to be playing a yard further forward as their coaching staff bayed at Daley and Atkinson to run into space behind United's full-backs. In the last quarter of the first half neither side could create much of meaning, the game increasingly fought in the centre of the pitch, with Keane and Ince jostling for possession and dominance with Richardson and Townsend. United right-back Paul Parker lashed a shot wide in the

38th minute before a jinking run from Daley just failed to set up Saunders at the opposite end. Villa's tactic of allowing United to play on to them before winning the ball back and breaking quickly was effective and seemed to surprise their opponents, who had often played the same way over the season. United felt they should have had a penalty as half-time neared, when Earl Barrett felled Gary Pallister, but as Keith Cooper blew the whistle on the first period, Ron Atkinson could address his charges pleased with what he had seen unfold. Accosted by ITV's Gary Newbon, Atkinson confirmed the plan to frustrate United tactically seemed to be working, acknowledging that his side's pace on the break looked crucial – although with a word of warning about 'being brave enough to use the ball when we win it back'. The message was clear: Villa needed to continue to play and pass the ball, as opposed to some sort of containment exercise. A slender Villa lead at half-time would make for a fascinating watch in the second 45.

As the second half commenced with no changes for either side, injured Manchester United captain Bryan Robson was interviewed by Newbon and over-simplified Villa's job as 'just needing to defend well'. It seemed unlikely that would be enough given United's strengths. It was United who got proceedings under way as Villa looked set to utilise the formation and shape that had served them so well in the first period, with Fenton and Atkinson looking to stretch their opponents on the counter. The first five minutes saw some probing, but Villa were sloppy on the ball and often overran opportunities. For United, Kanchelskis continued to threaten and only a superb sliding challenge by Shaun Teale stopped the winger bearing down on Bosnich's goal. The early stages were characterised by some battling from Villa's players – often from the likes of Daley and Atkinson, of whom that was not always expected. United responded by being more direct, with future Villa manager Steve Bruce making some searching 40-yard passes looking for Giggs and Kanchelskis, and Villa's defensive efforts dropped deeper with some added desperation.

McGrath marshalled proceedings expertly, ever the calm and commanding presence his side needed. McGrath's own story is well told, but as a player he was often underrated and in a different era his gifts may have been celebrated more vociferously. For Villa it was a case of just being thankful he was 'ours' – his reading of the game and communication making life easy for those around him, as many of his team-mates would attest in the future when asked the best player they had played alongside.

The first ten minutes of the second half were full of energy but neither team could fashion what might be described as a goalscoring opportunity – United's movement of the ball was quick but was matched by Villa's retention of shape. Alongside that, Villa remained a threat once they won the ball back – the pace of Barrett and Daley threatened on multiple occasions but there was no final output. It was difficult to argue with the ITV commentary team that the next goal was crucial. If United were to get it one could foresee a win for them, whereas a second Villa goal would have the opposite effect. On the hour mark Daley did manage to conjure up a shot on goal only to see it blocked. From the resulting corner a wild Barrett effort did little to trouble Les Sealey.

In the search for some inspiration, Alex Ferguson turned to Lee Sharpe, who had of course scored twice against Villa in the league at Villa Park in 1993, with the Halesowen-born winger replacing Ryan Giggs. The newcomer didn't look like getting much change out of Earl Barrett and these exchanges were now characterised by a deep-seated resilience from Villa that United didn't seem to be able to come up with an answer to. To a man Villa were outstanding, all willing to run and battle for their club in the sort of all-action performance that Ron Atkinson had often bemoaned the absence of over the course of the season. McGrath remained the colossus on which the overall effort was constructed, although the experienced centre-half's efforts were almost undone by a panicking Bosnich flapping at a cross that McGrath clearly had covered. The young keeper felt the lashing of a Dublin tongue. Sharpe started to move more central, with some profit, and he had a good chance just after 70 minutes which, bar a stunning diving intervention from Kevin Richardson, would surely have led to the equaliser. Soon after, Villa broke through Saunders and Fenton but again it came to nothing as the 19-year-old's cross ballooned out of play. As the game switched from end to end Sharpe and Hughes got in each other's way trying to turn in a speculative Ince cross.

With just a quarter of an hour remaining Daley, again jinking down the left, was callously upended by Parker to give Villa a free kick in a dangerous area on the edge of the United penalty box. As Daley received some treatment, a gang of Villa players seemed to be plotting something, with one of them – Dean Saunders – wheeling away quickly into the box. Richardson whipped a ball into the area directly where Saunders had run to. The Welshman stuck out a foot and to the apparent surprise of a flat-footed Manchester United rearguard, directed the ball into Sealey's net. Villa's hard work had reaped a reward, and at 2-0, maybe, just maybe it was time to believe.

As Villa had discovered in their 1992/93 title challenge, United under Ferguson were not beaten until it was impossible to come back. Steve Staunton, suffering with his season-defining injury, was replaced by Neil Cox – although the utility man slotted in at right-back with Earl Barrett moving to the opposite side. Cox was soon involved, curtailing a United attack, but he was unable to intervene as Hughes scrambled a goal for his team in the 73rd minute. Bosnich missed a cross, taking out Teale and McGrath in the process, and Roy Keane's first-time return was buried at the second attempt by Hughes. A queasy feeling of inevitability started to rise up in Villa fans as United incessantly poured forward in search of an equaliser.

Villa's defence coped relatively well but were reliant on their goalkeeper in a pivotal moment in the 88th minute. Eric Cantona knocked the ball down for Mark Hughes who snatched a volley towards the Villa goal, seemingly destined to nestle inside it for the equaliser. The maverick Bosnich, who had exhibited some odd errors of judgement in the match, threw himself to his left to make a diving save that, like many of his feats in a Villa shirt, seemed unfathomable. It was the moment that, in many ways, won the game, or at least secured Villa's footing in defending their lead. As he had throughout the Coca-Cola Cup campaign, Bosnich's theatrics between the sticks had come to Villa's rescue. Between him at one end and Dalian Atkinson at the other Villa had found their key match-winners, making interventions to either keep a goal out or score one, that sustained their challenge and ultimate trophy success.

Amazingly there was still more to come. Successive United corners were defended securely, and it became a reality that anywhere outside of their own penalty box would do. In the 89th minute, as Bosnich clutched the ball to his chest and urged calm, Villa fans found their breath. Bosnich kicked long, deep into the United half where Saunders knocked the ball sideways to Dalian Atkinson. Atkinson, looking left, saw an ocean of space in which to play the ball, ideally placed for the speedy Tony Daley to run on to. Daley slammed a shot against the post and then Atkinson's rebound was handled on the line by Kanchelskis. Kanchelskis saw red and Saunders hammered the resulting penalty right down the middle of the goal to put Villa 3-1 ahead. There would be no grand comeback from United on this March Sunday – it was Villa's day.

As Keith Cooper blew the final whistle, Villa's players on the field reacted with an exhausted elation; pure excitement given context by the superhuman efforts the team had put themselves through. Non-playing squad members and unused substitutes bounded on to the field to join the celebrations, while some – Kevin Richardson and Dean Saunders among them – consoled their vanquished Manchester opposition. Richardson knew the pain of defeat having been on the losing side of League Cup finals twice – with Everton in 1984 and Arsenal four years later. Ray Houghton hadn't seen action from the bench but collected a second winners' medal having also been victorious with Oxford in 1986. It was the other unused substitute – goalkeeper Nigel Spink – who adds weighty context to what had unfolded at Wembley that day, as Villa won their first trophy since the 1982 European Cup, a side Spink had been a part of. Squad members like Ugo Ehiogu and Dwight Yorke, gleefully celebrating on the pitch, could have had an inkling that their time was to come – but others, Bryan Small and Garry Parker among them, must have known this was probably as good as it was going to get in terms of their Villa careers.

Ron Atkinson was quietly emotional as was his chairman Doug Ellis looking on, with the manager acknowledging to Gary Newbon that the 'last ten minutes felt like an hour'. Kevin Richardson led his Villa team up the famous Wembley steps, followed by Mark Bosnich and the rest of the group where he also collected a richly deserved man of the match award, alongside the trophy.

Chapter 11

Reflecting on Cup Success and Seeing Out 1993/94

THE SUCCESSFUL Coca-Cola Cup campaign of 1993/94 will long be important in the annals of Aston Villa's history. It represented a return to trophy-winning success after a period of much change and transition, as the club saw relegation, promotion and title challenges come and go. It also represented for a generation of Villa fans a staging post in a consciousness of supporting the club that would define that generation of fans for many years to come. For those fans who hadn't witnessed the 1982 European Cup win, beating Bayern Munich in Rotterdam, events at Wembley in March 1994 were the equivalent. As Mat Kendrick, former football editor at the *Birmingham Mail*, has said, 'This was our Rotterdam.' It explains why, at the time of writing, 30 years on from that heady day in Wembley, Villa fans are still fondly talking about Atkinson, Teale and Müller and attending events where those players are lauded and celebrated as a crucial part of Villa's collective history but also those individuals' own personal histories.

Aston Villa's tactical discipline, effective counter-attacking, and utilisation of key moments allowed them to outmanoeuvre Manchester United at Wembley. United's inability to break down Villa's defence and their vulnerability to counter-attacks were crucial factors in the result. This victory marked a significant achievement for Villa, as they secured their fourth League Cup, drawing level with Liverpool and Nottingham Forest in the record books (all three sides, coincidently, had competed in six finals). There would have been some private vindication for Ron Atkinson, his ousting from Manchester United still lingering in his own mind, and for Paul McGrath and Mark Bosnich, who had played for the opposition earlier in their careers. For players like Andy Townsend and Shaun Teale, schooled on the fields of Weymouth, the cup win represented an ascent to the top of the English game that had been long and winding in its journey and duration. In a similar vein, for Tony Daley to win a major trophy with the club he would play over 230 times for was justly deserved, while for Nigel Spink it was a book end to a long and loyal commitment to Villa that had started at the fag end of the 1970s. The overarching concept here is that winning the 1994 Coca-Cola Cup truly *meant* something beyond simply winning a trophy. Would it still mean as much 30 years on had Villa gone on to win a series of other trophies? Perhaps not, but that can only be conjecture.

It was a cup campaign that glossed over some of the frailties around Ron Atkinson's side, but the ultimate trophy win was the final coat. The fine margins of success and failure in football are never more evident than when looking at the 1994 win – if Villa had lost the final this season would have been a mere footnote. Instead, we are attending events, writing books and buying retro Müller shirts. Memories are indeed made of this.

Three decades on, players involved demonstrate the importance in their own recollections. Shaun Teale and Tony Daley published retrospectives of their careers and for both the Coca-Cola Cup win is a centrepiece. Daley talked of being 'in heaven' at the final whistle, a feeling no doubt shared by everyone with a Villa connection. Teale, meanwhile, referred to being 'loud and proud', again echoing the feelings of supporters at the final whistle but also beyond as they went into work and saw friends and family sage in the knowledge that Villa were 'winners' again.

It was a campaign that spanned eight games in total, with only two coming at Villa Park (both of which were second legs in two-legged ties) with five away from home and the final beneath the twin towers of Wembley. Villa scored 16 times across the eight games and conceded seven. There were unconvincing big wins and utterly convincing successes that seemed to suggest scraping home. There was high drama and heroics from players who would form Villa's future as well as their present. Given Ron Atkinson's preference for consistent team selections, it is perhaps a surprise that only four players started all eight games – Dalian Atkinson, Paul McGrath, Kevin Richardson and Andy Townsend. Less of a surprise was the fact that the quartet represented the core spine of the team. When you add Mark Bosnich, Earl Barrett, Shaun Teale and Dean Saunders, who started seven games each, then the spine is genuinely established (and to be fair to Bosnich he also came on as substitute and saved a penalty in the one game he didn't start). Steve Staunton (due to injury) and Tony Daley (due to flirtations with Udinese) started five games of the Coca-Cola campaign that year, while Ray Houghton and Neil Cox started four each. Garry Parker, Gordan Cowans, Graham Fenton, Bryan Small and Guy Whittingham all started at least once, while Ugo Ehiogu and Steve Frogatt appeared as substitutes only. Strangely given his start at Villa, but ultimately as a result of injury, Dwight Yorke didn't have a single involvement across the cup run. While it was an increase on the 14 players that Ron Saunders had utilised in winning the 1981 First Division, Villa's squad was small enough to give the manager consistency but equally keep those not playing as much relatively happy.

Demonstrating his importance to the side and the ultimate final success, Dalian Atkinson scored six of Villa's 16 goals, followed by Saunders with four. Midfield generals Richardson and Houghton scored two each on the way to Wembley, with one each for defenders Barrett and Teale. Mark Bosnich was in the Villa net for every goal conceded, although that is outweighed by his penalty heroics at either end of the cup run, and a performance at Sunderland that beggared belief. Some of these names will be etched into Villa history in a way that other (better) players who won nothing won't. That trophy being lifted was transformative – a line in the sand for what Villa fans would hope was to come but equally a marker of what success felt and looked like.

The celebrations on Sunday evening after the game went long and hard into the early hours of Monday. Daley, despite being teetotal, siad it was what he imagined what it felt like to be drinking all night. Teale most likely was drinking all night, confirming, 'It was party time and boy did we do it well.' But the difference with the League Cup, as opposed to say the FA Cup, is that it is not a season closer, and Villa and Ron Atkinson had to prepare for a Premier League game in just three days – against Everton at Villa Park. For some time, the Coca-Cola Cup was held up as the one option to prevent the season petering out, but now the trophy was secured (and as a result European football for 1994/95) there was a sense the season would peter out anyway. Atkinson would not be satisfied with such a slide into the summer break, however.

Over 36,000 hardy souls turned out at Villa Park to welcome the team 'home' with the League Cup trophy. The fans serenaded the squad on the pitch before the Everton game, the players displaying a banner reading 'Thanks for Your Support'. Villa Park felt like a carnival, the tension of a big game or indecisive outcome removed, and just pure celebration allowed. Atkinson predictably made changes with Ehiogu, Houghton, Parker, Froggatt and Yorke coming into the side to freshen things up and hopefully fuel a celebratory performance. Persistent wind and rain whipping around Aston did not help but Villa were flat and struggled to create anything until the game was nearly at its halfway point, when Kevin Richardson smacked a long-range punt towards Neville Southall's goal. The club's official review of the season noted that 'winning the Coca-Cola Cup has proved to be an oasis in a desert of barren results' and while those at Villa Park bore the squad no ill will after finally providing them with a trophy, the stark realities of Villa's form and focus would be put to the test over the closing weeks of 1993/94.

A week on from Wembley, Villa paid a visit to Manchester City, who were marooned in the relegation zone. Their hosts' poor form and the harsh reality that Villa had sustained better results away from home gave Ron Atkinson hope that Maine Road could be a genuine place to start looking back up the table. Villa actually started well, with Ugo Ehiogu – finally getting a run of games – looking as commanding as the man he was covering for, Paul McGrath. Andy Townsend and Tony Daley were back in the side after sitting out the anti-climax of Everton. Against the run of play, though, City took the lead when a Peter Beagrie free kick took a wicked deflection off Kevin Richardson, deceiving Bosnich in the process. Moments later, the returning Daley was felled by Keith Curle as he sprinted towards goal – unbelievably the Manchester City defender was not penalised, never mind dismissed for a deliberate professional foul in stopping a goalscoring opportunity. Ron Atkinson described Daley as being 'mugged'. To rub salt into Villa wounds, one of the smallest men on the pitch, City striker Paul Walsh, was left unmarked in the Villa area to head home the second goal. City then made it three through Uwe Rösler in what was their best result since September 1993. A second consecutive 0-0 draw followed at Villa Park, against Norwich. Villa were slap bang in the middle of a bona fide goal drought, with the stark statistic that in the six league games either side of the Coca-Cola Cup win, none of their players had managed to find the net (the goal in the 2-1 defeat by Oldham was an own goal). While the season remained in credit, almost now entirely thanks to the League Cup, the run of form was concerning to an extreme. Questions were bubbling to the surface around the make-up of the side and how that personnel could cope with the rigours of a long campaign. Increasingly, the Wembley win was being seen as a 'last hurrah' for Atkinson's squad as opposed to a catalyst for future progression.

Villa failed to score again away at Blackburn as they slipped to tenth – their opponents cementing their second spot and status as the main challengers to Manchester United, a role Villa had played with aplomb 12 months previously. Some cautious optimism was restored against Sheffield United in the middle of April, albeit through some unusual personnel. With Dalian Atkinson and Dean Saunders on the treatment table, and Tony Daley banished to the bench, Atkinson started with a front three made up of Graham Fenton, Stefan Beinlich and Dave Farrell. The youngsters Atkinson drafted in created numerous issues for Sheffield United's defence, offering width and energy that hadn't been seen in claret and blue since lifting the League Cup. After falling behind, a Farrell cross ended up at the feet of Kevin Richardson before Fenton scored his first senior goal to secure a 2-1 win. The captain's goal marked the end of a run of a staggering 415 minutes without a Villa goal in the league, since that own goal scored by Oldham. Even more unbelievable was that it was 724 minutes since a Villa player had scored – Tony Daley's winner at Coventry.

The next three games firmly extinguished that cautious optimism as Villa lurched toward successive defeats. Farrell and Fenton stayed in the team for a visit from Arsenal, but it was the old-stager Ray Houghton who equalised Ian Wright's first-half penalty. Sections of the Villa public seemed content with a point against the Cup Winners' Cup finalists, but Wright was on hand again in the game's final minute. In many ways it was an Arsenal victory that was undeserved but there was a churlishness in that allegation from a Villa perspective, in that again any tenuous sense of positivity or optimism was only tweaking a veil over the reality the team were facing.

It would have needed to be a thick veil to disguise the fact Villa were, quite simply, eviscerated in their next two games – away at Newcastle and Southampton. German forward Beinlich opened his Villa account after ten minutes in the north-east, but the home side then scored five unanswered goals in what would be Ron Atkinson's biggest defeat as Villa supremo. Southampton came close to equalling that a few days later when putting four past the malingering Villa rearguard. Paul McGrath was back from another AWOL adventure, but Shaun Teale had been injured against Newcastle. Nigel Spink was sent off with around a quarter of an hour to go, forcing Neil Cox in goal, the defender rather inevitably conceding the fourth Southampton goal. Dean Saunders' 16th goal of the season in all competitions was scant consolation. To add to the all-round embarrassment several Villa fans invaded the pitch at The Dell and broke one of the goalposts, for no obvious reason than they sought some better entertainment than on the pitch. Villa languished in tenth, 30-odd points behind Manchester United in a seriously alarming drop-off from the previous campaign, Coca-Cola Cup or not. One home game remained to seek out some sort of solace at Villa Park and mark the end of an era with a rousing finale.

Chapter 12

The Holte's Last Stand

SATURDAY, 7 May 1994 saw the end of the Coca-Cola Cup-winning season, but it also saw the end of another longer-running era and initiated a change that would impact the fabric of Aston Villa Football Club for ever. The last home game of the season, versus Liverpool, would also be the last of the club's famous Holte End terrace, which would be knocked down over the following summer.

In the wake of the Hillsborough disaster in April 1989, which led to the deaths of 97 fenced-in Liverpool fans after the standing pens on the Leppings Lane terrace were over-filled, Lord Justice Taylor had been instructed to complete an overarching report into the disaster – both its causes and also recommendations as to how such a tragedy could be avoided in the future. Taylor's final report was published in January 1990, and although it decreed that the principle initiating factor was a 'complete breakdown of police control', the report would also have stark consequences for the future of standing up to watch football in England. Taylor did not find that standing was intrinsically unsafe per se, but he did conclude that there should be a shift in the balance of seated spectators to those standing, in favour of the former. In line with the already issued 1989 Football Supporters Act, which gave the government power to make stadia all-seated, Taylor's recommendation was clear, writing, 'The Secretary of State should ensure that spectators are admitted only to seated accommodation at matches played at sports grounds designated under the Safety of Sports Grounds Act 1975.' The caveat of the 1975 Act meant that smaller grounds were under different expectation, but for top-tier clubs like Villa the death knell for standing terraces had been sounded. Taylor confirmed his recommendation of all-seated stadia 'should apply with effect from the start of the 1994/5 season to all matches at grounds in the first and second divisions of the Football League'.

The Holte End, along with the other huge terraces of the time at Anfield, Ibrox and the like, had become entwined into the folklore of football. These terraces were overtly linked to the fervour of supporters and often acknowledged as a de facto 12th man, the swaying masses behind the goal creating iconic images of a yesteryear matchday experience. The Holte End ostensibly took its name from the Holte family – and specifically Sir Thomas Holte – a wealthy landowning dynasty who built Aston Hall between 1618 and 1635. The hall, of course, predates a football club in Aston but the Holte family and the grounds of the hall play an important part in the history of Aston Villa. The area where Villa Park is now situated was the former kitchen garden of Sir Thomas, with Aston Hall's ground stretching significantly further through the parish of Aston than now. By the time Aston

Villa Football Club came to the area, having previously played further north in Perry Barr, the former gardens were being used for Victorian pleasure pursuits and were known as the Lower Grounds. Whatever the genealogy of the area, these green spaces, Jacobean stately homes and pleasure grounds give a nod to the grandeur and prestige of the area.

The almost cathedral-like features of Aston Parish Church also give a nod to previous incarnations of Aston as a major rival to Birmingham itself, and there is considerable evidence that initially the 'Holte' End was known as the 'Church' End. It can be argued that Aston was even the more important site of work and trade as the conurbation grew up, and almost certainly had aspirations of city status. Much has changed and the parish of Aston and Nechells is now ranked 118 out of 12,382 (one being the lowest) in the Church of England's deprivation index. It says a lot that more people attend Villa Park every other week than live in the parish (circa 40,000 versus 23,808) and much is to be made of the decline of industry and employers in the area (Kynochs, Ansells) which has led to a population drift away from Aston. Many people associated with the parish church will readily point at the irony of the parish's biggest employer employing people from around the world on million-pound salaries, who don't live and aren't seen in the area apart from on a matchday.

Nonetheless, the naming of the Holte End has ensured that the club's (at least) historical links to the area are noted and celebrated. In its early days, the Holte End was an open, unroofed terrace, typical of many English football stadiums at the time. This basic structure was made of earth embankments, laid in 1914, often with simple wooden or concrete steps to accommodate standing spectators. It was a time when football grounds prioritised capacity over comfort, aiming to fit in as many fans as possible. During the interwar period, particularly in the 1930s, the Holte End saw significant upgrades. The terrace was restructured with reinforced concrete, which improved both safety and capacity. The new concrete terracing allowed for a more organised and stable standing area, capable of holding a large number of fans, enhancing the matchday experience and safety. The mid-20th century was a golden era for many traditional English football grounds, including Villa Park. The Holte End became renowned for its passionate and vocal supporters and in 1962 they were given a roof to cover them at a cost of £40,000. It was following this period that the stand earned its reputation as a fortress, a place where the roar of the crowd could intimidate opposing teams and inspire the home side. The terrace was one of the largest single-tier stands in Europe, capable of holding a staggering 29,000 people at its peak. The atmosphere in the Holte End was electric, with supporters tightly packed together, creating a wall of sound. This era was marked by the rise of football as a cultural phenomenon, and the Holte End became a symbol of this growing culture, known for its vibrant and loyal fanbase.

It is that history and context that made the Holte's 'last stand' in May 1994 so poignant for many, as a deeply ingrained part of the club's and individuals' history was to be ripped down. Amazingly, the Holte housed 19,210 people that sunny May afternoon against Liverpool, approaching half of what was then the Premier League's biggest overall attendance of 45,347. Each entrant into the famous old terrace was issued with an *Evening Mail*-produced certificate to note the occasion, although I often wonder how mine found its way back home with me after several hours in a seething mass of bodies. The huge numbers who wanted to take their small place in a historic end of an era for the club only goes to demonstrate the collective consciousness of football supporters. Those fans afforded the team an atmosphere that belied the terrible end to the league season, with recent hammerings by Newcastle, Southampton and Manchester City firmly in the rear-view mirror. Instead, a parade of former iconic players and the Coca-Cola Cup making another appearance meant all was well in Aston.

Despite the party atmosphere, Villa fans remained desperate for a win to celebrate on the momentous occasion, and equally serious in their desire to see a goal at the Holte End. A chance to celebrate one more time in a way they would never do again in that timeless terrace. To aid that cause, Mark Bosnich was back in goal and managed to fend off several Liverpool attacks single-handedly. He was helpless on 17 minutes, however, as the effervescent Robbie Fowler put the away side ahead in a clear threat to Villa's ambition of an era-ending outcome to cherish. Villa would attack the Holte in the second period, and Ron Atkinson made two changes at the break, throwing on Dwight Yorke and Bryan Small. It had been a frustrating season for Yorke, making only two league starts, but he grasped the nettle here and delivered the Villa public what they yearned for. Twenty minutes into the second half a

Dean Saunders cross-cum-shot landed at the feet of the Tobagan to side-foot home. Villa had an equaliser and the Holte seemed to glow with an electric sense of possibility. With ten minutes remaining, some sterling endeavour by Ray Houghton crafted a second chance for Yorke, and a second goal. As farewells go, it couldn't have come to fruition any better.

The end of an era in terms of Villa Park was confirmed as the demolition teams moved in and by December 1994 a new, all-seated megalith of a stand would exist in its place, still the Holte End in name but not always entirely in spirit. To this day it remains the noise-generating focal point of the matchday experience but the addition of corporate type hospitality spaces in supporters' hallowed ground has caused friction, along with increased prices to further ignite passions. The reality is that the move to all-seated facilities – although crystallised as part of the aftermath of Hillsborough – was and is just another element of the changes to football as a modern consumable product. Two seasons of the embryonic Premier League had begun to tell that story, and the pulling down of terraces was just another in a long list of things that people would miss with the inception of 'modern' football.

On the pitch, while not quite an end of an era, it once again felt like Aston Villa needed some fresh impetus. The Coca-Cola Cup win had been intensely important but not as a great signpost to future progress. Many of the side were experienced but didn't give the sense they would go again more successfully next time around. For Ron Atkinson and his tenure, it was beginning to feel that the triumph was the crescendo to his reign as opposed to a spark. The twin moments of pure elation – Wembley and the last day of the Holte – would cement 1993/94 into Villa fans' consciousness for ever, but they were standalone moments that could not completely disguise the trepidation that many felt going into the 1994/95 season.

Chapter 13

An Interlude: USA '94

SUMMER FOR football fans is a strange time – going from the dog days of analysing the season just finished to looking hopefully towards what happens next. The pulling down of the Holte End offered some sombre reflection, but the heady days of Wembley in March, and the 3-1 victory over Manchester United to lift the Coca-Cola Cup was still being replayed in minds and on VHS alike. The endless rumour mill plays out as we enjoy the sunshine and some time off work while, actually, all we are waiting for is the Walsall away pre-season friendly.

Often, thankfully, we have a major international tournament to distract us. The summer of 1994 saw the World Cup take place in the USA. A strange one to say the least as most people's perceptions of the USA was a country that very much saw 'soccer' as a less important staple than their main sporting offerings. Not that Thom Meredith, former communications director of US Soccer, agreed, saying, 'Anyone who thinks that football isn't a part of the fabric of American life is either an idiot or not paying attention.' But more was at stake than met the eye.

We have already heard in these pages how Italia '90 began a turning of the tide in terms of the perception of football in the wider public consciousness – it might have been a bad tournament for Aston Villa, but it set in motion a process that was, four years on, now in the hands of US Soccer. As Matthew Evans, in his superlative account of the tournament, *USA 94: The World Cup that Changed the Game*, says, 'The fate of the game's globalisation rested on the shoulders of the 1994 World Cup.'

As we have seen, Graham Taylor had left the Villa manager's job to take over the England national team and had led them to an underwhelming Euro '92 in Sweden, where the main headlines focussed on Taylor's substitution of freewheeling frontman Gary Lineker, thus denying the striker his last chance to beat England's all-time goalscoring record. It was a neat summation of Taylor's torrid time in charge of the Three Lions; having drawn the first two group games against France and Denmark, both 0-0, he was in desperate need of a goal against Sweden to salvage something from the group. Lineker hadn't scored or looked overly fit across the tournament so a substitution, even if it was Arsenal's Alan Smith, was not the most inspiring choice. Either way England didn't score and crashed out, the blame laid squarely at Taylor's door. The campaign to qualify for USA '94 went even worse for Taylor and his England side. Away losses to Norway and the Netherlands largely put paid to any idea that England would finish in the top two qualifying spaces, even though they were quite easily dispatching minnows like San Marino. England finished third in their group, never able to capitalise on a strong goalscoring record from David Platt, again working under his former Villa manager. With much ignominy and strife, Taylor had failed to get England to the World Cup for the first time since 1978.

As a Villa fan all was not lost. Jack Charlton, as a player a World Cup winner for England in 1966, had led the Republic of Ireland to the USA. Charlton had taken over Ireland in 1986 and guided them to the European Championship of 1988, where thanks to a Ray Houghton goal they had beaten England. At the 1990 World Cup Charlton again worked his magic, drawing with England on the way to a quarter-final defeat to host nation Italy. Perhaps the Irish high point in the tournament had come in the previous round when they defeated Romania in a penalty shoot-out having worked tirelessly to keep their exciting opponents at bay, despite the unique talents of Gheorghe Hagi. Villa defender Paul McGrath had been central in marshalling Hagi and ensuring the Irish kept a foothold in the tie. Fast forward four years and one Villa representative in Charlton's squad had become four – McGrath now joined by Andy Townsend, Ray Houghton, and Steve Staunton. Given that all four were regular starters for Villa and ostensibly what might be described as fan favourites, following the Republic's fortunes that summer became an extension of following Villa.

Ireland's campaign began against Italy at a sweltering Giants Stadium – a repeat of the 1990 quarter-final – and due to the number of Irish fans who had somehow obtained tickets it felt like an afternoon on the Dublin craic. It wasn't certain that all four Villa men would start – McGrath had been hampered with a shoulder issue since the 1994 Coca-Cola Cup Final and there was a level of expectation that

Houghton would be ceded in the side by the younger Jason McAteer. As it was, all Villa's stars did commence minute one of the game and played an integral part in what was ultimately a 1-0 win for the Republic. After 12 minutes our own Ray Houghton scored what would be the only goal – his tumbling celebration foreshadowing an equally important goal for Villa the following season. Charlton had his doubts about the 32-year-old's worth, but this was the kick-start the Irish needed against a backdrop of huge Irish support in New Jersey.

Paul McGrath was two years Houghton's senior but was central to an Irish rearguard action that protected the lead. Quite simply, McGrath confirmed to the world what every Villa fan already knew and loved. Republic midfielder Roy Keane wrote of McGrath's 'courage' that day and how 'he presented a final, insurmountable object when Italians got sight of the goal'. In clear discomfort and finding it difficult to fully extend his left arm, from official figures, McGrath made an astounding 21 interventions to prevent a goalscoring opportunity, perhaps the best when blocking a rancorous goal-bound effort from Roberto Baggio. The Irish squad famously met the Pope in Italy during the 1990 tournament and his Holiness would surely have approved of Villa's own 'God'. As would happen in the 2022 World Cup with Emi Martínez and Euro 2024 with Ollie Watkins, Villa fans felt huge pride in their own players, no matter their national allegiance.

The Irish moved on to Florida to play Mexico in their next game and again the four Villa players started. They struggled in the heat of Orlando, however, and could not follow up their famous victory – slumping to a 2-1 defeat, although John Aldridge's 'consolation' goal would prove to be more important than at first thought. In his account of the tournament, *Andy's Game*, Villa midfielder and Irish captain Andy Townsend wrote extensively of the impact of the heat but also of the intense disappointment that the team couldn't back up the Italy result. As much as being a Villa fan lent me pride and resonance with the Italy result, the Mexico game similarly meant sympathy in Aston with our Villa boys melting in the heat of Orlando.

It wasn't a surprise that the Villa contingent all started Ireland's third game against Norway back in New Jersey. It was dire – and having watched some highlights before writing this I can confirm it has aged even less well. Nevertheless a, 0-0 draw was enough for the Republic to advance to the knockout stages. Again, a strong defensive performance was marshalled by Staunton and McGrath. Norway manager Egil Olsen described McGrath as quite simply 'the reason we couldn't score a goal'.

Ireland's reward for finishing second in the group was a tie against the Netherlands, back in the humidity of Florida. Again, it wasn't a great game and the Dutch eased to a 2-0 win. From a selfish Villa-related perspective, again all four of Townsend, Staunton, McGrath and Houghton started. At the death two of them combined for what *would* have been a sensational World Cup goal. McGrath controlled a high pass from Houghton by sweeping his leg high in the air and then sliding the ball into the Dutch goal. Alas, McGrath was deemed to have collected the ball dangerously as he had also made contact with Frank Rijkaard's head.

It's fair to say that Ireland's 1994 World Cup campaign petered out after the jubilation of Houghton's winner against Italy. Roy Keane, never slow in coming forward in criticism of his country's attitude, felt that Ireland's tournament was 'over' the minute Italy were defeated. Instead of using the win as a spark to top the group, Ireland seemed relieved, that they hadn't disgraced themselves to the point they relaxed meaning there was a pervading sense of unfulfilled potential. Famous stories of Guinness taps being installed in hotel rooms and Gary Kelly and Jason McAteer reminiscing on Sky Sports that the six weeks in the USA had been like 'the best stag do ever' perhaps says it all. The tournament as a whole was rather a damp squib, but it says a lot for club connections that an interest in Ireland's progress was sustained by the presence of those four Villa players. All four were great servants to the club and their country and exemplify that links and resonance to Villa often transcends the obvious ways we support our club. A 'Villa summer' indeed filtered through Irish eyes.

Chapter 14

1994/95: Pressured Beginnings

WHILE HIS Irish players may have been having the time of their lives Stateside, one can imagine even the seemingly unflappable Ron Atkinson may have been starting to feel the pressure over the summer of 1994. Over the previous two seasons, Villa had lurched from second to tenth, albeit with the hugely credible Coca-Cola Cup success as a sweetener to that slide. As Atkinson reminded anyone that listened, that was a first major trophy for the club in over a decade and had secured another season of European football. The manager's arguments for his own case were valid, but there was a growing sense around Villa Park that something had to give somewhere, with particular attention focussed on the age of the squad and the fact that scoring goals had dogged Villa's development over the whole of Atkinson's tenure, despite sporadic periods that would suggest otherwise. Atkinson's position wasn't up for tangible debate over the summer but looming in Villa's rear view (and every other Premier League side) was a change to the format that would apply additional pressure. The Premier League had made a decision that over the

1994/95 season the competition would be reduced from 22 to 20 teams. The upshot would be that in May 1995 four clubs would lose their Premier League lives, as opposed to three. It wasn't that Villa were under any more threat than anyone else, but the decision spread an uneasiness across the league especially before a ball had been kicked. Added to that mysterious mix was news that refereeing reviews would likely lead to more stringent management of games; a cracking down on physical defence and an increase in red and yellow cards being doled out.

If others were worried about the age of the Villa squad, Atkinson didn't seem to concur. As with the previous summer, the squad was tweaked in the off-season but categorically not overhauled. Indeed, many of those who did leave could have been deemed as younger, future options while those who the naysayers were designating as past their best appeared to be as central to the manager's plans as ever. In terms of incomings, the arrival of John Fashanu from Wimbledon was an outright shock, the physical striker seen by Atkinson as offering some ballast to a potentially different approach. Over the past season, once Cyrille Regis had departed, none of Atkinson's striking options – Dean Saunders, Dalian Atkinson, Dwight Yorke and Guy Whittingham – offered an option of strong hold-up play, often three of the four playing in an all-too-similar and predictable forward line. Fashanu certainly offered something different, his intensely physical and often menacing style having been honed within Wimbledon's 'Crazy Gang' culture and he had come to embody some of that craziness, along with the likes of Vinnie Jones, never more so than when he broke

Gary Mabbutt's skull and eye socket in an aerial challenge. That kind of caricature belied Fashanu's skills and abilities, and uncultured bruisers don't score 107 goals in 267 games, including an FA Cup win. While that caricatured reputation may have preceded him, Atkinson's pursuit made sense in terms of offering alternatives, although as if to prove a point that he was unconcerned about age, Fashanu was already 30 when he signed. Another incomer, Phil King, was slightly younger and Atkinson saw his former Sheffield Wednesday charge offering versatility, but also experience, in defence. Atkinson's other summer signing was young Ghanaian Nii Lamptey, who was something of a phenomenon in Europe as a teenager with Anderlecht and PSV Eindhoven, and for his country in multiple FIFA Youth World Championships where Pelé himself touted him as, well, 'the new Pelé'. King, and to a lesser extent Lamptey, would have their moments over the season to come, but as a triumvirate of new signings the pulses were not overly set racing among the Villa faithful.

Outgoings were not extensive, and the arrivals of King and Lamptey were directly linked to replacing the attributes of those who had left. Neil Cox and Dariusz Kubicki had moved on to Middlesbrough and Sunderland respectively, meaning full-back cover was impacted, meaning the King addition made sense. Kubicki had barely played in the first team since Earl Barrett had arrived, but Cox was more utilised, and came on as a substitute in the 1994 League Cup win. He clearly felt that he should be playing more, however, and a Villa career plagued by his own flexibility came to an end. As a winger, Lamptey was intended to fill the gaps left by the departures of

Tony Daley and Steve Froggatt to Wolves. The two wide players were at contrasting stages of their careers, with Daley bringing down the curtain on a hugely impactful spell at Villa, while Froggatt, like Cox, clearly wanted to prioritise consistent and regular playing time. German duo Stefan Beinlich and Matthias Breitkreutz also left for Hansa Rostock.

An argument could have been made for Cox, Froggatt and Beinlich to be part of Villa's future plans rather than consigned to the past, but Atkinson and the club clearly felt they were unlikely to reach the levels required to get the game time they desired, and the newly moneyed world of English football meant they commanded attractive fees. To underline the lack of ostensible change over that Villa summer, one only has to look at the Coca-Cola Cup-winning side and reserves – Mark Bosnich, Earl Barrett, Paul McGrath, Shaun Teale, Steve Staunton, Dalian Atkinson, Andy Townsend, Kevin Richardson, Graham Fenton, Dean Saunders, Nigel Spink and Ray Houghton all remained as central figures at the club, with only Daley and Cox having sought pastures new. Even the tracksuited squad members that day at Wembley largely remained; Ugo Ehiogu, Dwight Yorke, Bryan Small, Garry Parker and Guy Whittingham all seemingly part of a plan, with again only Froggatt having gone elsewhere. Returning to that idea of pressure, however, the lack of squad transition meant the focus remained squarely on Atkinson to manage the team and squad he had created over the previous three years. It very much felt like *his* team and squad, and he would have to reap the reward or bear the cost.

Atkinson took the squad – minus McGrath, Townsend, Staunton and Houghton as they had some extra recuperation time post World Cup – to HMS *Raleigh* in Torpoint, Devon, a Royal Navy training camp that was well geared up for fitness work and pre-season focus, in mid-July. The Irish contingent excepted, the majority of core players from 1993/94 were in attendance, along with some additional youth players looking to make an impact, such as Scott Murray and Gareth Farrelly, and several youngsters who had seen action the previous season, in Graham Fenton and Dave Farrell.

One senior player conspicuous by their absence was central defender Shaun Teale. There had been some rancorous undertones between Teale and his manager since the end of the previous season. Despite an injury in the hammering by Newcastle, Teale had been named in a provisional England squad, chosen by Terry Venables, to play in some friendlies during England's non-World Cup summer. Atkinson informed Venables early on that Teale would not be fit for the games so the squad was formed without him, but then almost simultaneously Teale was informed by his boss that he would be captaining Villa on a post-season trip to South Africa. It's a narrative that clearly does not sit well with Teale to this day, as despite having the honour of meeting Nelson Mandela and introducing the team as captain, he clearly felt it was the best chance he would ever have to represent his country. The salt in the wound, from a selfish perspective, was that Earl Barrett and Kevin Richardson were selected by Venables and played in the fixtures.

It was on the South Africa trip that it was agreed Teale would take the extra time Villa's Irish contingent would have, in order to have and fully recover from a nose operation and also a double hernia procedure on his groin, therefore missing the camp in Torpoint. The issue seemed to arise – for Atkinson – when Teale, alongside the medical engagements, also went on a family holiday to Florida, Big Ron seeing that as not part of the agreement made, and in Teale's words being 'fixated on the holiday and nothing else'. It's fair to say that, true to their characters, both defender and manager would maintain a steadfast position on these events and refuse to back down. Either way, Teale missed the start of pre-season, Atkinson wouldn't forget the perceived slight and their relationship would never be the same.

Alongside their exertions with the Royal Navy, Villa played two friendlies against local opposition. First, they crossed the county border to Cornwall to defeat Falmouth Town 3-1 with goals from Garry Parker, Dalian Atkinson and Scott Murray. Murray was then rewarded with a start against Torpoint Athletic as Villa eased to a 9-1 win. Murray scored again, alongside a Guy Whittingham hat-trick and one each for Ugo Ehiogu, Dwight Yorke, Dean Saunders, Dave Farrell and Gareth Farrelly. As is often the case in pre-season, Atkinson wouldn't have read too much into these processions, but the training camp – issues with Shaun Teale aside – had served a purpose in terms of building spirit ahead of an important campaign.

As the calendar clicked into August the Irish players started to return and Villa played an array of friendlies in locations almost bizarre in their inconsistency. A 3-3 draw at Oxford United (in benefit to former Villa player and Oxford trainer Ken Fish) was followed by a 0-0 draw away at Atlético Madrid, settled by a penalty shoot-out in which the newly arrived Phil King, in a moment that would foreshadow future events, scored the winning penalty. With the exception of King, Atkinson's team selection entirely resembled what had come before in the previous season, a trend that then continued across a game with Coventry, for Steve Ogrizovic's testimonial, with the addition of Nii Lamptey, who looked impressive on his debut. Villa then made a short trip to Ireland to play Drogheda United (led out by Steve Staunton's brother David) where Lamptey scored his first goal for the club. Shaun Teale was back in the fold, although one of the most instructive lessons from pre-season seemed to be the selection and performances thereof of Ugo Ehiogu, who seemed on track to fulfil every bit of promise that he had shown during sporadic involvement previously. John Fashanu was finally unveiled before Villa's final warm-up against Rapid Bucharest at Walsall's Bescot Stadium. There was some irony in the fact Fashanu failed to score in an 8-0 cakewalk, with his half-time replacement Dwight Yorke notching four goals. Ehiogu and Lamptey sparkled again, both scoring, as the comprehensive win against the Romanians gave some clues to Ron Atkinson's plans for the impending top-flight season.

Villa opened up at Everton with only Fashanu of the new signings starting. A line-up of Bosnich, Richardson (albeit at right-back), McGrath, Ehiogu, Staunton, Houghton, Parker, Townsend, Yorke, Fashanu and Saunders was pretty much 'as was', with Lamptey nowhere to be seen despite impressive warm-up outings. Ehiogu's selection over Teale did confirm what pre-season had seemed to suggest in terms of a changing of the guard, as did Yorke's starting berth over Dalian Atkinson. With Earl Barrett recovering from surgery, the selection of Richardson at right-back ahead of Phil King felt like a very Atkinson selection, preferring to have his favoured players on the pitch no matter their position. King did come off the bench, replacing the injured Steve Staunton, and changed the game – assisting, via a right-wing corner, John Fashanu's first Villa goal (a quintessential booming Fash header) and then setting in motion a move that resulted in Dean Saunders slotting in the second. A 2-2 draw was deemed 'satisfactory' by Atkinson, who was most pleased or relieved by the fact both his strikers had opened their account for the season. King retained his place in the home opener against Southampton. Another draw, this time 1-1, saw another Saunders goal played out in front of the steel framework for the new Holte End. Villa's third game – and second at home – against Crystal Palace could only summon up another draw with Staunton scoring direct from a corner. If an opening draw was seen as satisfactory, only taking two points from six at home was starting to seem a little less so. Some of the issues that haunted Villa previously under Atkinson – failing to score and then conceding late – seemed to remain unaddressed, although the manager didn't concur, reminding everyone that in the process of finishing second in 1992/93 Villa had also drawn their opening three fixtures.

If Atkinson's narrative was born out of a stubborn defence, he was able to be more on the offensive after the next game, away at Coventry. An early Dwight Yorke goal from Andy Townsend's cross, was enough to secure a win, and with six points from a possible 12, and the fact Villa remained unbeaten confirming Atkinson's best start to a season with the club. The *Birmingham Post*'s Andy Colquhoun struck some reality into proceedings by reminding his readership that, despite that 'record', Villa's display was 'limp and error-strewn'. Colquhoun may have been grudgingly more impressed by a 2-0 home win against Ipswich, although Atkinson wasn't there to see it. With the manager in Milan watching Villa's UEFA Cup opponents Inter, Jim Barron took charge and selected a team that gave some sense to that upcoming Inter tie and the UEFA rule at the time that only three 'non-national' players could be selected. Villa were unbeaten in the first five and sat seventh, a reasonable if not entirely secure return, and focus could now shift to Europe.

Chapter 15

Inter Milan and UEFA Cup Glory

ASTON VILLA had been drawn against Inter Milan in the first round of the 1994/95 UEFA Cup, to be played over two legs on 15 and 29 September. Inter were the holders, having defeated Austria Salzburg over two legs in April 1994, but had only finished 13th in Serie A, and owed their participation this season solely on the basis of being able to defend their title. There was a growing interest and awareness in Italian football in the UK, stemming from the launch of *Football Italia* on Channel 4 in 1992. Marketed as a free alternative to the subscription-based service Sky Sports, the show attracted at its peak over three million viewers. Host James Richardson's segments reviewing the *Corriere dello Sport* over a cappuccino in a sunny piazza lent the show a luxurious feel, all of which was supplemented by the antics of Paul Gascoigne, freshly arrived at Lazio.

Football Italia, and its magazine show partner *Gazzetta*, had changed the perception of Italian football from one of dull defensiveness, a legacy perception that had gained popularity through the 1960s as coaches such as Helenio Herrera had popularised a tactical system known as *catenaccio* – literally 'door bolt' in Italian. What unfolded on Channel 4 every week was certainly not *catenaccio*, and viewers were treated to an array of international stars. While this idea may seem commonplace now, the still embryonic Premier League was not littered with foreign talent – although English clubs were subject to the same 'non-national' rules as everyone else, the main issues usually sprang from numbers of British players as opposed to too many Italians or Germans. *Football Italia* thus played an important part in building anticipation for Inter v Villa to go beyond the confines of Birmingham.

Inter and Villa already had their own shared history. As the 1990/91 season dawned, English clubs were, after a five-year hiatus following the Heysel disaster, allowed back into European competition. UEFA had decreed it still too early for English champions Liverpool's own re-admittance after their fans' guilt five years earlier, so it was Villa, as runners-up the previous season, who were one of England's two representatives – they entered the UEFA Cup and Manchester United would play in the Cup Winners' Cup. Led by Dr Jozef Vengloš, the club's first foreign manager, Villa had defeated Baník Ostrava 5-2 on aggregate to set up a second-round tie with Italian giants Inter. The draw initially left Villa facing a trip to Milan for the first leg, but after AC Milan were also drawn at home in the European Cup the legs were swapped to avoid a clash for the two San Siro tenants.

We shall never know if that switch made any difference, but the first leg on 24 October 1990, instead taking place at home, remains for many supporters, quite simply, the quintessential European night at Villa Park. When you look at the line-ups the perceived difference in quality is stark – Inter's three 'foreigners' were Lothar Matthäus, Jürgen Klinsmann and Andreas Brehme, all of whom started the season on the back of winning the World Cup with West Germany. They were joined by Italian stalwarts Walter Zenga, Nicola Berti and Giuseppe Bergomi. Andy Colquhuon in the *Birmingham Post*, meanwhile, described the Villa side as a 'more modestly concocted collection of Football League professionals'. David Platt, himself on the back of a wildly successful Italia '90, was Villa's star, backed up by familiar names like Gordon Cowans and Tony Daley, along with some more forgotten players – the likes of Andy Comyn, for example.

Villa won the first leg 2-0. Kent Nielsen unleashed an unbelievable 30-yard volley to open the scoring before Platt, assisted by an otherworldly diagonal pass from Cowans, made it 2-0. For the 36,461 in Villa Park that night the second goal sparked wild celebrations. It was a timely result given English clubs' transition back to European football and would go some way to beginning a restoration of reputation. As Venglоš said post-match, 'I think it proves that everybody in Europe has to have respect for English soccer again.' The second leg, inevitably, failed to live up to the expectation of the first as Villa were soundly dispatched 3-0 in front of 75,000 in Milan, albeit with the help of some dubious refereeing decisions. Inter's second goal came from a debatable free kick, while the third could have been disallowed for myriad reasons, with the ball appearing to be out of play and then players in offside positions. Inter manager Giovanni Trapattoni praised Villa effusively after the game, alluding to the fact that their performance had shown him 'how much English football has changed for the better'. The reality was that Villa were beaten by a strong Inter side who would go on to win the whole competition, as opposed to having been cheated out of a famous victory, but the opportunity to redress some of that balance in 1994 was welcome.

Inter Milan of 1994 remained a strong proposition, with the German axis being replaced by a Dutch one of Wim Jonk and Dennis Bergkamp, supplemented by the effervescent Uruguayan Rubén Sosa. That non-national spark was built upon a solid Italian foundation, one that still contained the likes of Bergomi and Berti from the clubs' previous UEFA Cup showdown. For Villa, Nigel Spink and Paul McGrath were the sole survivors from four years prior, and Ron Atkinson's team selection was troubled by the UEFA non-national ruling meaning no place for Dwight Yorke in the squad. There may have been some debate about Mark Bosnich's inclusion, although, perhaps conveniently, he had been suffering with injury, meaning Spink could start and Atkinson avoided having to make a decision about another non-English player. After the enforced change four years earlier, the first leg of the 1994/95 iteration was played at the San Siro. Amazingly, only 23,000 were there due to a heady mix of electrical storms, torrential rain, and public transport strikes in Milan. The poor attendance, plus rumoured rancour between coach, player and fans, buoyed Villa fans alongside the dangerous perception that Inter did not have the strength of four years previously. The presence of Bergkamp and Sosa gave lie to that assumption, as did the fact they were defending the UEFA Cup as holders.

Although Atkinson's team selection wasn't especially evolutionary, and he maintained a status quo built around his core of Kevin Richardson, Steve Staunton et al, Phil King and John Fashanu started at the San Siro which suggested there may be a new dawn of flexibility under consideration. What was more revolutionary was the contrast between the two Villa sides of 1990 and 1994 – the gulf in appearance, aesthetics and personnel. The dual Inter ties represent the shifting of the sands in English football, partly crystallised by the inception of the Premier League but set in motion by Italia '90. It is almost like reviewing two different eras when in fact they were separated by less than half a decade. The kits are a fine example of the moving aesthetics, a move from Umbro to Asics, and Mita to Müller as mentioned earlier, pointing to a globalisation of the game that would continue unabated. Even the cut, material and shape of the kits points to a new world of sportswear as a marketable asset and saleable product. In 1990 Villa wore short-cut blouson blue shorts with their shiny, albeit iconic, white away shirt with a black and blue stripe, but by 1994 the Asics top appeared better-fitted and more matte in visual presentation. The personnel for Villa seemed to also shift, with a more rugged, physical player being exchanged for some added finesse – Tony Cascarino and Kent Nielsen in 1990, Dalian Atkinson and Ugo Ehiogu in 1994. Same era, but through my eyes worlds apart.

In Italy, Villa would have to fight for their lives. Paul McGrath and Ugo Ehiogu were superb in central defence, the former playing his hits of USA '94 for Ireland against Italy, and the latter learning from the best. For long spells, Dean Saunders represented the only out ball, and for all his industriousness Villa couldn't gain any long period in possession. With a quarter of an hour remaining, an onrushing Spink was adjudged to have made contact with Sosa for an Inter penalty, which the ever-calm Bergkamp dispatched without concern. In a very Nigel Spink way, the goalkeeper was quietly furious after the game, saying, 'There was no physical contact, the gentleman fell over.' There was no doubt that ending 0-0 would have been the preference but given some of the context Villa were very much in the tie as they headed home.

The second leg would follow two weeks later; quite simply a huge game both in terms of immediate progress but also historic standing. As Ron Atkinson noted in his matchday programme notes, 'It's the kind of match we want constantly at Villa Park.' The manager made just one change from the San Siro 14 days earlier, with Ray Houghton, scourge of the Italians for his national side in the World Cup over the summer, replacing John Fashanu. That change began to feel inspirational in the 42nd minute when Kevin Richardson's aerial pass was deflected off Inter defenders and dropped neatly for the Irishman to drive home the aggregate equaliser. It was eerily reminiscent of the goal he scored for Ireland in New York to defeat Italy, and was easily the midfielder's defining moment for Aston Villa, a fact Atkinson agreed with as he admitted that the 'little man had never played better for me'. The second half was only intermittently ignited by any chances – Spink saved well from Bergkamp, and Davide Fontolan somehow missed a gilt-edged chance, before Guy Whittingham, on for a cricked Dean Saunders, almost made it 2-0 on the night with a deft chip. Ultimately there were no more goals, and the tie would be settled by a penalty shoot-out, encapsulating the drama of the two legs into the endgame of all endgames.

The penalty shoot-out was of course a format to which Villa had become accustomed during the successful 1994 Coca-Cola Cup campaign, although their agent provocateur, Mark Bosnich, was still missing against Inter. Bosnich's record against penalties was exemplary and there was categorically some wringing of hands around the Australian's absence and the potential impact on Villa's chances. As it was, ironically, his replacement Nigel Spink did not indeed make a save as Giovanni Bia, Bergkamp and Andrea Seno all scored for Inter, matched by Garry Parker, Steve Staunton and Andy Townsend for Villa. At 3-3 Spink was still not required as Fontolan, he of the missed chance in normal time, missed again in the shoot-out. Guy Whittingham, in what could have been the chance to really kick-start his Villa career, stepped up knowing that if he scored, Villa were in the ascendancy. The ex-soldier missed. Rubén Sosa, reserved for the final penalty for reasons of technical accuracy and reliability, could only smash his effort against Spink's crossbar. The gauntlet was passed to Phil King, on the surface an unlikely choice but lest we forget that penalty shoot-out in Madrid in pre-season. King wandered to the spot, relaxation personified, and cracked it down the middle to the extreme delight of Villa Park. The Inter goalkeeper that night, beaten by King in defeat, was Gianluca Pagliuca who famously is an Aston Villa fan with tattoos to prove it. Not many goalkeepers who lose a penalty shoot-out go on to describe their emotion at playing in this 'wonderful stadium' in the aftermath.

Atkinson quipped that King had thought Villa were playing against Wigan Athletic because of the blue and black stripes, but the manager knew the vital importance of the result for him and his Villa legacy, and also to settle the nerves that had started to fray as that legacy seemed to be being tainted by inconsistency. Atkinson told the *Birmingham Mail* that he had never enjoyed a match as much in his career, and the newspaper could see why explaining that Villa's 'technical ability' matched Inter's as well as their 'wholehearted effort'. It was a heady brew that success had been built on, and when Atkinson effusively said 'the match was something I will treasure for ever' he wasn't alone.

Chapter 16

Defending the Coca-Cola Cup and the Story of Nii Lamptey

SANDWICHED WITHIN the Inter Milan epic were two league games, both of which Villa lost. Another late defensive lapse allowed Tony Cottee to score a late winner for West Ham in a 1-0 defeat that, although it was Villa's first reverse of the season, felt endemic. Ron Atkinson kept a brave face, joking through gritted teeth that he had played his three Bulgarians against the Hammers – Couldov, Wouldov, Shouldov. He was more dispirited after a 3-1 reverse away at Blackburn Rovers, where Villa were thoroughly outplayed with only a last-minute Ugo Ehiogu goal, his first for the club, to take back down the M6 in consolation. Alongside a stuttering Premier League programme, Villa also opened up their defence of the Coca-Cola Cup between the Inter Milan legs, and once again that storied competition would offer some succour for Atkinson and his side.

A draw against Wigan Athletic, languishing near the foot of the Third Division, was appetising for a team needing goals and a comforting home win. In a two-legged tie, Villa would commence in Birmingham giving them the ideal opportunity to make a statement, even though only 12,433 supporters made the journey to Villa Park. Five months on from the win against Manchester United at Wembley, there is some instruction in looking at the team that faced Wigan in opening Villa's defence compared to the winning side from March. Mark Bosnich, Earl Barrett, Shaun Teale, Andy Townsend, Dean Saunders and Dalian Atkinson all started both matches, although Teale only played due to a Paul McGrath injury, and the fact Ehiogu was named as captain illustrated an undeniable changing of the guard in the centre of the defence. Kevin Richardson presumably would have played if fit, and League Cup winners Graham Fenton and Steve Staunton, dogged by injuries, were on the bench. Ultimately for the fans who did attend the game, it was only the presence of Nii Lamptey in the starting XI that prompted a sense of excitement in terms of novelty at least.

In an era before the *FIFA* video game and the internet, little was known of Lamptey. He had featured relatively heavily in pre-season, and scored goals, but once the season proper commenced he was very much on the periphery. Despite having played for relatively important European clubs – Anderlecht and PSV – his arrival was largely unheralded until some old headlines were discovered with Lamptey being described as 'the new Pelé' by the original one himself. It was that headline that gives the title to Jorius Kaper's book on Lamptey, the cautionary tale of a young and naive footballer which transcends his limited time in claret and blue.

Pelé had burdened the young Lamptey with his blessing during the 1989 U-16 World Championship, hosted in Scotland. Ghana were a relatively new federation but the 'Black Starlets' as the team became known impressed and the 15-year-old Lamptey was at the forefront. By the time the Starlets returned for the 1991 competition, Lamptey was an Anderlecht player and Ghana won the trophy, with Nii named player of the tournament. While he was never a fixture at Anderlecht his star was clearly rising – all against a backdrop of a difficult childhood; Lamptey's father was especially cruel at points, often stubbing cigarettes out on his son. It was no wonder that when Nigerian captain Stephen Keshi helped engineer a move to Anderlecht, Lamptey was happy to travel under a false passport that stated he was Keshi's son.

Lamptey went on to further success with Ghana, winning an unprecedented bronze medal at the 1992 Barcelona Olympics. Although they lost to a Spain team including Pep Guardiola in the semi-final, there was immense pride in Ghana being the first African team to win a football medal at the Olympics. In an understated tone that is a constant of the player and his reflections, Lamptey merely said, 'That was something to be proud of.' Following the summer Olympics, Lamptey still struggled to be a regular starter for Anderlecht and moved to PSV Eindhoven in 1993.

According to Kaper's work, it was a transfer encouraged by fellow future Villa player Luc Nilis, who also moved from Belgium to PSV a year later. At PSV, Lamptey had a strong record with ten goals in 22 games, having the fortune to learn from seasoned campaigners such as Erwin

Koeman, and seemed to be fulfilling that early, much hyped promise.

And so to Villa, and an opportunity to shine against Wigan. Lamptey impressed from the off, keenly demanding the ball and seemingly desperate to show Ron Atkinson he was ready to be involved. Football fans are no strangers to overreaction where new, young players are involved but Lamptey felt different, displaying an energy and probing that had only fizzled with previous wing experiments like Steve Froggatt. As the clock ticked into the 74th minute, Lamptey gladly accepted the ball on the edge of his own penalty area and proceeded to skip and jink past all in front of him, nudging his shot into the net despite being felled to the turf. An electrifying somersault celebration followed as Lamptey captured some claret and blue hearts under the Villa Park floodlights. Lamptey's goal was Villa's fourth of an eventual five that night – with a Dalian Atkinson brace, plus one each for Dean Saunders and Dwight Yorke making it a predictably comfortable night, but still one that lifted the club, at least in part to the emergence of Lamptey. Lamptey would score two more in the away leg, helping secure an 8-0 aggregate win, although the Ghanaian's brace was less spectacular than the 'smasher' as his manager decreed it in the home game.

Villa had made a successful start to defending their League Cup crown, but despite the part Lamptey played in that it would be a difficult journey onwards for him. It's unfortunate in hindsight that Lamptey felt he 'went to England at the wrong time', especially given the excitement of those Wigan games. Nine appearances, with just three of them from the start, tells its own story, but there is a sense that Lamptey was a little ahead of his time in terms of English football and, perhaps, for the tutelage of Ron Atkinson. Interestingly, Lamptey is critical of the style of play in England at the time, lamenting that 'he wanted to get the ball from defence but before I could even ask for the ball it had already been kicked forward'. For all of Atkinson's praise of the mazy run for Lamptey's first Villa goal, a chance born out of that very desire to collect the ball in a deep area, it seemed unlikely Atkinson was about to sanction that type of swashbuckling approach on a regular basis.

Lamptey wouldn't last at Villa beyond the 1994/95 season which, albeit through rose-tinted glasses, seems a missed opportunity at the very least. A move across the Midlands to Coventry City was possibly even less successful, and what followed was a long and many-staged career around leagues as diverse as China, Italy and Argentina. Lamptey talks fondly of his football career, but again the overriding sense is one of tragedy and misfortune – financially and personally. There seems little doubt that his then agent pocketed any signing-on fee from Villa, for example, and Lamptey lost two children at birth on his global travels. To top it off, Lamptey discovered more recently that his surviving children were not his. It is a cautionary tale and one that could have some resonance for young players of any generation.

For all the potential glamour, takes of young men being surrounded by the wrong people are not limited to Nii. His is an extreme example – made even more depressing by that 'new Pelé' tag. There is a lesson here in how we build up young players and pin our hopes on them.

Lamptey's story also helps us consider how multitudes of players have placed themselves (or not) in the Villa historical lineage and will continue to do so. This is a man who made a handful of appearances over a single season, but he is remembered with as much fondness as many other players of that Müller-adorned era. Is that pure nostalgia? Possibly. But nevertheless, reflecting on Villa's opening games of their Coca-Cola Cup success, those fleeting moments from Lamptey against Wigan are part of the story of Villa in this era and us as fans. It's to his immense credit, given the turbulent experiences he has had to endure, that Nii Lamptey has survived to tell the tale himself.

Chapter 17

The End of Big Ron

WITH THE UEFA Cup campaign on hiatus following the late-night penalty drama against Inter Milan, Ron Atkinson had to rouse his side for a quick return to Premier League action. Atkinson refused to be drawn on the idea that the Inter game would lead to an immediate slump as players struggled to shrug off the emotive end to that tie. He was very much of the opinion that the UEFA Cup was merely part of the job, and a professional approach was needed with league leaders Newcastle next up at Villa Park. Villa started well, despite missing Mark Bosnich, Kevin Richardson, Dean Saunders and Dalian Atkinson completely and Steve Staunton only being fit enough for the bench. It was a slightly unusual line-up with Garry Parker once again summoned from the periphery, and Graham Fenton and Guy Whittingham dovetailing with Dwight Yorke up front. Parker was central to some enterprising passing football but that nagging Atkinson trait of flowing build-up not being finished with goals again reared its head. For all their attributes, Fenton, Whittingham and Yorke were not for the moment what might be described as natural goalscorers, not that the missing Saunders and Atkinson had been prolific either. Add that to the fact John Fashanu was about to go under the surgeon's knife, and the lack of goals was an obvious issue. This had been the case for long spells under Atkinson, despite interventions in the transfer market, but he had always been able to turn it around with a string of results. It remained to be seen whether he would be able to continue repeating the trick.

Newcastle punished Villa's own profligacy with two goals of their own in the final quarter to cement their position at the top of the Premier League, while pushing Villa down to 12th. Two wins from eight was damning enough, but that statistic was enabled by another that was even more concerning – in those eight games Villa had scored just eight goals. To provide a contrast, Newcastle were top with 22 points, having notched 25 goals in their opening eight.

A trip to fifth-placed Liverpool was hardly the tonic that Villa might have requested in a bid to stop a run of three consecutive losses, although Bosnich, Staunton and Saunders did all return. Uncharacteristic mistakes hamstrung Villa at Anfield, where firstly Andy Townsend's slip resulted in a free kick which Neil Ruddock drove into the net, and then Paul McGrath failed to clear, a rebound dropping to the feet of the deadly Robbie Fowler. Going two goals down after 26 minutes saw Villa's heads begin to drop as a fourth consecutive defeat seemed to be a stark reality. Guy Whittingham, seemingly finally earning a run in the side, pulled one back but another mistake – this time from Bosnich – undid the striker's good work and allowed Fowler to reinstate the two-goal lead. A late Steve Staunton goal skewed the final score slightly, but Ron Atkinson was fuming about the period after Whittingham's goal, feeling his side were too passive in taking advantage of a momentum change. The manager had a point, but again it was down to missed chances, the stellar example being Dean Saunders heading over from a pearl of a Staunton cross when it seemed easier to score. With the fourth loss in a row confirmed, Villa dropped another two places to 14th and the nerves were firmly starting to jangle.

In an outcome symptomatic of Villa's league struggles, they fell a further place seven days on despite a Saunders goal securing a point at home to Norwich. Atkinson was relieved to finally get off the nine-point mark after those four consecutive defeats, but a tally of ten in ten was hardly vindication of a corner turned. A flat display on the pitch was matched by a flatness in the stands, with many critics suggesting an upcoming UEFA Cup trip to Turkey to play Trabzonspor was taking priority psychologically. If there was a preoccupation with European adventures, any drop-off didn't seem to make a difference. The league-based goalscoring issues pervaded into Turkey as Villa dominated the first half but failed to convert any of some appetising chances, with Whittingham and Ray Houghton the key culprits. The oldest lesson in football is proved that if you don't take your chances when on top, your opposition will have their own period of dominance and you could be punished. And so it unfolded on the edge of the Black Sea as the home side crafted a winner late on, an Orhan Kaynak header sneaking past Nigel Spink. It was difficult to argue with Atkinson's terse summary that in the second half 'they were considerably better, and we were considerably worse'. In terms of the tie, Atkinson knew that there was much to play for, but in the arc of the season as a whole it was another loss characterised by a failure to score.

Predictably, Villa drew another blank back in Premier League action, this time at home against Nottingham Forest. Atkinson tinkered again with his forward options, Saunders and Yorke this time tested as a striking pair to little avail. Whittingham was back on the bench while the manager's namesake Dalian was nowhere to be seen – seemingly punished for a lack of a league goal since January. A 2-0 loss condemned Villa to an unwanted record of just one point taken from the previous 18 available, and it was no surprise that relegation was mentioned for the first time by the manager and the press corps. Despite allusions to 'the drop', Atkinson remained bullish post-Forest, although that was a harder act to sustain after Villa repeated the 2-0 loss trick at Queens Park Rangers to send themselves spiralling down to 18th. Atkinson was forced to admit that his team's self-destructiveness meant 'we're in deep trouble now'. It was Mike Ward, in the *Birmingham Post*, who provided perhaps the key summary of where Villa were at and must have chimed with Atkinson's private thoughts if not his public utterances, 'As ever Villa's rich tapestry of passing, movement and manufacture of chances was a delight to watch. But, just as typically, they displayed a cutting edge that would not have sliced through a cherry trifle. All the more galling was to see Villa ripped apart by their own defensive errors as grotesque as any to unfold before the *Match of the Day* cameras this season.'

Ward's damning words read like an obituary for Ron Atkinson, even without mentioning his name. The themes within – of failing to score goals while making errors at the back – had too often scarred Atkinson's progress. Atkinson knew he was on the ropes – he had been in the game too long to be naive on that score – but there was one redemptive night up for grabs, as Villa played their second leg against Trabzonspor at Villa Park.

Dalian Atkinson was recalled, another attempt at twisting the formula up front, and he rewarded the decision with a display full of physical power and pace. It was the best version of Dalian, not seen often enough, frustration stemming from fans that knew that it was there. As the clock ran towards 80 minutes and the aggregate score was still marooned at 1-0 to the visitors, Villa won a penalty. Steve Staunton's effort was beaten out, initiating a goalmouth scramble that saw Ugo Ehiogu's shot cleared before Atkinson slammed in the opening goal of the night. As the striker wheeled away in the resplendent white Asics kit, never to be worn again, Villa Park breathed a sigh of relief; Dalian Atkinson returning to the glories of 1993/94 and rescuing Villa at the death. The relief was short-lived, however, and Ron Atkinson must have felt his emotions veer from 'one last reprieve' to 'the end is nigh' as Trabzonspor fashioned a goal from nothing, Kaynak driving home despite multiple defenders in close proximity. Although Ehiogu managed to score soon after, it was only half of what Villa needed and they were vanquished on the away goals rule. Atkinson was indignant, telling the *Daily Mirror* that Villa had come second in 'a one-horse race', pointing to the multiple chances that his team had as they swamped their Turkish visitors. It was an all too often used narrative however, and the stark reality was that UEFA Cup progression was gone and there would be no continuing adventure to smooth over the mounting fears of a relegation battle.

After the disappointment of Europe, Villa faced Manchester United at home, desperate to get the season back on track amid the sharp scrutiny of being in the lower reaches of the Premier League table. Ron Atkinson selected the same team as against Trabzonspor, at pains to point out that Villa had won that game and clutching for some sense of momentum shift. The side that would face United, and had played in midweek, was curiously also the XI that had beaten Inter Milan at Villa Park – anyone connected with the club would happily take any spurious signs of fate they could get. It was unfortunately the same old story for Big Ron and Villa as passing pressure was left unfulfilled, despite Dalian Atkinson putting his side ahead on the half-hour, his first league goal of the season. As is often the case with struggling teams, luck evaded Villa and in contrast seemed to seek out United, the ball falling conveniently to Paul Ince to equalise before Andrei Kanchelskis fortuitously got one through Phil King's legs past an unsighted Nigel Spink and into Villa's goal. Atkinson's demeanour post-match was now lacking any of his usual bullish, wry humour with his side isolated in 19th place with just ten points from 13 games. 'I suppose soon they will call for changes in personnel, be it me or the players,' he said. It seemed a long time since Atkinson reminded all who would listen that the opening four games represented his best ever start as Villa manager.

Atkinson could only go game-to-game by this stage, with chairman Doug Ellis twitchily reviewing next steps as the prospect of a serious relegation battle, in a season where an extra club would suffer, became reality. And thus Atkinson took his troops to London to play Wimbledon and offer one last effort at turning things around before it was either too late or before his chairman decided the risk was too big. Despite falling behind, Villa then summoned up one of their performances of the season. Dwight Yorke laid one on a platter for Garry Parker, and Dean Saunders returned to goalscoring action before half-time to make it 2-1. Villa even seemed to survive an Andy Townsend sending-off, Saunders scoring again to open up a two-goal cushion. Surely, this was the beginning of something more positive; if not a corner being turned then at least an indicator being flicked on. Uneasiness started to settle in after Neal Ardley pulled one back just after the hour but hope pervaded that the dire nature of Villa's situation could precipitate a holding out. When Vinnie Jones's speculative effort deflected off Paul McGrath's boot for the equaliser, attention turned to the value of a point gained, but as the game drew to a close Øyvind Leonhardsen's winner for Wimbledon was the sucker punch of all sucker punches. Defeats had become all too frequent, but this was something else – a spirit-crushing conclusion to a horrible run of form.

It's fair to say there was no overwhelming clamour from Villa fans for Atkinson to be dismissed in the wake of the dreadful position the club found themselves in. Inevitably, supporters were disappointed that a second-placed finish and a Coca-Cola Cup win had deteriorated into an apparent relegation dogfight, but the cup success particularly would seem to give Atkinson time and patience that others might not have had. Doug Ellis, it seemed, had other ideas, haunted by the extra relegation place that put in jeopardy the new-found riches of the Premier League. No chairman, even one without the reputation of Ellis, could countenance this and as a result Atkinson was summoned to a board meeting where Ellis summarily sacked his manager in a conversation that lasted less than five minutes. The decision just went to show the power of the new football world in owners and chairmen making decisions that, however drastic, could somehow ignite a team into pulling away from danger. The cost-benefit analysis was just too great in terms of the former – the risk of relegation was one that was not worth taking. While it was quite rare for speculation to be outpaced by the action itself in these type of situations, a statement Ellis released to the *Birmingham Evening Mail* reminded fans subtly that the garden hadn't always been rosy under Atkinson: 'We know the players have had some bad luck, but the law of averages prevails and the buck stops at the manager who had complete control of the playing staff, including those he bought and sold in the last three and a half years. He was never refused money and during last summer I prompted him to buy but he declined, choosing to stand by the existing playing staff.'

Ellis's words felt like a veiled criticism of Atkinson's loyalty to a core of the squad who some would argue was past its best. The fixation on the term 'complete control' was similarly blunt in its conclusion that Atkinson was paying the price for a lack of consolidated progress. Either way, Ron Atkinson found himself dismissed from his role of manager at Aston Villa Football Club on Thursday, 10 October 1994.

Atkinson's overall record was strong and underlines why many Villa fans were taken aback with the timing of Ellis's decision – the overriding sense was that given some more time, Atkinson could have turned things around. A win rate across three and a half seasons of 43 per cent does suggest there is a grain of truth in that belief, but the bigger faith in Atkinson had been created by a triumvirate of achievements rather than an enduring period of success.

The 1991/92 season can be seen, for Atkinson and the club, as one of consolidation and got the team heading in the right direction again, after the missteps of Dr Vengloš. Villa had done exceptionally well to finish second in 1992/93 but there were fans aplenty who would argue that a lack of goals in the run-in gave away their best chance to win the league championship for the first time since 1981. That season was littered with staggering highs but also some dreadful lows, especially when the pressure began to tell. The 1993/94 league campaign was in contrast a disappointment as Villa failed to maintain any sort of consistency. What it did bring of course was a Coca-Cola Cup win that will ever enshrine Atkinson in Aston Villa folklore, his tactical tweaks outsmarting Manchester United in an iconic final. It is the League Cup win, alongside the Inter Milan victory at Villa Park, that will ever define Big Ron's tenure and the very reason many Villa fans hold him in exalted company in terms of the club's many and varied managers. The harsh reality was that 1994/95 had been a disaster thus far, and particularly once Villa had crashed out of Europe, Atkinson was facing an ever-quickening battle against the inevitable as one dispiriting loss followed another. The manager may have gone, but Villa had a season, and a future, to save.

Chapter 18

The King is Dead, Long Live the King: The Return of Brian Little

THE SEARCH for Ron Atkinson's replacement began immediately, as did the speculation of who might be next up in the manager's office at Bodymoor Heath. An initial front-runner was former Villa player Bruce Rioch, who was having some qualified success at First Division Bolton Wanderers having led them to an FA Cup quarter-final in 1993/94 and had them competing well in the title race at the time of Atkinson's dismissal. Ultimately, any interest in Rioch wouldn't materialise, and he led Bolton to promotion and a Coca-Cola Cup Final before departing for an ill-fated spell at Arsenal.

There were myriad other names in circulation, some prompted by the managerial merry-go-round that had been triggered by Osvaldo Ardiles's sacking by Spurs ten days before Atkinson's. Ardiles was replaced at White Hart Lane by Gerry Francis, who was replaced at Queens Park Rangers by Ray Wilkins. Ardiles's availability was probably a red herring, however, and again no concrete exploration happened from Villa's point of view. The first post-Atkinson game was against Tottenham, in what would be Francis's first match in charge, but Villa would be led by Big Ron's assistant Jim Barron and coach Dave Sexton while the search went on.

As is so often the case with a team whose manager has been sacked, Villa found a response, perhaps playing with a little more freedom generally, albeit with the same personnel that Atkinson would have picked. Barron did bring Graham Fenton into the team and was vindicated with a two-goal salvo from the young Geordie. The fact that Dean Saunders and Dalian Atkinson both scored as well was chalk and cheese compared to the goal drought of Ron's dog days, although Spurs scoring three in reply meant issues at the other end would remain a concern for whoever took over the side over the longer term. The three at White Hart Lane, coupled with the four at Wimbledon in Atkinson's farewell, and the two against Manchester United, meant Villa had conceded nine goals in the past three games. There was plenty to work on.

By the time the whistle had blown against Spurs, the appointment of a new Villa manager seemed to be progressing. Another former Villa player, Brian Little, had emerged as the new front-runner, but the situation was complicated by his current employment. Little had joined Leicester City as their manager in 1991, leading them to a play-off final with a place in the about-to-be-established Premier League up for grabs. It set off a remarkable chain of events for Little and Leicester in a battle to reach the top flight, although that was thwarted at the end of the 1992 season by Blackburn Rovers, who won at Wembley to secure promotion. In 1992/93 Little galvanised his side again to reach Wembley in the play-offs 12 months later, defeating Portsmouth in a semi-final before losing to the odd goal in seven to Swindon at Wembley. Amazingly Little went again, and in 1993/94 Leicester reached their third consecutive play-off final, beating neighbours Derby County to finally secure promotion to the top tier. Rightly so, Little's achievements were hugely regarded by Leicester fans and the club and there was quiet confidence he could lead them into the Premier League and create some stability at the top table. At the time Villa's keenness for Little was becoming clear, Leicester had won just two of their 13 Premier League fixtures and looked doomed, not that Little's own future at Filbert Street was in question. That explains why Villa's interest was so angrily received by Leicester's board and chairman; they felt that they had a strong relationship with Little and had stood by him over a long but ultimately successful period. Moreover, they were keen to point out that Aston Villa were also in a relegation battle in the same division.

There was some inevitability that Little would be intrigued by Villa's interest. Although born in Newcastle, Little's playing career was centred in Birmingham and he left an indelible mark on Aston Villa. From his early years, Little showed immense promise and his journey through the ranks began when he joined the club as a youth player. His talent was quickly recognised, and he made his first-team debut in 1971 at just 17 years old. That marked the beginning of a decade-long association with Aston Villa, where he would become a fan favourite and one of the club's most influential players during the 1970s.

As a forward, Little was known for his exceptional pace, technical skill, and an uncanny ability to find the back of the net. These attributes made him a constant threat to opposition defences and earned him a key role in attack.

Little's impact was immediate and he quickly established himself as one of the most exciting young talents in English football. His breakthrough came in 1974/75, a pivotal year for both him and the club. That season he played an instrumental role in Aston Villa's successful campaign to win the Second Division, securing their promotion to the top tier. His 20 goals that season were a testament to his emerging status as a top forward, and his performances helped Villa return to the First Division after an eight-year absence.

The following seasons saw Little continue to rise in prominence. In 1975/76 he became the team's top scorer, solidifying his reputation as one of the most dangerous forwards in the league. However, it was the 1976/77 season that would for ever etch Brian Little's name into Aston Villa folklore; he was the driving force behind the League Cup success. In the final against Everton, Little delivered one of the most memorable performances of his career. After the first match ended in a draw, the final went to a replay where Little scored twice to secure a 3-2 victory for his side. His heroics not only won the trophy but also made him a hero among the Villa faithful. That same season, Aston Villa achieved a fourth-placed finish in the First Division, their highest in many years, with Little's contributions being a significant factor in their success.

On the international stage, Little's talent did not go unnoticed. He earned his first and only cap for England in

1975. Although his international career was limited, this cap was a recognition of his ability and the impact he was having at the domestic level. However, competition for places in the squad was fierce, and Little was up against some of the best forwards in the country. Unfortunately, just as he was reaching the peak of his powers, injuries began to take their toll. Little's career was plagued by persistent knee problems which started to severely limit his playing time. Despite various attempts to overcome these issues, the injuries became too debilitating, and in 1980, at the age of just 26, Little was forced to retire from professional football.

The early end to his playing career was a significant loss to English football as Little had the potential to achieve even greater heights. However, his impact during his playing days was undeniable. At Villa he is remembered not just for his goals and skill, but for his passion, dedication, and the joy he brought to the fans. His flair on the pitch, combined with his crucial role in some of the club's most memorable moments of the 1970s, has ensured his place as one of Aston Villa's all-time greats. Even once enforced retirement drew playing to a close, Little's links with the club did not abate. While waiting for insurance premiums to come through after the spell of injuries, Little worked for the print shop that produced the Aston Villa matchday programme. He also worked for what was then called the Development Association, which sold various Villa-related scratchcards and prize funds, many of which were overseen by Little, driving around Birmingham in a Mini Metro adorned with claret and blue Aston Villa branding. Amazingly, Little even worked in the club shop after his retirement, the sort of story from late-1970s football that would make current players' and young supporters' eyes pop today. Tony Barton, Villa's supremo when they won the European Cup in 1982, then gave Little an opportunity to manage and coach the youth team, a role he held until a falling-out with new manager Graham Turner in the summer of 1984. Any young, ambitious manager with such explicit links to a club with the history and prestige of Aston Villa would surely find it hard not to at least be intrigued by what Doug Ellis had to say.

In fairness to Little, in testament to the relationship he had built up with Leicester and the city's footballing community, he felt genuinely 'torn as to whether I should take the job'. Little's assistant at Leicester was another former Villa player, John Gregory, who in the manager's account encouraged him to go for the job 'as you may never get the opportunity again'. One former Villa player to another, both aware of the standing of the club and their personal histories within it; it was an argument that made sense. Whether Gregory was instrumental or not, Little seemed to decide that Villa was where his future lay, and in his words, 'When I make my mind up about something, that's what I am going to do.'

Leicester seemed unlikely to easily engage with Little's desires, however, making a statement which read, 'Villa will never be given permission to speak to the manager. If he walks out with 30 months left on his contract there is no way he could manage Villa.' For Leicester that threat was unenforceable, and the way they put forward their own views would have made the stubborn Little even more likely to want out. In Little's memory, he told the Leicester chairman that he would 'pack in management' if he wasn't allowed to speak to his old club, although this became twisted in some sections of the press that Little said he 'wouldn't go to Villa if he left Leicester'. One can understand Leicester's frustrations but the realities of standings of football clubs were not wholly different 30 years ago in that loyalty is not overvalued by any party. Little had become determined to 'prove I was worthy of the position of Aston Villa manager'.

With the acrimonious situation between Leicester and Villa festering, Little held a press conference to tell people that 'at this stage in my life I have to do something else'. The Leicester board placed on record their sincere thanks to Little, repairing some of the damage to a relationship that had been wholly positive as he had transformed the club's fortunes. No mention of Villa was made as Little's Leicester managerial career had a line drawn under it, but just three days later he was announced at Villa Park. He was followed by John Gregory, who resigned immediately, telling Little, 'I am coming with you.' Slightly unusually at the time, Little had two assistants, the other being yet another man entrenched in Villa folklore: Allan Evans. Evans, a member of the 1982 European Cup-winning team and with over 380 appearances across a 12-year stint, would join his fellow alumni but with a slight delay after he took charge of Leicester's game with Arsenal.

A new era had begun – one that was intrinsically linked to Villa's heritage.

Chapter 19

Settling into Survival Mode

BRIAN LITTLE was not afforded any significant time to settle in before his new Aston Villa side were back in Premier League action. Villa faced Sheffield Wednesday at home in Little's first game as the calendar prepared to tick into December and given the lack of any lead-in it was no surprise that he fielded the same team Jim Barron had picked against Tottenham Hotspur a week earlier. Although Little had inherited a team languishing in 20th place, Wednesday were also rooted in relegation trauma, so the game presented a decent opportunity for the new manager to hit the ground running. Villa started well, Little's new charges apparently keen to impress their new boss and hope sprung eternal in the Villa Park stands when Dalian Atkinson, after good work by Garry Parker, put them ahead. Ten minutes later Villa could have gone 2-0 up when Graham Fenton sent in a rasping shot only for a sprawling Kevin Pressman to somehow prevent a goal. That was about as good as it got as Little watched his team drain of energy and impetus, seemingly running out of ideas despite the bright start. Nobody was surprised when more haphazard defending led to an equaliser. A 1-1 draw would have left Little in no doubt that there would be much work to be done, and he alluded to adjustments to come post-match, acknowledging that the first half was strong but the drop-off in the second was a concern and rating the performance as 'nine out of ten in the first, five or six in the second'. It was clear that Little was serious about his task and that, in time, there would be changes in method and personnel, saying, 'I'll do what I have to do to improve things.'

If the Coca-Cola Cup had been some solace for Ron Atkinson, it was more of a distraction for the new man, whose sole focus was now on survival. That said, for a fourth-round tie with Crystal Palace (Middlesbrough had been beaten 1-0 in the previous round, towards the end of Atkinson's reign) Little named a strong side, with only winger Dave Farrell a slight outlier. Everything went wrong after the team was selected – Ugo Ehiogu was sent off before the half-hour mark, and although Atkinson put Villa ahead soon after, the goalscorer then limped off with a pulled hamstring. Four goals in 40 second-half minutes for Palace seemed a sad way for Villa to give up their defence of the cup they had secured in such an exhilarating way just a few months prior. If the victory against Manchester United had been built on firm foundations of pace and power, the defeat to Palace represented as limp and disappointing a display as had been seen for some time. The contrast between winning the competition in March and crashing out in November exemplifies the steep slide Villa had made – again, Little was reminded that getting away from trouble in the league would be no cake walk.

While the personnel could still be effective and show quality, they seemed to have lost the optimism that came with winning games, and it increasingly felt like a cultural change was needed to move things forward.

Even in these early days of his Villa managerial career, Little was aware of the differences between his former roles at Leicester and Darlington, compared with a club of the scale of Villa. He reflected, 'I was now dealing with top-quality footballers who naturally had their own opinions on the game and responded in different ways.' Little knew he had to exercise his views and methods on to the squad, but even in these early exchanges some were less engaged than others; Dean Saunders and Dalian Atkinson shied away from group possession sessions, for example, preferring to focus on their own finishing.

Little was a coach in a different sense to Ron Atkinson – he wanted to be involved and showing his charges the vision of his tactics and style. While Atkinson enjoyed joining in five-a-sides, there is no doubt his sessions were more light-hearted compared to the 'serious' approach of Little in getting his ideas across no matter the views of players, senior or otherwise. Little had just undergone serious back surgery prior to his appointment so was not physically able to lead sessions at Bodymoor Heath as he hoped. He was clearly concerned by this, and it meant setting the tone early was difficult, especially when he was trying to change habits among many of those senior figures. Little was firm from the outset, saying of his players, 'They may not want to do it this particular way, but it was the best way of doing it.' It was clearly an approach that was going to rankle with some of Atkinson's established core.

In Little's third game, an unfortunately timed return to Filbert Street to play Leicester City, he demonstrated with clear intent that he was in charge. Mark Bosnich and more sensationally Paul McGrath were named on the bench – for the latter, the first time in his Villa career he had been a substitute. How serious a message it was is debatable, especially as both players would prove central to Little's Villa side, but the changes were an overt nod to others that he was prepared to make difficult decisions. That decision would have paled into insignificance in terms of difficulty when Little arrived in Leicester for the game. A febrile atmosphere turned hostile quickly, and he was greeted with homemade banners reading 'Liar' and 'Judas'. Barracking Little throughout, there was no doubting the Leicester public's feelings, and even decades on the official Leicester website described the 'sense of betrayal and hurt when Little walked out on the club 18 years ago this week was palpable and very deeply felt'. On the pitch, Shaun Teale was back in the side after missing the past dozen games, and Bryan Small made his first appearance of the season, with Guy Whittingham given a chance to show his new manager he had a part to play. It was Whittingham who earned Little and Villa a point and drew a line under the acrimony.

Having secured a draw at Leicester, Whittingham started again, at home against Everton, in what proved to be the third consecutive league draw since Little's appointment. It also proved to be Whittingham's last game for the club, drawing a blank in a 0-0 draw that represented Villa's first clean sheet in the Premier League for three months. Whittingham was used as a makeweight in Little's first transfer business for the club, in which he brought in a player who would prove integral for him and several other future Villa managers, Ian Taylor. Born in Birmingham, Taylor was a Villa fan who had sneaked on to the Holte End as a child but had worked his way up through the leagues via Moor Green and Port Vale to Sheffield Wednesday, so wasn't especially known to supporters. What Little saw though was a high-energy midfielder whose commitment would provide the side with new impetus compared to the likes of Kevin Richardson and Ray Houghton. It was the first sign of a gradual changing of the guard within the squad. For Whittingham, it was always going to be tough to replicate his goalscoring feats at Portsmouth at the top level and a new challenge seemed to make sense. Little was clearly beginning to divide the squad into those who would meet his expectations and those who would not.

Taylor missed a sloppy defeat to Southampton before making his full debut in a home draw with Arsenal. It still felt like Little was tinkering in an attempt to work out his best side, with John Fashanu back in the fold but lacking impact. Andy Townsend had returned from a six-game suspension but was sent off again, and the fact that Little replaced Dean Saunders with Paul McGrath with 20 minutes to go said everything about Villa's priorities and the importance of a point in their perilous predicament. The 0-0 draw left Villa in 20th but Little had stopped the rot that had set in during the last weeks of Ron Atkinson's time and in doing so seemed to have laid some foundations on which to build the mission for survival.

Just two days after Arsenal, Chelsea came to Villa Park and what unfolded further moved the barometer to positive. Played out in front of the newly, fully opened Holte End, Villa were unrecognisable, irresistibly pouring forward, driven by the newly added Ian Taylor. In a storybook ending, Taylor scored a thumping header to add to goals from Dwight Yorke and Steve Staunton (via Frank Sinclair) to secure a first home win since September. Little was relieved but couldn't resist wryly acknowledging, 'To merely scrape a win would have been pleasing enough but to do it with such style was just what we needed.' 1994 drew to a close with a comeback draw against Manchester City, leaving Little with a league record of five draws, one win and one loss in seven. It was a fair return and most pleasingly given the ongoing battles to come, was characterised by a resolve that had gone missing pre-Little's arrival. This resolve was characterised by the signing and resultant influence of Ian Taylor, meaning Villa fans approached the new year with, if not expectation, then certainly hope, that avoiding relegation was absolutely achievable.

Chapter 20

One Step Forward, Two Steps Back

1995 BEGAN as 1994 had finished, with another draw, this time at home to Leeds. Played out in treacherously icy conditions, there was little to write home about other than the continued defensive solidity that Brian Little appeared to have instilled – the clean sheets the new boss had overseen was double Ron Atkinson's tally for the season. Despite Little's positive style as a player, it was clear to all that he had set about turning things around by building a firm defence as a priority, knowing that not losing games initially would settle the ship.

Although the Leeds game felt like more of the same medicine, there was another tweak which was more instructive as to how Little would look to set up for the longer term and mould his squad. Against Leeds, Little started Shaun Teale, Ugo Ehiogu and Paul McGrath for the first time together, who along with Earl Barrett and Steve Staunton at times formed a back five – the full-backs seen more as wing-backs in attacking phases. Atkinson had used Staunton further up at times, but this felt different especially in transition and pointed to a different approach, that while commonplace now was less so in 1995 as managers felt less confident in deviating from a traditional 4-4-2. It was with wing-backs in mind that Gary Charles was signed on 6 January 1995 from Derby County for just under £1.5m. Charles had emerged initially under Brian Clough at Nottingham Forest, where his manager had described him as a 'gazelle', and he had won two England caps during his time at the City Ground but was more often remembered for being the victim of Paul Gascoigne's challenge in the 1991 FA Cup Final that led to Gazza being taken from the field on a stretcher. A move to Derby was a success and Charles built a reputation as a modern, attacking full-back, being selected for the 1993/94 PFA Team of the Season. Little clearly saw Charles as an upgrade on Earl Barrett, who although had a similar style was slightly older and lacked the raw pace of Charles. The deal for Charles was actually a joint one with his Derby colleague Tommy Johnson also joining Villa. Johnson had come to public attention at Notts County where he scored a commendable 47 league goals in 118 games, and he had a solid record at Derby. For Earl Barrett in Charles's case, read Dalian Atkinson for Johnson's – the new additions were both 24 with those they were earmarked to replace nearly four years their senior.

Neither Charles nor Johnson were involved in a diversion to FA Cup action away at Barnsley, although both watched from the stands as the experiment with three centre-backs flanked by wing-backs tentatively continued in a professional 2-0 Villa win. Johnson started next up at Villa Park, against Queens Park Rangers, although ironically it was the lesser-spotted John Fashanu who opened the scoring. Villa seemed ill at ease with Little's new formation, with Dwight Yorke forced into midfield alongside Ian Taylor and failing to influence a stop-start display. A booming Ugo Ehiogu header secured three points and, crucially, finally edged Villa out of the relegation zone. Little confirmed what everyone else was thinking though when he said, 'It wasn't a great performance – we would like to play with a little more style, but at the moment we are result-orientated.' The manager also alluded to his tactical shift and team set-up, acknowledging that as Villa were in essence having to practise in-game there were bound to be teething issues, as opposed to having a pre-season to iron out difficulties.

Little was, as we have seen, a steadfast character and if he believed in something he was going to see it out, and results (broadly) had shown a reward for his persistence. Those rewards were greatened with another win – and Little's first away from Villa Park – against Nottingham Forest where another Fashanu goal set the team on their way. The Forest victory exemplified one of the knock-on benefits from selecting three centre-halves, in that Steve Staunton was able to impact play further forward, especially in getting into positions to cross the ball. The Irishman had a wand of a left foot, and laying on goals for Fashanu and then Dean Saunders was testament to what he could bring to the team beyond being a perfectly effective 'traditional' left-back. The win catapulted Villa up to 14th and began to neuter some of the darker fears of a drop out of the Premier League. It was evidence of the fraught nature of the relegation battle that season that two wins in a row could suddenly flip a team's perspective, but equally with four to go down, the opportunity to get sucked in was ever present.

As it was, Little oversaw a third consecutive win, against Spurs, that further consolidated Villa's new-found position of relative safety, the team inching up to a barely credible 12th place. Little garnered considerable attention for the perceived turnaround, even winning the Premier League Manager of the Month award for January. The new defensive system continued, but the midfield was bolstered by the return of Andy Townsend, who instantly created a better balance in the side. A truly memorable Dean Saunders thunderbolt had put Villa in the ascendancy, but the game would be better remembered for a shocking incident involving Spurs and Germany superstar Jürgen Klinsmann. Mark Bosnich had initially been dropped by Little but had managed to fight his way back, partially aided by some poor health for Nigel Spink. Since his return, though, Bosnich had been erratic to say the least, mixing his usual acrobatics with some incomprehensible 'rush of blood to the head moments'. The same was to be the case here as Klinsmann ran through the middle chasing a long ball, only to see Bosnich careering out of his goal, beyond the penalty area, and flying through the air into the striker. It was a dangerously ugly error of judgement that left Klinsmann out cold and stretchered off the pitch, while the Australian somehow escaped any card-related sanction. If it wasn't for another severe lack of judgement that night, as Eric Cantona kung-fu kicked his way into the stands at Selhurst Park, Bosnich may have come under more scrutiny for his own flying kick.

If Villa needed a reminder that short-terms gains hadn't completely removed peril from their position, two visits to Manchester in a week proved to be just that. Firstly, the blue side of the city knocked Villa out of the FA Cup and then their red-shirted neighbours inflicted a first defeat in nine games on Brian Little's side. Sandwiched between the games was the sale of Earl Barrett to Everton, a piece of business that was barely a surprise, but the way the right-back's situation had progressed was peculiar. It had absolutely seemed that Gary Charles had been acquired from Derby to replace Barrett, and yet in the nearly four weeks since Charles signed he hadn't started a game with Barrett being selected in them all. That intervening period appeared to be lessening the chance of Barrett going, only for him to make the move to the north-west anyway. Barrett had been an outstanding contributor for Villa, across over 140 league and cup appearances, including the 1994 Coca-Cola Cup Final. He had coped well with Ron Atkinson moving him from the centre of defence to right-back, and as his Villa career progressed his flexibility reaped great reward for Atkinson and the team. The fact he had kept his place even after Charles's signing is testament to his professionalism and quality, although ultimately a change would have to come so it made sense to explore options. The departure allowed Charles to make his first start, at Old Trafford, and he impressed defensively and offensively in a game that Villa could never quite gain a foothold in, despite some scintillating attacking play. Tommy Johnson had his most promising appearance in a Villa shirt albeit to no avail. Not for the first time, a new Villa striker needed a goal.

Johnson's first goals would come against Wimbledon at Villa Park, in a game that was the clear high point of Brian Little's early reign. The 7-1 win was Villa's highest league margin of victory for over 30 years, and while it was not a surprise that it was their record Premier League win, it did match the previous highs in the embryonic competition. This being the Villa-verse, they went 1-0 down but immediately responded and carved Wimbledon open at will. Johnson got a 16-minute hat-trick, all three goals being the sort of poacher's finish that Villa had often missed under Ron Atkinson, while the new man's positioning also freed Dean Saunders up, and the Welshman scored a brace of his own. An exquisite Dwight Yorke chip rounded things off and an elated Villa found themselves up to 11th, with the supporters having witnessed potentially the team's best league performance of the 1990s thus far.

The excitement of a big win and the securing of, for now, mid-table status glossed over some more changing of the guard in terms of personnel which marked the fact that the dismantling of Ron Atkinson's team was reaching fruition. Before the evisceration of Wimbledon, Garry Parker had been sold to Leicester City and a few days later Kevin Richardson was also moved on, joining up with Atkinson again at Coventry City. Parker's impact had always felt fleeting at Villa, often failing to string a run of performances together despite his obvious skill and talent when passing the ball. Nevertheless, he had been a big part of the past four years and although he didn't take the field in the 1994 Coca-Cola Cup Final, he had played in that run and was seen as an important squad member.

Along with Richardson, however, in Little's eyes Parker was representative of how Atkinson had let the squad run stale and perhaps not pushed the envelope of change when it was needed. Richardson has more of a lasting legacy at Villa, backed up by 180 appearances and captaining the winning team at Wembley and being named the man of the match. For Richardson, the image of him lifting the trophy will for ever be enshrined in Villa history, and his commitment was total, an ever-present in the league across 1991/92 and 1992/93, and only missing two games in 1993/94. Little acknowledged that Richardson took the decision to let him go badly, and the sight of the former captain sat as an unused substitute against Wimbledon, and then never to be seen again, was a sad denouement for a great servant to the club.

Interlinked to Garry Parker's departure to Leicester was the arrival of winger Franz Carr from Brian Little's former club. Carr began an underwhelming spell at Villa on the bench against Sheffield Wednesday, where their play was described by club writer Dennis Shaw as 'quick, penetrative and exhilarating', a set of terms that could often be applied to Ron Atkinson's time in charge. The key difference under Little was that Villa were scoring goals consistently. At Hillsborough, another Dean Saunders brace was enough, in the striker's 100th game for the club, and elevated Villa to their highest position of the season – ninth. Villa appeared upwardly mobile, and with Little given the time and scope to alter the playing staff his vision seemed to be, as every week went past, ever closer to being realised. What followed the win against Wednesday was a sliding doors moment of the season and on reflection a key moment in defining what could have come after, and what actually did.

As February 1995 drew to a close, Leicester were the visitors to Villa Park, Garry Parker among their number. While hardly harmonious, the vitriolic reaction to Brian Little's departure had calmed, with the visitors more concerned about their own issues, entrenched in the relegation zone and beginning to despair. Villa lined up with what Little had settled on as his preferred team: Mark Bosnich, Gary Charles, Ugo Ehiogu, Shaun Teale, Paul McGrath, Ian Taylor, Andy Townsend, Steve Staunton, Dwight Yorke, Tommy Johnson, Dean Saunders. They started like a train, Saunders scoring after just eight minutes, after Steve Staunton's long-range effort deflected off him. Staunton scored himself before half-time to make it 2-0, collecting a pinged cross-field pass from Yorke to drive the ball in from 20 yards out. Yorke scored a third on the hour, and although Mark Robins pulled one back for Leicester, when Tommy Johnson made it 4-1 with a stunning lob the game seemed to turn into a procession. Of course, Leicester, wounded and in deep troubles of their own, were in no mood for rolling over any further and once the Holte End started greeting Villa passes with gloating 'oles' the visitors added anger to their anxiety. Firstly, Iwan Roberts made it 4-2 before substitute David Lowe scored twice in the last ten minutes to somehow force a 4-4 draw.

If Leicester deserved some credit, Villa deserved consternation as they capitulated through a mixture of arrogance that the game was won and panic once there was any doubt cast in that. As an isolated outcome on a wet Aston night, it was a tough one to take, but there now lingers a feeling that the result represented a pivotal moment for the remainder of the season. Had Villa held on they would have sat seventh with 40 points, having won three on the bounce. As it was, a morale-busting Leicester comeback had not only limited points gained but seemed to sow a seed of doubt in the Villa ranks that just maybe there was still cause for concern.

That argument was given weight over the next four games, in which Villa undid much of the good work that had settled their position since Brian Little's arrival. Title-chasing Newcastle had a wonderful recent record against Villa, and they continued that trend with a 3-1 win, a result that was compounded by another loss to Blackburn at Villa Park. Both opposition sides were involved at the top of the table but given the progress under Little there was a disappointment that nothing could be taken from either game, especially as a return of zero points saw Villa slip back down to 11th. Worse was to come as Ron Atkinson and Kevin Richardson returned to Villa Park for a stupor-inducing 0-0 draw and then an average West Ham side dispatched Villa 2-0. The West Ham result was especially galling given that they started the game five points behind Villa and finished it two adrift – losing to sides at the top was one thing but losing to those around you only results in being pulled right back into trouble. Little didn't mince his words, admitting that the West Ham showing was the worst since he took charge: 'We have been sucked right back into trouble and it all started the night we gave a 4-1 lead away against Leicester. The honeymoon is over for myself, and I have to work as hard as the players to put it right.'

The West Ham game marked the debut of left-back Alan Wright, signed from Blackburn for around £1m, and also the last time Ray Houghton would be seen in a Villa shirt, moving on shortly after to Crystal Palace. Wright was largely an unknown factor and hadn't been first choice at Blackburn, but Little clearly saw the dynamism he wanted on the left side. The departure of Houghton was not a shock given Little's dismantling of Ron Atkinson's midfield, and the Irishman would have wanted to garner as much playing time as he could elsewhere. Houghton would be best remembered in claret and blue for the winner against Inter Milan at Villa Park, but he contributed much and often across 100-odd starts, including important goals in the 1994 Coca-Cola Cup campaign, although he was an unused substitute at Wembley. Little's personnel changes continued at pace but they were not being backed up with results and consolidation of safety.

Sometimes, teams deep in the mire need a piece of unwarranted good fortune to stem the tide, and as April 1995 dawned Aston Villa got just that against Ipswich Town at Portman Road. The hosts, even further down the table than Villa, had their own issues and as a result the match was cagey and tight with neither team wanting to give an inch. For his part Little started with Ehiogu, McGrath, Teale, Charles, Wright and Staunton, giving a sense of what was to come. As the dour exchange approached the final whistle, Gary Charles made a rare foray up field before crossing hopefully into the Ipswich box. Dean Saunders and Dalian Atkinson had both been substituted and their replacements, Dwight Yorke and Graham Fenton, seemed surprised by Charles's application and were too deep. Inexplicably, Ipswich defender Chris Swailes headed the cross past his own goalkeeper to give Villa a 1-0 win. An undeserved three points maybe but Little didn't care a jot, saying that he 'made no apologies, I don't mind how we get them'. The win edged Villa back up to 13th, and an equally cautious and anxiety-ridden 0-0 with Crystal Palace – whose team included the recently departed Ray Houghton – nudged them even further away from danger to 11th. On one hand, surely Villa had become pragmatic and had done enough to secure their Premier League safety, but on the other they were still only five points clear of the first relegation place. As the season had taught them, nothing could be assumed.

There was deep irony that at 4-1 up against Leicester, most Villa fans and pundits would have concluded that Little had solved the team's long-standing issue with consistent goalscoring. Yet since then, a Villa player had only scored once in the next six games – Andy Townsend's goal against Newcastle, with the isolated winner at Ipswich having been an own goal. There was some truth in the fact Little had retreated tactically to a position where Villa were hard to concede against and hard to beat, but the ever-recurring issues of goals just couldn't seem to be escaped. Six became seven as Little oversaw a 1-0 loss to Chelsea, a result that saw the Londoners leapfrog Villa. Arsenal at Villa Park followed in what was a genuine moment of questioning of Little by supporters as he abandoned the defensive mindset. It hadn't been pretty, but an extra central defender had at least kept things tight, and while no fan desperately yearns for solidity, neither do they want their team relegated. Against Arsenal, Dean Saunders, Dalian Atkinson, Dwight Yorke and Tommy Johnson all played, with a more traditional back four in place albeit with Ugo Ehiogu at right-back. If it was an attempt by Little to try and carve open Arsenal and initiate some attacking progression, it was a spectacular failure as the Gunners eased to a 4-0 win. It was the worst result at Villa Park in four seasons and Little seethed afterwards, talking of indiscipline and 'heads dropping', especially after Dean Saunders had missed a penalty at 2-0. More worrying was that Arsenal started the day only three points clear of Villa, so were not as daunting a prospect as the eventual scoreline might suggest. Everyone connected with the club seemed dumbfounded as to what was unfolding, not least the manager himself, who couldn't fathom that 'two months ago I couldn't do anything wrong and even picked up an award for winning football matches' and yet now 'couldn't pick a team that can win a game of football'. Amazingly, Villa would now have a clear 12 calendar days before their next game, away at Leeds, for Little to take stock and try and instil some renewed fight in his team, who lay in a perilous 16th place.

The gap saw Little go back to the defensive solidity model that seemingly had borne some fruit, and Villa scrapped for their lives at Elland Road. It was the sort of game built for Shaun Teale, who got something in the way of everything he could, whether it be in the air or on the ground. In front of him, Ian Taylor continued to justify his transfer, and then some, getting from box to box in a relentless demonstration of commitment to the cause. Still though Villa could not score a goal, the drought extending to eight games and 12 hours of football. Disaster then struck late on when Mark Bosnich was sent off for a second bookable offence, pushing Carlton Palmer in the chest after the Leeds midfielder had upended Teale. Nigel Spink was brought on but was motionless as Palmer sent a wonderful long-range effort past him and into the net. A 1-0 loss clutched from the jaws of a 0-0 draw was hardly the most inspiring of aspirations but given Villa's lowly position that point lost seemed crucial, and in fairness the team had strived hardily for it. With just three games to play, Villa slipped to 17th and nerves were no longer jangling so much as booming.

For their run-in, Villa would face Manchester City and Liverpool at home (not quite the proposition it is today) before making an away trip to fellow strugglers Norwich. If Villa could win their home games, it would mean no need for last-day drama in East Anglia, but winning them – especially in the midst of a stupendous goal drought – was not going to be easy, so a tally of five points across the three might have seemed more realistic. Against Manchester City, an early Ugo Ehiogu goal broke the eight-game famine, the defender heading/handling the ball past City keeper John Burridge to salve the worry around Villa Park. As a footnote, impressively Burridge was 43 years of age and had played for Villa a whole two decades previously. A surprisingly open game was squared up just after the hour by Uwe Rösler, and Villa seemed content with a point, which could have been none if not for the supersonic Bosnich somehow denying Peter Beagrie.

The draw essentially made the visit of Liverpool a 'must-win' encounter.

A year earlier, Villa fans had serenaded the last day of the Holte End with a standout win against Liverpool. Although the result was not as vital that day, it reminded the 40,000 who made the journey to Villa Park that the team was capable of producing when necessary. Whereas that result was important as it allowed the Holte to be celebrated and remembered in the right way, a victory against the same side 12 months on would go a huge way to securing top-flight status. Villa's approach was aggressive and on the front foot, the time for caution removed by necessity, and Liverpool, with Europe secured having taken over from Villa as Coca-Cola Cup winners, were ripe for the taking. Peculiarly, the game had some direct similarities with the encounter a year before, chiefly in the goalscorer. Villa had said goodbye to the Holte End with a 2-1 win, Dwight Yorke coming off the bench to score twice. This time around Yorke started and scored two first-half goals to put Villa 2-0 up in glorious sunshine. On these moments do football seasons and careers turn – the anxiety of relegation seemed to melt away while for Yorke it also felt a fundamental moment, finally in his Villa career being used as an out-and-out striker, and a precursor for what would come in the 1995/96 season. Villa slithered up to 15th and on to 47 points and knew that a point away at the already relegated Norwich on the season's final day would be enough to ensure safety and send Crystal Palace down.

If Villa needed some sense of fate or fortune leading into the Norwich game, they got it with the announcement that

Keith Cooper was to be the referee. Cooper had also been the man in the middle for the 1994 Coca-Cola Cup Final, not a bad omen if one was needed. Those Villa fans who made the trip east, plus over 7,000 watching from the Holte End on a newly installed jumbo screen on the Villa Park pitch, craved an early goal. Arguably Villa's standout and most consistent performer of the season – Steve Staunton – delivered that after just seven minutes, scoring a valuable if rare headed goal from an Andy Townsend delivery. Little did Villa fans know that Ruel Fox had also put Newcastle United 1-0 up against Crystal Palace just a minute earlier, a lead that was extended to 3-0 by half-time, meaning an extraordinary swing would be required to relegate Villa. But football is never entirely straightforward and in the second periods Palace pulled two goals back, including one from Ray Houghton, and Norwich one of their own, but Villa were never seriously in peril. In fact their build-up play and attacking verve belied the position they were in and, in not entirely novel goings-on, they should really have made the game more comfortable but as was so often their wont, chances were spurned.

It was with a mixture of gratitude and relief that the whistle blew on the match, and a difficult, often traumatic nine months. Villa were safely ensconced in 18th place, hardly cause for jubilation but ultimately a relative success in the context of the season. The 1994/95 campaign had everything: the ups and downs of sacked managers and controversial replacements, record wins and staggering defeats, exciting new faces and sad farewells.

The change in manager felt central to the season, and although the initial promise of Brian Little evaporated into a relegation battle he thought he had avoided, there was enough to see in his work on and off the pitch that Villa could look forward with optimism. Little had started to overhaul what was an, if not old, then 'ageing' squad and injected some freshness within their ranks. He had also continued Ron Atkinson's development of Ugo Ehiogu into a fine defender and leader, while bolstering Dwight Yorke's involvement as a central striker. The experiment with a back five seemed to have evolved into Plan A, having the potential to get the best out of a squad without natural wingers, and simultaneously harnessing the energies of Ian Taylor and Andy Townsend in the middle of the park. That said, Doug Ellis would have made it painfully clear to his manager that relegation battles were not the done thing around Villa Park, and that progress back up the table would need to be swift and obvious. There would also be problems to solve in terms of goalscoring (the regularity of it), a conundrum that had stumped successive Villa managers since Andy Gray had scored 20 in the 1977/78 season. There was much for Brian Little and his team to ponder as they approached their first pre-season at Aston Villa.

Neil Cox battles for possession against Birmingham City (October 1993)

Mark Bosnich was in spectacular form as Villa defeated Sunderland in the Coca-Cola Cup third round (October 1993)

Ray Houghton celebrates scoring against Sunderland

Dalian Atkinson powers home against Tranmere in the Coca-Cola Cup semi-final (February 1994)

Mark Bosnich saves the crucial penalty from Tranmere's Liam O'Brien to send Villa to Wembley (February 1994)

Ugo Ehiogu celebrates with fans in the aftermath of the Tranmere victory (February 1994)

Dalian Atkinson scores the opener in the 1994 Coca-Cola Cup Final

Surprise inclusion Graham Fenton battles with Manchester United's Denis Irwin

Dalian Atkinson, Dean Saunders and Tony Daley celebrate Villa's second goal in the 1994 Coca-Cola Cup Final

1994 Coca-Cola Cup winners

The Two Atkinsons – Dalian and Big Ron with the trophy

Tommy Johnson played a key role in the 1996 Coca-Cola Cup campaign

Dwight Yorke was at his electric and prolific best across the 1995/96 season

On the way to Wembley – Milosevic, Ehiogu and Townsend

Ian Taylor – from Holte End to Wembley winner

The three goalscorers in the 1996 Coca-Cola Cup Final – Yorke, Milosevic and Taylor

Brian Little celebrates a unique double – League Cup winner as player and manager

1996 Coca-Cola Cup winners

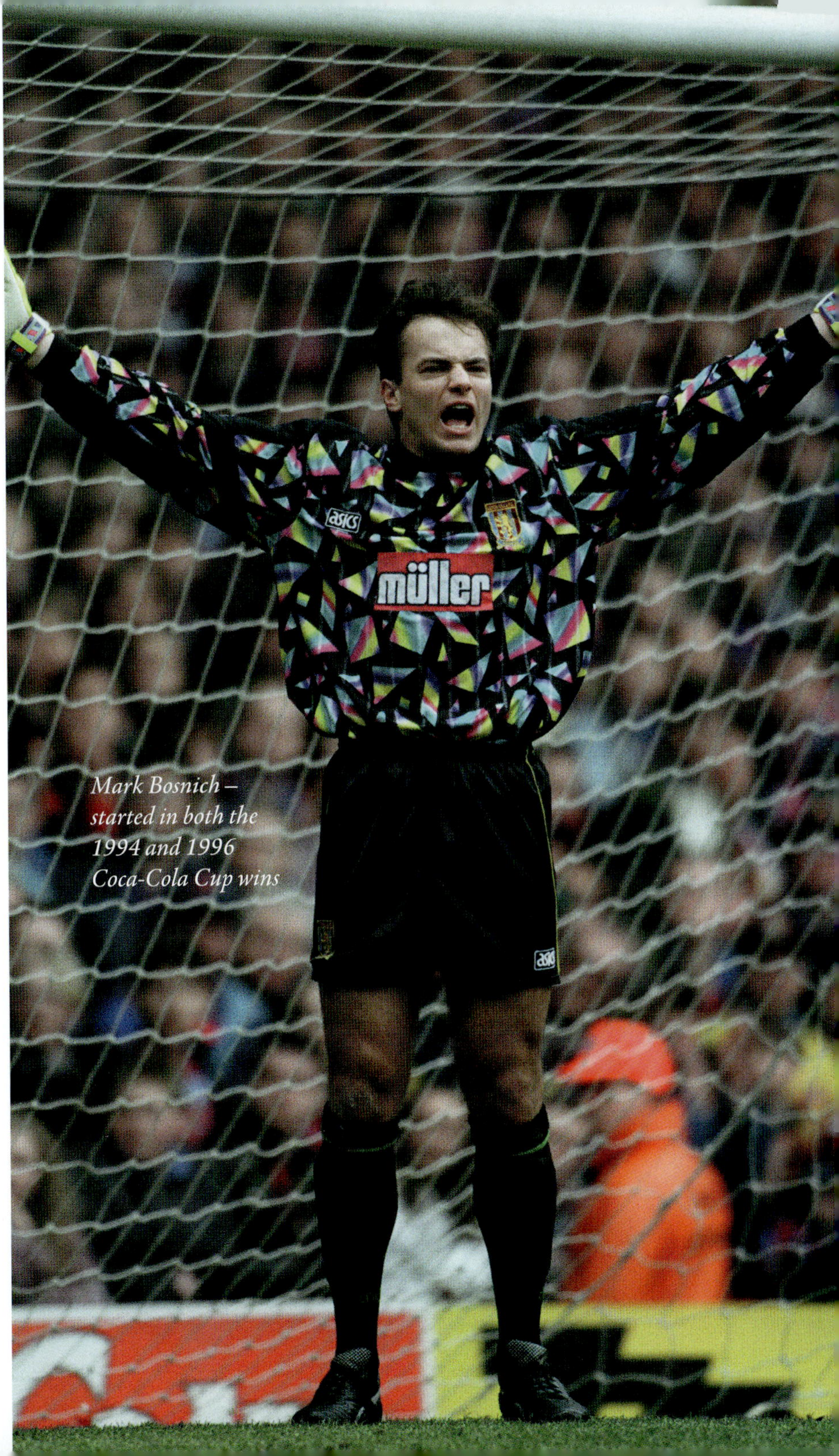

Mark Bosnich – started in both the 1994 and 1996 Coca-Cola Cup wins

Paul McGrath, Pure Genius – started in both the 1994 and 1996 Coca-Cola Cup wins

Andy Townsend – started in both the 1994 and 1996 Coca-Cola Cup wins

Nii Lamptey may not have won either the 1994 or 1996 trophies but his story sums up why we love football and our club

Chapter 21

Summer 1995: All Change

THE PRIME objective of survival secured, Brian Little could focus on the final stages of his rebuilding of Villa's squad and tactical approach. It's important to remember that these were very much the final stages of that transition, after Little had already taken a hatchet to Ron Atkinson's playing personnel in the midst of the 1994/95 season, while simultaneously adding his own flavour along the way. Gary Charles, Alan Wright, Tommy Johnson and Ian Taylor had all arrived during the course of the previous campaign, and all had made a strong impact and looked set to be key starters in 1995/96. Franz Carr had also been added as a wide option but hadn't been involved to any degree and was destined to be a squad player at best.

Alongside those incomings, the exit door had been opened (not always ceremoniously) for several of Atkinson's core side – Earl Barrett, Kevin Richardson, Ray Houghton and Garry Parker all left for pastures new. Guy Whittingham, brought in by Little's predecessor to solve the ever-continuing goalscoring problems, had also departed as part of the Ian Taylor deal. While that extensive transfer business hadn't always borne fruit in terms of results, it would materialise in terms of developing a way of setting up the team and how Little would work tactically. It seemed that incoming business over the summer of 1995 would be targeted on certain key positions.

The first of those was at centre-back, where Little had long held some reservations about the age and mobility of the defenders he had inherited. The apparent move to three at the back made this even more pertinent an area to strengthen, with the initial choice being Crystal Palace's Chris Coleman. Eventually, it was another Palace player who joined Villa's ranks, and one who hadn't always played at centre-back – Gareth Southgate. Villa paid £2.5m for Southgate, a player who had scored several times against them from midfield, including a double in a 4-1 League Cup defeat at Selhurst Park early in Little's reign. Little also had his eye on midfield, where despite the evisceration of the options Atkinson had built there he still felt short. The key seemed to be having another option to play alongside Ian Taylor and Andy Townsend, a berth that had sometimes been filled by Steve Staunton in the previous season. Mark Draper was signed from Leicester City for £3.25m and would go on to become a fixture of Little's team. A cultured midfielder, with a powerful shot and dead-ball delivery, Draper had come to people's attention at Notts County, where his final season had seen him score 14 goals from deep and initiate a move to Leicester City where his manager had been, of course, Brian Little.

The third and final area of focus was, inevitably, a striker as Villa approached another new season caught in the quandary of who could contribute goals on a consistent basis. Summer 1995's option was more left-field than previous iterations, and Serbian striker Savo Milošević was signed from Partizan Belgrade in a deal worth £3.5m. Milošević arrived with a strong record in Belgrade, where he had scored 65 goals in just under 100 appearances, 30 of those coming in the previous season as Partizan won their domestic title. Savo also arrived with a bandana, much being made of the suggestion that at Partizan he had 'apparently' played in it. Villa's commercial team went into overdrive with branded bandanas available for sale to mark the arrival of the club's new striker. With a faint air of inevitability, the Premier League were having none of it, telling Villa that headwear couldn't be worn on the pitch, meaning despite the initial fanfare Savo's bandana never saw the light of day in a competitive match.

The purchase of Milošević pointed to the ongoing growth of English football, and a change in attitudes and awareness that had been precipitated by the inception of the Premier League three summers previously. Villa fans had never known a signing like this, a player who trod a fine line between obscure and exotic and arrived with a supermodel wife and a bandana. It's trite to fixate on foreignness as the key marker of this change, but it had a key bearing on how the Premier League was opening up its markets and footballing borders. The global growth of English football, starting to manifest itself through televised Premier League games, not only allowed a new monetary impetus for clubs to look abroad, but also meant that foreign players were more willing to move to England. Milošević was just one example of a growing trend of foreign imports to the Premier League that summer – with superstar additions such as Dennis Bergkamp at Arsenal and Ruud Gullit at Chelsea joined by, like Milošević, lesser-known players such as Regi Blinker at Sheffield Wednesday and Faustino Asprilla at Newcastle. Even David Platt, who since leaving Villa had spent the entirety of his peak years in Italy, was tempted back, joining Bergkamp at Arsenal. At a local level, the contrast was telling. Twenty-four months previously, Villa had tried to solve their infrequent goalscoring by plucking Guy Whittingham from second-tier Portsmouth for £1.8m and a year previously John Fashanu had been deemed the answer, joining from Wimbledon. The addition of Milošević represented a vastly different approach and was representative of the now transformed face of English football.

The outgoings would also continue apace. Fashanu retired in July 1995, dogged by injuries and having never made a telling impact with Villa, with just a handful of goals. In retrospect, he is a slightly incongruous footnote in the annals of the club's attacking history. Dalian Atkinson, in contrast for ever enshrined in Villa's history, also left, joining Fenerbahçe in Turkey. Atkinson's departure was no great shock, given he had only sporadically been involved under Little and had been open about a desire to move abroad. Of more surprise was the departure of 1994/95's top goalscorer Dean Saunders, who joined his former strike partner in Turkey, the Welshman joining up with Galatasaray. Saunders, although never prolific, had scored a decent amount of goals for Villa with a total of 49 across all competitions, but he seemed surplus to requirements in terms of how Little wanted to play, not only through Milošević's arrival but also the re-emergence of Dwight Yorke as a central striker. The same can be said of Shaun Teale, who joined Tranmere, sidelined by the dual threat of the emergence of Ugo Ehiogu and the acquisition of Gareth Southgate. Last to leave that summer was Nii Lamptey, joining back up with Ron Atkinson at Coventry City, a move that felt tinted with a sense of what might have been.

With the dust on business dealings settled, Villa's first-team squad for 1995/96 was as follows:

Goalkeepers
1 – Mark Bosnich
13 – Nigel Spink
30 – Michael Oakes

Defenders
2 – Gary Charles
3 – Steve Staunton
4 – Gareth Southgate
5 – Paul McGrath
12 – Phil King
14 – Alan Wright
16 – Ugo Ehiogu
20 – Riccardo Scimeca

Midfielders
7 – Ian Taylor
8 – Mark Draper
11 – Andy Townsend

15 – Graham Fenton
19 – Gareth Farrelly
22 – David Farrell
24 – Scott Murray

Forwards
9 – Savo Milošević
10 – Tommy Johnson
12 – Steve Froggatt
17 – Franz Carr
18 – Dwight Yorke
23 – Neil Davis

A review of that list when compared to the squad that won the 1994 Coca-Cola Cup is instructive of the huge change that had occurred in 16 months. Of the starting XI that day in March 1994, only Mark Bosnich, Steve Staunton, Paul McGrath, Andy Townsend and Graham Fenton remained, with only Nigel Spink from the substitutes' bench still at Villa. Given that many of the names that had departed were, at the time, seen as integral players it's clear that Brian Little was desperate to put his own mark on the squad, and in essence to break up the ageing but established Ron Atkinson team. Of the non-playing squad members who celebrated on the Wembley pitch, Dwight Yorke and Ugo Ehiogu had – as predicted – gone on to establish themselves as key players, but the rest were long gone. Such a wide-ranging transition within the playing staff over such a short time is phenomenal, particularly given the relative success of 1992 to 1994. We are all used to seeing players come and go from our clubs, but these changes felt more like one era closing and another beginning, despite the change occurring over such a small window. The sense of a new era was reinforced aesthetically with a change in kit manufacturer to Reebok, and in the new front of shirt sponsor, AST Computers. The Asics/Müller era, for ever associated with Ron and Dalian Atkinson, Dean Saunders, Kevin Richardson, Shaun Teale et al, was consigned to the dustbin of nostalgia.

Little's first pre-season was a strange brew but gave strong indicators of how Villa would set up and look to play once the season commenced for real. Villa first played West Bromwich Albion at The Hawthorns in a game that was delayed due to crowd congestion, the home side clearly surprised that nearly 17,000 wanted to come and see a pre-season friendly. The team Little picked was representative of what was to come, although Shaun Teale was still around and started at the back alongside Southgate and Ehiogu, before being replaced by Paul McGrath at half-time. Gary Charles and Steve Staunton started in the wing-back positions, with Draper, Taylor and Townsend in midfield. Dwight Yorke and Savo Milošević embarked on their new strike partnership, although neither could score as Villa lost 1-0. The team selection and substitutes who came on – Alan Wright, Tommy Johnson and McGrath – even at this early stage, showed fans what would become Little's core and trusted personnel. Shape work gave way to fitness work for the next friendly, as Little selected two different sides, one for each half away at Northampton Town. Ugo Ehiogu was the only Villa player to play the full 90 in a game that saw action for the likes of Riccardo

Scimeca, Gareth Farrelly and Phil King and also saw Savo score a first goal in Villa colours. If Northampton offered fewer clues than West Brom, then Portsmouth further muddied things as Ian Taylor started as the right-sided wing-back. All the new signings impressed, however, in a more vibrant display, including another goal for Milošević.

It was the final friendly, against Partizan Belgrade, a week before the season was due to start that gave fans the clearest sense of how Little was intending to line up. The game, arranged as part of the Milošević transfer deal, was unusually played at Villa Park, not often used in pre-season, although only 12,177 were in attendance, in part limited by work on the Doug Ellis Stand. Villa's line-up on a sunny afternoon in Birmingham was Mark Bosnich, Gary Charles, Alan Wright, Ugo Ehiogu, Paul McGrath, Gareth Southgate, Ian Taylor, Mark Draper, Andy Townsend, Savo Milošević, Dwight Yorke. It was a team that would be replicated in many more important games to come. Also foreshadowing what was to come was a Yorke goal that exemplified his new confidence as an out-and-out striker, trusted to lead the line and be Villa's main goal threat.

As pre-season drew to a close, Brian Little and his assistants could be in a positive state of mind. Transfer business – both in and out – had been concluded early and satisfactorily, meaning the squad and projected team were settled and had the chance to work together in pre-season. That pre-season had also given a sense that the more positive elements of 1994/95 had been retained, for example the continued establishment of Yorke and Ehiogu as first-team stars, while some of the issues of conceding goals had been addressed. The wholesale move to five at the back had influenced this, as had the hard-working midfield three. Little drew on his own Villa history to explain the importance of Taylor and Townsend at the heart of the midfield, comparing their aesthetic with Des Bremner and Frank Carrodus as players who had 'boundless energy and just ran for fun'. Little was also aware of the reinvention of Paul McGrath in his three-centre-back model, saying he believed that with 'Gareth and Ugo alongside him, Paul was given a new lease of life and an extra season playing at the highest level, which he might not have anticipated'. The embryonic Yorke–Milošević partnership, with Tommy Johnson champing at the bit on the bench, also gave hope that some of the inconsistency in terms of goalscoring could be consigned to the past.

All in all, Villa prepared to open 1995/96 in good shape, confident that their occupation of the lowly positions the previous season was strictly a one-off.

Chapter 22

Early Promise in League and Cup

IF BRIAN Little, or indeed anyone connected to Aston Villa Football Club, could have penned a script for the opening day of the 1995/96 season then it may well have read exactly in line with what unfolded at Villa Park on Saturday, 19 August 1995. In the midst of a heatwave, Villa welcomed Manchester United for the first opportunity to see the extent to which Little's overhaul in tactics and personnel could come to fruition and what indicators it might give for the season to come. On the back of four league wins in a row against Villa, United had undergone their own transition having finished second in the Premier League in 1994/95. Eric Cantona was still suspended after his foray into the crowd at Selhurst Park, and seasoned Alex Ferguson campaigners Mark Hughes, Paul Ince and Andrei Kanchelskis had been sold. To much consternation, Ferguson had made no significant signings by the way of replacements, instead opting to put his faith in a well-regarded but inexperienced set of academy graduates.

The United side that day was not quite as youngster-orientated as history would have you believe, with Peter

Schmeichel, Paul Parker, Denis Irwin, Lee Sharpe, Gary Pallister, Brian McClair and Roy Keane all starting. For context, that core had all been part of the squad that Villa had beaten in the Coca-Cola Cup Final in March of 1994. That said, the team also included Nicky Butt, Gary Neville, Paul Scholes and Phil Neville, with David Beckham on the bench, all constituent parts of what was to become known as the Class of '92.

For all the relative uncertainty around some of United's starters, Villa's team mirrored that which was picked in their final pre-season game a week before against Partizan Belgrade: Mark Bosnich, Gary Charles, Alan Wright, Ugo Ehiogu, Paul McGrath, Gareth Southgate, Ian Taylor, Mark Draper, Andy Townsend, Savo Milošević and Dwight Yorke. That continuity of selection seemed to pay early dividends with Villa starting furiously, backing up their manager's pre-match assertions that this version of the team would be 'quicker and hungrier'. Before the quarter of an hour mark was up, Dwight Yorke and Andy Townsend combined well in midfield, with Yorke's cross then evading everyone before finding Gary Charles on the right-hand side. Charles's low cross was met by an onrushing, stretching Ian Taylor to put Villa 1-0 up in the sunshine, resplendent in their new Reebok kit. Villa's second goal was even more representative of the speed and ferocity that Little had clearly engendered since the end of the previous season. A tenacious Alan Wright broke up some intricate United triangular patterns, before feeding Mark Draper at pace, the midfielder then progressing the ball to the already mobile Yorke. With United's defence floundering in a desperate attempt to catch up with play,

Yorke fed Milošević, who with sleight of touch nutmegged Roy Keane to play in Draper who, having continued his run, gleefully dispatched past Schmeichel. Milošević was then central to a third goal, winning a penalty which Yorke slotted home to, somewhat unbelievably, put Villa 3-0 up after just 36 first-half minutes.

The football in that opening half was extraordinary and represented a sea change from some of the displays that had characterised the end of the previous season, as Little had (correctly) prioritised survival. United were quite simply blown away by the verve and spirit of Villa's display, prompting, famously, Alan Hansen to prophesy on *Match of the Day* that United 'can't win anything with kids'. United were better in the second half and David Beckham scored a mere consolation with the kind of finish he would become globally famous for. Post-match, Ferguson suggested that without the interventions of Mark Bosnich his side may have got something from the game. Although Bosnich had been at his stupefying best, the *Sports Argus*' judgement that 'Vibrant Villa' were the outstanding team was almost impossible to counter. For Ron Atkinson, a 3-1 victory against Manchester United had confirmed his legacy but, in hindsight, it had been the high point of his era as Villa manager. Whereas the League Cup win had begun a managed decline for Atkinson, for his successor, one could only hope that a similar 3-1 victory was just the beginning.

Unchanged from the United game, Villa doubled down next in north London, defeating Spurs 1-0. Ugo Ehiogu scored the only goal, rising insistently to power in Mark Draper's pitch-perfect corner. Villa's approach placed more emphasis on solidity than on the opening day, by nature of being away from home perhaps, with the back five and midfield three again superb in controlling the game. Ehiogu's goal meant a 100 per cent record after the two opening Premier League matches and a hugely positive start to the season. Brian Little was naturally pleased although moved to dispel some early ideas that his side lacked width and would not always be able to break teams down. 'Our system at the back is working well,' Little said. 'People talk about a lack of wingers but with three centre-backs, if you pick your full-backs right, you can still have width.' In a peculiar act of symmetry, 17 years previously to the very day, Villa had played Spurs at White Hart Lane and beaten them 4-1. And who was on the scoresheet that day for Villa? None other than the current management team of Little, Allan Evans and John Gregory.

Along with Villa, Newcastle, Wimbledon and Leeds had all won their opening two fixtures, and it was to Elland Road to play the latter that Villa travelled next. Little was forced into his first change, Gary Charles ruled out with a tooth infection, an absence that saw Ian Taylor deployed in Charles's right-sided wing-back position with Tommy Johnson making his first start of the season in an attacking midfield role. Ostensibly, as credible a cover option as Taylor was, it weakened the system slightly in that Johnson lent the side a more attacking dimension and therefore increased pressure on Mark Draper and Andy Townsend to control the middle of the field.

An early Gary Speed goal placed the onus squarely on Villa to make the running, but despite a high proportion of possession, they couldn't really manufacture a chance of serious note. By the time David White scored, his goal as late as Speed's had been early, Villa looked well beaten by a side that would sit top of the nascent Premier League table with three wins out of three. Little acknowledged that 'everyone could have played a little bit better' but was certainly not downhearted with the loss, especially within the context of the opening three games placed together.

That positivity was enhanced further with a second home win of the season, and a second clean sheet after a 1-0 win against Bolton. Dwight Yorke's header deep into the second half was enough to move Villa to nine points from 12, their best start of a league season since they won the old First Division in 1980/81. The only slight concern among Villa fans was the fact that Savo Milošević had yet to score a league goal, although the counter to that concern was again that he had played satisfactorily and, indeed, crossed the ball for Yorke's headed winner. There was no doubting that the Premier League was a huge step up for Milošević from his previous domestic league. Little chose to ignore questions about the striker's early form, instead focussing on the differences to the previous caampaign, 'Last season we tended to let go and we might have ended up at 1-1 or even losing. Three wins out of four is a satisfying first phase.'

Little was right to keep his counsel as Milošević opened his Villa account in a 1-1 draw at defending champions Blackburn Rovers. Off the back of an international break which allowed the striker some time at home, Milošević's sweetly struck 20-yarder prompted him to run the length of the Ewood Park pitch to celebrate with the Villa fans, in a mixture of relief and elation. Villa then followed up with a 2-0 home win against Wimbledon, where a fantastic (albeit non goalscoring) performance from Dwight Yorke put them up to third in the table. Yorke laid on goals for Draper and Taylor as Villa attacked with an effusive confidence and defended stoutly. Wimbledon had started their own Premier League campaign strongly, so it was a pleasingly routine win to follow up a tough away point at Blackburn. What was also pleasing – and telling – was that Brian Little named the same starting line-up for the fifth time in six games, with even the substitutes the same for three matchdays in a row. It pointed to a process of development of permanency by Little and his staff – a team proficiently drilled in the tactics demanded and becoming increasingly adept at executing them on the pitch.

With a lofty league position pocketed, attention could turn to the Coca-Cola Cup, a competition that surely represented a genuine opportunity for Little to cement some trophy-based success and back up that 1994 victory. As per that campaign, Villa's participation began in the second round with a two-legged tie, this time against Peterborough United, with the first leg taking place on Wednesday, 20 September. Despite playing against lower-league opponents, the Villa side demonstrated an early commitment to the competition, as Little lined up his team as follows: Mark Bosnich, Gary Charles, Gareth Southgate, Paul McGrath, Ian Taylor, Mark Draper, Tommy Johnson, Andy Townsend, Alan Wright, Ugo Ehiogu, Dwight Yorke. The substitutes were Nigel Spink, Graham Fenton and Gareth Farrelly.

With Savo Milošević away with Yugoslavia, scoring in a 2-0 win against Greece, Tommy Johnson started only his second game of the season, and came out of the blocks with the air of a man aiming to stake a claim for regular involvement, testing Peterborough goalkeeper Jon Sheffield twice in the first four minutes. Sheffield had no chance whatsoever after 12 minutes when Mark Draper summoned up a moment of unadulterated majesty. A slaloming Dwight Yorke had been felled by Billy Manuel in the D of the penalty area, giving Villa a clear shooting opportunity. Andy Townsend, now installed as de facto permanent captain of the side, flicked the ball up to Draper who, after controlling the ball on his thigh, volleyed the ball directly into Peterborough's goal. The visitors simply couldn't cope with Villa's direct running, encapsulated by Yorke and Townsend, the latter being fouled in the box in the 16th minute with the former nonchalantly converting the resultant penalty. If the pressure of being 2-0 down wasn't enough, Peterborough hamstrung themselves further when former Villa youth player Lee Williams was sent off after a verbal exchange with a linesman. They would have hoped just to limp to half-time and regroup, but more direct running from Villa, this time Johnson, and more ill discipline from Peterborough led to another penalty, again calmly dispatched by Yorke. Villa were 3-0 up at half-time, and as the ITV Central news commentary concluded, 'It's so easy.'

A fourth goal, despite Villa's absolute authority, took a while to materialise, with Yorke missing a golden opportunity for a hat-trick before Johnson reaped his reward for a sterling night's work after 67 minutes. A raking Ehiogu pass had evaded Yorke but was picked up by the ever-willing Townsend, who squared for Johnson to rifle in a left-footed shot. Another direct but crafted Ehiogu ball led to Villa's fifth, Johnson again running behind the Peterborough defence before crossing for Alan Wright to chance his arm from outside the box. Wright's shot was deflected in off Gary Heald and deemed an own goal, denying the wing-back his first Villa goal. Yorke rattled the crossbar before Gareth Southgate did score his first goal in claret and blue, persistently wriggling through bodies in the box to scrape home. The *Birmingham Post* described the evening as being a 'massacre', although, as ever, Brian Little was more contrite, stressing that although he was 'very pleased' the focus was on the competition as a whole and its 'importance' in the season as a whole. An intention had been made clear – the Coca-Cola Cup was again high on Villa's agenda.

Despite his hard-running, goalscoring performance in the Coca-Cola Cup, Tommy Johnson was dropped for a return to league action against Nottingham Forest, with Savo Milošević recalled into Little's 'standard' side. Townsend gave Villa the advantage in a tight game, set up by an impudent Yorke back-heel, before then being sent off to initiate a grim rearguard action which Villa couldn't sustain. Right-back Des Lyttle snuck in to score an equaliser as time was running out, meaning Villa slipped down to fifth. Fifth rapidly became second a week later with a 3-0 posting of Ron Atkinson's Coventry City at Highfield Road. Steve Staunton made a welcome return to fitness, and the starting XI to replace the stricken Paul McGrath, but had hardly managed to get a sense of his surroundings before Yorke scored after just 13 seconds. It was a goal that equalled the record for the fastest in the Premier League, and enabled Villa to maintain a foothold despite some consistent Coventry pressing. Mark Bosnich, who'd had a relatively quiet start to the season, was at his absolute best, denying Peter Ndlovu with a flying save that brought back memories of his former manager Atkinson describing his Australian goalkeeper as a 'trapeze artist'. It wasn't until the final five minutes though that Villa could put the game to bed through two welcomed and needed Milošević goals.

With a 6-0 aggregate lead in their possession, the second leg of the Coca-Cola Cup tie with Peterborough took place on Tuesday, 3 October and saw Brian Little name a surprisingly strong team: Mark Bosnich, Gary Charles, Gareth Southgate, Paul McGrath, Ian Taylor, Mark Draper, Savo Milošević, Andy Townsend, Alan Wright, Ugo Ehiogu, Dwight Yorke. The substitutes were Nigel Spink, Graham Fenton and Steve Staunton.

Little's intentions were most likely rooted in momentum and consistency, but Villa found it difficult to raise themselves to the levels of the first leg, with progression in essence already secure. Dominating the ball, Villa lacked the energy and ruthlessness that the early running of 1995/96 had demonstrated in spades. For much of a tepid affair it looked like they might contrive to, embarrassingly, lose – Gary Martindale had put Peterborough 1-0 up in the first half and nothing much looked like changing. Little's replacements did make a difference, however, Graham Fenton adding some enthusiasm and Steve Staunton scoring late on to square up the game and afford Villa a 7-1 aggregate win. The indifferent performance was met by indifference by Little, who merely said with a shrug, 'These things happen.' It was clear that nothing had changed in terms of the Coca-Cola Cup being a clear target for Villa, and a draw that gave them Stockport County at home in the next round would categorically endorse that.

Chapter 23

Doubling Up

THE LOSS to Leeds in late August had been Villa's sole defeat in ten league and cup games, a satisfying return that vindicated the time and resources Brian Little had been given. Inevitably, however, as with the rhythms of any football season, a slump was incoming. With Andy Townsend suspended against his former side, Chelsea arrived at Villa Park in tenth but imbued with a sense of glamour by the installation of Ruud Gullit as a roaming sweeper. Gullit was yet to be representative of a wider globalisation at Stamford Bridge, Glenn Hoddle's team being built on a foundation of British grit, with the Dutchman offering a sprinkling of fairy dust. It was not dissimilar to how Villa's squad was shaped after the addition of Savo Milošević, with the core of British players still the norm but with some more quixotic foreign signings thanks to the Premier League's moneyed status.

Gullit had been more of a quantifiable success than Milošević, who still hadn't scored at Villa Park, poking the nervous weak spot of many Villa fans who had become scarred by a lack of consistent goalscoring over the decade. As it was, it was an example of Chelsea's less-fashionable assets, Dennis Wise, who scored the only goal in a 1-0 defeat for Villa. A trip to Arsenal followed, the Gunners adorned with their own Dutch delicacy, Dennis Bergkamp, although again Villa were undone by England internationals Ian Wright and Paul Merson. Merson's goal came from a disappointing Mark Bosnich error as he dropped an innocuous-looking cross, a moment of lunacy that Little described with no sympathy as a 'clanger' and the moment that 'the whole thing went to pieces'. A second consecutive loss put Villa down to seventh, and also saw some tweaks by Little that, while potentially needed, hadn't initiated the intended outcomes. Milošević had been relegated to the substitutes' bench for the first time, but surprisingly wasn't replaced by Tommy Johnson, with Steve Staunton instead being drafted in. It wasn't unique for Staunton to be employed further forward by Little, as indeed Ron Atkinson had, but it changed Villa's attacking dynamic with Dwight Yorke at severe risk of isolation up top. It was clear that Little was aware of that risk, given that Milošević, Johnson and Graham Fenton were all on the bench, with neither a defender nor a goalkeeper in sight.

The Coca-Cola Cup third round encounter with Stockport County, which unfolded on Wednesday, 25 October, now represented a clear opportunity for Villa to get back on track after a faltering week in the Premier League. Milošević was back, alongside a first start for Riccardo Scimeca in place of the injured Paul McGrath: Mark Bosnich, Gary Charles, Gareth Southgate, Ian Taylor, Mark Draper, Savo Milošević, Andy Townsend,

Alan Wright, Ugo Ehiogu, Dwight Yorke, Riccardo Scimeca. The substitutes were Michael Oakes, Graham Fenton and Tommy Johnson.

Scimeca, born in Leamington to (as lovingly documented in an issue of *Claret and Blue* magazine) an Italian restaurant-owning mother and father, had seen an astronomical rise. As an even younger player he had been deployed as a target man-type forward, but a move to defence had started to prove a masterstroke, especially as Scimeca fitted the profile of what Brian Little wanted as a centre-half – good on the ball, progressive, a good reader of the game but with the solidity more common with the position. Having made his league debut as a brief substitute on the opening day, this was a deserved but important opportunity for the young defender and represented the first time Little had promoted a homegrown player to the first team for a full debut.

After the previous round's 6-0 victory against Peterborough, Brian Little had talked about that type of game being difficult until you get the first goal, but once you did then players calmed and took control. Against Stockport it took Villa a while to get going, and even though the Hatters played their football two leagues below a nervousness was sparked when all was level at half-time. Ehiogu, Draper and Milošević all had good chances, but Stockport, set up to be resilient and chance-limiting, defended robustly. Villa did get their inertia-busting goal after half-time, with Ugo Ehiogu powerfully heading in Andy Townsend's left-wing cross. As Little would have predicted, Ehiogu's goal freed Villa up. Alan Wright, in a show of purpose reminiscent of his role in Draper's goal against Manchester United in August, won the ball on the left and released Dwight Yorke. The shimmering Yorke danced his way down the touchline before veering inside, a slipstream of Stockport defenders in his wake, before slotting in a measured effort from the edge of the penalty box. Whoever the opposition, Yorke's goal was a thing of outstanding aesthetic gorgeousness and offered further proof of the step up Yorke had made under Little. Throughout his Villa career he had always impressed, but now, as the main man in the forward press, he was brimming with the confidence that Little's full trust had given him. A sixth goal of the season was a rich reward, and his manager was satisfied that another hurdle in the competition had been jumped.

Coca-Cola Cup progress proved to be a catalyst for a renewed period of success in the league as Villa faced five games in advance of the next round. Yorke was at it again in a late home win against Everton, using all his athleticism to manoeuvre Draper's cross and secure a needed three league points. The Everton game saw the debut of Carl Tiler in the centre of defence, a knee-jerk signing driven by the injury concerns for Paul McGrath and Steve Staunton. Signed for £750,000 from Nottingham Forest, there was great irony when Tiler was himself stretchered from the field injured to be replaced by Riccardo Scimeca. There were rumblings of impending business elsewhere, with Graham Fenton being lined up by Blackburn in a £1.5m deal, cynics suggesting that Little was boosting the coffers in readiness to strengthen again up front given the malaise surrounding Savo Milošević. The Serbian still hadn't scored at home, and there was a growing awareness

– as ever – that Villa would need to score more goals to compete at the top end of the Premier League. Statistics bear this out – after beating Everton, Villa lay seventh behind Newcastle in first, equitable goals conceded but the leaders were outscoring Villa 2:1. In that context Villa were blessed to have Dwight Yorke in such sparkling form, as Little enthused, 'We allow Dwight licence to give full expression to his talents and he has a complete range of them. We pointed him in the right direction, and he has responded. He has two good feet, he's good in the air, he can turn defenders, has genuine pace and is an excellent finisher. He may not be the biggest striker around, but opposition defenders are finding he's deceptively strong.'

Yorke was certainly the fulcrum of Little's side and was finally fulfilling the promise of the cheeky Caribbean teenager who had arrived at Bodymoor Heath in 1989. Tony Daley tells stories of Yorke doing 100 consecutive keepy-uppies with his head while standing in a dustbin which sums that early version of the forward up, although he made a real impact as early as the 1991/92 season, when as we have seen he was joint top scorer with 17 in all competitions. Between the start of 1992/93 and the end of 1994/95 Yorke suffered from a combination of injury, being played out wide and being a victim of Ron Atkinson's often intransigent team selections. Seven, three and eight goals across those three seasons tells its own story, but the mould had been smashed under Little as full faith would be put in Yorke to set himself on the road to becoming one of the league's best strikers.

Goals arrived away at West Ham in a display which had Villa fans scratching their heads as to why they had been concerned about where the goals were coming from. A brace for Milošević, and one each for Johnson and Yorke cut West Ham to pieces, on a ground where Villa hadn't won for a decade. Edged up to fifth, the *Birmingham Post* described Villa as 'ragingly competitive and brilliantly resourceful'. Johnson justifiably kept his place in the side away at league leaders Newcastle and scored again in a commendable draw. The point lifted Villa into the top four but was more important as a statement performance against a side who were threatening to run away with the league, albeit one that still left them 11 points back. They were beginning to look the part and the demonstration of progress was apparent for all to see.

Things got better for Villa and Johnson in another win, this time away at Southampton, another ground where they had suffered for some time – Johnson secured their first win there for 13 years. It was Johnson's third goal in three games and moved the team up to third. They couldn't replicate the trick at Manchester City a week later, where the Southampton scoreline was reversed into a 1-0 loss. Around the City game were concerning signs that the relentlessness of the league programme, allied to Brian Little's consistent team selections, meant that players seemed jaded and in some cases were picking up injuries. Andy Townsend had been absent for a trio of matches and although the loss of the captain was glossed over by the fact his replacement, Tommy Johnson, scored three in three in his stead, Ian Taylor was also injured in Manchester. That pointed to a certain lack of depth in the squad – Fenton had gone to Blackburn and Phil King had also departed to West Bromwich Albion on loan. Little's standard bench was Nigel Spink, Steve Staunton and Riccardo Scimeca – solid enough but lacking players who could change a game or provide impact should Villa be, for example, behind.

As was becoming increasingly true across this period, and not for the first time in the 1995/96 season, the Coca-Cola Cup offered Villa a chance for respite and to start building some momentum again. Andy Townsend, to some relief, was back for a fourth-round meeting with Queens Park Rangers at Villa Park on Wednesday, 29 November: Mark Bosnich, Gary Charles, Gareth Southgate, Paul McGrath, Mark Draper, Savo Milošević, Tommy Johnson, Andy Townsend, Alan Wright, Ugo Ehiogu, Dwight Yorke. The substitutes, unsurprisingly, were Nigel Spink, Steve Staunton and Riccardo Scimeca.

Villa started very much on the front foot, with the aim of getting ahead and forcing their visitors to open up, in opposition to their seemingly protective mindset. Johnson was at the centre of Villa's early probing, putting an effort wide after an exchange with Yorke and then dropping an ambitious overhead kick on to the roof of Tony Roberts's net. As QPR placed their whole XI behind the ball, Villa seemed to miss Ian Taylor's drive in an overcrowded centre of the park, especially as Andy Townsend had clearly been rushed back from his injury (he would acknowledge after the game that it was still a 'wee bit of a problem'). It was also a testament to the impact Taylor had made since Little brought him down from Sheffield Wednesday, the midfielder now firmly established as a quintessential fan favourite – a local Villa fan who was a driving force in the team.

In a staid game that appeared to be petering out towards a replay, it was the returning Townsend who provided a moment of inspiration. Paul McGrath lofted in a hopeful long ball which Yorke adeptly controlled on his chest, laying it into the path of his captain, who launched a left-footed wonder strike past Roberts. Soon after Townsend broke the deadlock, Yorke, via Roberts, hit the bar but ultimately Townsend's intervention was enough to settle the game, which never threatened to ignite.

Suddenly Villa found themselves looking forward to a Coca-Cola Cup quarter-final, a time which Brian Little felt 'any club starts believing they are capable of going all the way'. Yet, in contrast to the 1993/94 run under Atkinson, the progression to a quarter-final had felt a little muted and undercooked. By the time Villa played Spurs in the 1994 quarter-final they had defeated Birmingham City, Sunderland and Arsenal. The first of those games, by nature of the fraught local-ness, would always be fondly remembered and the win against Arsenal felt like a statement victory. Even the Sunderland win, four goals crafted in adversity with Mark Bosnich the standout headline grabber, had a memorable slant. The 1995/96 vintage had seen wins against Peterborough, Stockport and QPR which presented as more underwhelming, and lacked an iconic moment even in comparison to Nii Lamptey's goal against Wigan in late 1994. Not that Brian Little would have cared a jot – a major trophy last-eight to go with a top-four position in the league meant that, as December 1995 dawned, Villa could move forwards from an incredibly positive standpoint.

Chapter 24
League Lessons

DECEMBER 1995 saw no cup action at all, meaning that with a Coca-Cola Cup quarter-final locked in, Brian Little and his squad could concentrate on consolidating their position in the Premier League. The five league games that would be played over December and New Year's Day 1996 would, however, give important lessons for the cup opportunities to come and provide an insight into how Little continued to see his squad, tactics and the club's ambitions.

Team selection over this period was, as had been the manager's wont, fundamentally consistent, with Little asking a core of players to go to the well again and again. Mark Bosnich, Gary Charles, Gareth Southgate, Mark Draper, Savo Milošević, Tommy Johnson, Alan Wright and Ugo Ehiogu started every one of these five games, with Dwight Yorke starting four. Andy Townsend, Ian Taylor and Paul McGrath started three each, with Riccardo Scimeca making two appearances from the off. Operating with such a small squad can lead to varying consequences, both positive and negative, and Villa would see, as a distillation, the breadth of those over these five games. There is no inevitability that injuries are a factor when team selection is so consistent, but that consistent selection can impact different players in different ways – the three appearances made by McGrath, Taylor and Townsend were not consecutive, suggesting that players were brought back in through necessity but perhaps lacking full fitness, which meant ailments were exacerbated.

Closer inspection bears this out, with McGrath playing in games one, three and four, Taylor in games two, three and four and Townsend in games one, four and five. There is also a knock-on effect on depth of squad by nature of the fact that a manager in essence picks the same team every week, in that players not in that elevated company will tire of not getting a chance. That had been the case with Graham Fenton, for example, and led to a scenario where the only options Little had were young academy players such as Riccardo Scimeca, Gareth Farrelly and Lee Hendrie, the latter making his first appearance on the bench in this period of games. In essence managers can paint themselves into a corner, stuck in a vicious circle of wanting to be consistent in selection, but in doing so having no option but to be.

None of these factors, at least publicly, were debated at the time by Little, who clearly valued the togetherness that a consisten team selection meant. There is no doubt that the fact players such as Draper and Milošević, even when suffering dips in form, remained in the team was a huge boost to their confidence and confirmed the faith the manager had in them. Both would repay this faith over this period. As we have seen, Little had clear tactical ideas for his team, which had started to be bedded in at the tail end of 1994/95 and came to fruition from August 1995. As Little has said, 'I saw no benefit in chopping and changing the line-up just for the sake of it,' and the continuity meant that his tactical ideas and shape would also gain continuous development and improvement. It's an explanation as to why Little would pick the same team, outside of this period of games, against Peterborough away with a 6-0 aggregate lead. Little was a firm if measured manager who wanted to utilise every opportunity to get his ideas across and then see how his preferred team could translate them on the field. It was difficult to argue that the twin benefits of togetherness and tactical understanding were there for all to see, given Villa sat in fourth and awaited a Coca-Cola Cup quarter-final.

It was around this time that Villa filmed the content for what would become a VHS release called *The Squaddies*. Ian Taylor, in one of the opening segments of the film, directly references the 'togetherness' of the squad which could sound like a platitude had he not also referred to the previous season when they weren't. The relaxed nature of the production had clearly put the players at ease and a naturalness emerged that had seemingly been engendered by Little and the size of his squad. *The Squaddies* is actually an amusing watch, with poor Savo Milošević struggling with questions and answers in English, never more so than when being asked if he was a good player when he was a 'little boy' to which he replied, 'I don't know.' At least the production company spelt Milošević's name correctly – his strike partner was listed as Dwight York.

Mark Draper came in for a fair amount of stick from his team-mates, Gareth Southgate saying that 'the lads are holding a stewards' enquiry' into whether the midfielder possessed any O-Levels, a claim backed up when a straight-faced Draper himself said that he'd like to play for an Italian club, like Barcelona. Southgate had picked up a nickname of his own, 'Harry', due to the fact that Little's assistant John Gregory recalled that there was then a constituency in London called Enfield and Southgate. Other nicknames were less imaginative – 'The Beak' for Andy Townsend and 'Jurassic' for Ugo Ehiogu – and some references are now just inappropriate, Tommy Johnson staggeringly describing Alan Wright as looking like Tom Hanks from *Philadelphia* (Hanks played an Aids victim). Gregory's role in *The Squaddies* was interesting, not solely that he was the assistant manager, but more so that manager Brian Little was barely involved. This was instructive of the personality Little was and also how Gregory portrayed himself – the manager more serious and measured compared to his assistant's cocky banter. They worked relatively well together, although how things would unfold in the future would test that theory.

The first league game in December 1995 was a visit from Arsenal, who on their last journey to Villa Park had smashed their relegation-threatened hosts 4-0. Arsenal sat a place above Villa so the game represented another staging post in the team's development under Little in terms of how they could continue to compete and keep pace with those around them. It also represented a first return to Villa Park for former cult hero David Platt, who had left in July 1991 to play for Bari. Platt's time in Italy can be seen as a qualified success, and in an age when many English players struggled to assimilate abroad he adapted and contributed well. Bari were relegated in Platt's first and only season there, although he played regularly and scored 15 goals across all competitions. A move to Juventus followed, where Platt struggled to establish himself to the level he would have desired, although as was his nature he still made crucial contributions. Platt would only spend one year in Turin, but he won the UEFA Cup, playing in both semi-final legs against Paris Saint-Germain and scoring the winning goal against Panathinaikos in the second round. Sampdoria were next for the ex-Villa midfielder, where he spent a further two years, winning the Coppa Italia under Sven-Göran Eriksson. Platt had also established himself as a key starter for England, which further demonstrated the trajectory everyone at Villa knew he would take when he first left. Inevitably he scored the opening goal on his return with a diving header that threw up fond memories of claret and blue days past. More importantly, though, Dwight Yorke levelled things up five minutes later with an equally stunning diving header, to mirror the impact of his old team-mate. Little was understandably delighted, saying that 'coming back like that felt just like winning', and Villa could be thrilled at the fact that those dual aims of competing and keeping pace with the likes of Arsenal was achieved for the moment.

Yorke scored his tenth goal of the season away at Nottingham Forest to open the scoring, although a late Jason Lee leveller dampened the mood slightly as Villa slipped to sixth. The fact that there seemed little room for error as far as league position was concerned demonstrated the strength of the Premier League and the nip and tuck that would pervade the season as a whole. There would be no room for error for Villa or anyone else. Villa, playing in their well-regarded navy blue away kit, were missing the Republic of Ireland contingent Andy Townsend, Steve Staunton and Paul McGrath who were on international duty – another relic of 1990s football compared to modern iterations of the game where league programmes are halted for ten days to accommodate 'international breaks', and another factor in the injury record of these players and their availability to Little.

Villa were back on song and back in fourth with a bubbling 4-1 win against Coventry City, a game that finally saw Savo Milošević break his home goal duck in some style. Tommy Johnson scored the first for Villa, an exquisite finish after beating three defenders, before ex-Villa captain Kevin Richardson was sent off, which changed the game as a contest. Milošević took over from that point, scoring a second-half hat-trick that certainly temporarily abated some of the doubts circling around the young Serbian. It should not be forgotten that Milošević had only just turned 23, living in a new country and playing in a new league – so a return of eight goals was respectable in that context, although the never-ending pressure of English football meant there was no time to rest on laurels.

It was a case of one step back and one forward in the last two league games before a return to cup action. Just before Christmas, Villa made a trip to a freezing Loftus Road to play Queens Park Rangers. The result ended up being a direct reverse of the Coca-Cola Cup tie which Villa had won 1-0 through an Andy Townsend goal. This time it was QPR's Kevin Gallen who scored the decisive goal, albeit in controversial circumstances, Villa being convinced that the striker's header hadn't crossed the line. More ignominy was to follow as Lee Hendrie, making his debut as a first-half substitute for Mark Draper, was sent off for two bookable if minor offences. Again, the game was instructive in terms of how stretched Villa could be in terms of personnel, not only in the fact Hendrie was even involved, but that when Ian Taylor was stretchered off late on he was replaced by goalkeeper Nigel Spink. Two goalkeepers on the pitch was unique enough, but this ultimately being Spink's final appearance for Villa after such a lengthy and celebrated career would in hindsight add to the peculiarity of the situation.

Also peculiar was the fact that Villa then had two home games postponed – against Liverpool and Sheffield Wednesday – at the end of December as wintry conditions set in around the country. The frustration was that other teams managed to get matches played having dealt with equitable snow, ice and the like, suggesting that Villa Park hadn't quite moved with the times in terms of modern innovations such as undersoil heating. By the time Villa did play again, it was New Year's Day 1996, meaning that they would in the second half of the season have two games in hand on the majority of other teams – the cost-benefit analysis of such a situation would remain to be seen. The unintended extended break did, however, give time for some fitness issues to be resolved, with only Paul McGrath and Ian Taylor missing from Little's first-choice squad for a trip to Middlesbrough. A first Villa goal for Alan Wright and another for Tommy Johnson secured a 2-0 win and consolidated the team in fifth, even having played those two games fewer.

Eight points from 15 was a reasonable if not remarkable return over December, and certainly made the ambition of European qualification perfectly justifiable. There were rumblings of concern though about the squad depth and how injuries could curtail progress. That was the lesson of this period of league games as 1995 drew to a close – how to best manage the squad and their fitness to maintain a European place in the league, while continuing to exploit the FA Cup and Coca-Cola Cup challenges on the horizon.

Chapter 25

Curios and Coca-Cola Cup Quarter-Finals

BEFORE THE serious business of a Coca-Cola Cup quarter-final could be considered, Villa had a genuine curio on their hands which represented a unique moment in their modern history. Villa had been drawn away to Southern Premier League side Gravesend & Northfleet in the third round of the FA Cup, but with some consternation Gravesend made a decision to play their 'home' tie at Villa Park. There was some logic in the decision given that the Kent side's ground, Stonebridge Road, held at a push only 3,500, meaning the move to Villa Park would open up the game to more fans but also bigger gate receipts. In moving, though, Gravesend were largely giving up any hope of an upset that playing in their own backyard may have given them. In more modern times this type of switch wouldn't happen – lower-league sides are more likely to play at their own home and hopefully gain a competitive edge, but ultimately Gravesend decided the other way.

Cynicism aside, some 5,000 Gravesend fans made the journey and enjoyed the day as if it were a cup final as opposed to the third round. No stranger to cynicism, Villa chairman Doug Ellis caused a modicum of controversy when he decided to move home season ticket holders from their usual seats for the game, proving that ticketing debates are by no means an invention of the 2020s. So Villa set about a cup tie that was played at their ground, but they were the away team, and in the process embarked on a game that was almost no-win. Anything other than a convincing victory, in their navy blue away kit given the context of the game being switched, would have been ill received. Villa's start suggested they had got the memo, Mark Draper scoring after just two minutes when his long-range effort somehow escaped the attention of the 'home' goalkeeper – the 20,000 or so non-Gravesend fans inside Villa Park would have imagined that Draper's goal was the start of a landslide, but it remained 1-0 at half-time, and Gravesend were not starved of possession. Fortuitously, Villa started the second period as they had the first, when Savo Milošević scored early on from a cross-cum-shot which made it almost impossible to imagine the lower-league side coming back. Yet still the avalanche of goals did not arrive, and when Tommy Johnson made it 3-0 in the 72nd minute it felt more of a damp squib, with Johnson looking almost apologetic that valiant Gravesend's big day out had been ruined. Brian Little was pragmatic afterwards, absorbed with the 'right result' and the fact that Villa hadn't had to exert themselves ahead of a big month. The proud Gravesend boss, Chris Weller, could be more light-hearted and referenced the match being switched when wryly pondering, 'Had we played it at our place we might well have got a draw.' The *Birmingham*

Post was not amused, a rather damning coda from Adrian Milledge opining that 'this was [Gravesend's] Wembley – Villa's, on this showing, is some way off'.

Little was right that a big month lay ahead, and a Coca-Cola Cup quarter-final just three days after the Gravesend game indicated that actually Villa were pretty close to Wembley. On Wednesday, 10 January 1996, Wolves arrived at Villa Park with a semi-final at stake in an eagerly awaited West Midlands derby. The anticipation of success in the competition was building among the Villa faithful, proved by the swelled attendance – 39,277 compared with 24,951 in the previous round against QPR. The local rivalry belied the fact that Wolves were a decidedly average First Division outfit, and as with the previous rounds it was a game Villa were expected to win.

As ever, Little's team selection verged on the predictable: Mark Bosnich, Gary Charles, Gareth Southgate, Paul McGrath, Mark Draper, Savo Milošević, Tommy Johnson, Andy Townsend, Alan Wright, Ugo Ehiogu, Dwight Yorke. The substitutes were Nigel Spink, Riccardo Scimeca and, returning from injury, Ian Taylor.

Although Wolves were struggling in the second tier, for West Midlands football fans of a certain vintage their side still contained some iconic and recognisable names – Mike Stowell, Mark Venus, Mark Rankine, Don Goodman and, of course, Steve Bull. Wolves manager Mark McGhee had initiated a man-marking system to counter Villa's mobile front three, with Rankine assigned the task of following Tommy Johnson wherever he went. It was a tactic that worked initially as Villa grew frustrated and sent long-range pelters towards Stowell's goal, although the crowd above and behind were more troubled than the Wolves stopper. One after another, Ugo Ehiogu, Dwight Yorke and Savo Milošević all sent shots careering high and wide, the opportunity for either side to get the ball down and play made nigh-on impossible by a horrible, cut-up Villa Park pitch. In the ITV coverage Alan Parry and Jimmy Greaves echoed one another by saying the 'game needs to slow down' and 'there's a lot of hurrying and scurrying but no end product'.

Inevitably for a derby there were some industrial challenges, with Bull and Ehiogu particularly going at it, the Wolves striker being booked before escaping his claret and blue shadow and testing a tracksuited Mark Bosnich. Johnson then extended the theme of shanked long-range efforts and Milošević, from a deep, hanging Alan Wright cross, skewed a header when he should have scored. Greaves was prompted to describe the striker's effort as 'terrible', just as referee Martin Bodenham blew the whistle on what Parry described as a 'hurly burly sort of first half'. It was difficult to know whether the commentator was being sarcastic or factual when he described the best chances as having fallen to Milošević, but 'of course' they had been missed.

The second half started in a similar vein, but the visitors grew in confidence and aptitude to take the ascendancy. Mark Rankine was the driving force, Bosnich having to be near his best to push a shot wide, before Wright cleared a header off the line from Don Goodman. Wolves came again, switching play trying to stretch Villa, and Wright made an even better goal-line clearance from Dean Richards, before Goodman brushed Bosnich's right-hand post with a shot across goal. Wolves were dominant, seemingly freed from a concept that they needed to show Villa, as their league level superiors, respect – although they were coming up against the team with the meanest defensive record in the Premier League at the time, and Villa held their nerve. At the other end Andy Townsend flashed a shot wide, before a sparkling move involving Ehiogu, Gary Charles and Milošević that seemed alien to the match as a whole, ended with a flying Dwight Yorke header barely missing the target. Top scorer Yorke would have been disappointed not to have scored but was integral in the move that led to the first goal of the game, playing in Charles again down the right to cross first time. The right-back's delivery was met by Johnson with a downright awful connection which could have even squirmed wide had it not hit Stowell and deflected into the net. It was the sort of scrappy goal the match deserved and an emotionless Brian Little watched the celebrations stoney-faced, more than aware that Johnson had struck firmly against the run of play. Wolves weren't cowed by going behind, however, and Bosnich had to spread himself again to deny Bull. Ian Taylor made a late substitute appearance for the goalscorer to shore things up, but almost scored a game-clinching second, and should have done, after Stowell parried a Milošević shot.

As the final whistle blew, Alan Parry acknowledged that Villa owed a huge debt of gratitude to Alan Wright and his two-goal saving interventions on the line but ultimately, as with the Gravesend FA Cup tie, the result was all that mattered for Brian Little and Aston Villa. The manager didn't quite buy into the idea that he was 'relieved' to have gone through, telling Parry that he went through a range of emotions, pleased and relieved just two of them. Little did charitably give Wolves 'credit' for their performance, but increasingly he was fixated on the tasks in front of him, rather than getting drawn into any particular analysis of games that had come and gone. As a personality Little was fascinating, his often emotionless, stoic demeanour on the sidelines of pitch and when facing the media in direct opposition to his flamboyance as a player. It was clearly a managerial persona he had crafted and worked on, and exemplified how he saw his role within a tactical structure where the onus was on players to deliver and get results within that structure.

For Villa, it meant a then record tenth League Cup semi-final, and their second in three seasons. It was a strong vindication of the transition Little had overseen, a semi-final being a tangible sign of the intent to re-establish Villa after the dalliances with relegation in 1994/95. While Villa had been labouring past their Black Country neighbours, Arsenal had beaten Newcastle through two Ian Wright goals, and would be their opponents in a two-legged semi-final, with the first leg in north London. It was an enticing prospect, but such was the progress under Little that Villa had some other serious irons in the fire, so unlike 1993/94 focus couldn't shift entirely towards the Coca-Cola Cup.

Chapter 26

The Quest for Europe

BRIAN LITTLE was clear that although progression in the Coca-Cola Cup, and in a more emergent sense the FA Cup, was to be celebrated, the 'bread and butter' of the Premier League still offered the most influenceable opportunity to achieve the season's primary goal of European qualification. So, three days after the Wolves quarter-final success, Villa returned to Premier League action with – in a situation that was no longer any sort of surprise – largely the same team, with only Dwight Yorke (away on international duty) being replaced by the fully fit again Ian Taylor to face Manchester United at Old Trafford.

The benefit of that consistency of selection was most evident in terms of defence. United sat second before the game, with Villa in fifth, but it was notable that Little's men had conceded 12 fewer goals. The three-centre-back axis was the rock that record was founded upon; Ugo Ehiogu, Gareth Southgate and Paul McGrath were slowly being acknowledged as the best in the league. It says much that Mark Bosnich, so often the headline-grabbing centre of attention, hadn't been at the forefront as in his first seasons at the club, a huge testament to what stood firm in front of him. A 0-0 draw at Old Trafford meant a fourth consecutive clean sheet and a miserly seven goals conceded across the past 15 games. Alex Ferguson, seemingly forgetting that Villa had taken four points from his side over the season, saw fit to criticise their approach as overly defensive and 'unentertaining'. Ever the diplomat, Brian Little resisted any temptation to bite back, pointing out that Villa had been 'very adventurous' at times over the season while simultaneously, with a wink in his opposite number's direction, admitting, 'I didn't find today's game entertaining.' The point wasn't enough to stop Villa dropping to seventh, although they remained only six points behind United in second, with those two Christmas games in hand.

Trinidad and Tobago's short-lived participation in the Gold Cup was to Villa's gain as Dwight Yorke returned to the side at home against Tottenham Hotspur, making a swift impression on proceedings. The game represented a significant opportunity for Villa to make ground on Spurs, who sat in fourth, and a big crowd and fast start bore that out. A dashingly inventive scissor kick from Yorke led to a magnificent McGrath goal – always a popular goalscorer, this was met with loud and boisterous celebration, in spite of or perhaps because of the fact he hadn't scored in nearly three years. Even Little, usually reserved, allowed himself a wee leap on the touchline. A Ruel Fox equaliser pegged Villa back, but it was Yorke again who seized the initiative, beating several defenders before shooting past an advancing Ian Walker in the Tottenham goal with exquisite precision.

It seemed Yorke's precociousness knew no bounds as Villa deviated slightly to FA Cup matters against Sheffield United. In an uneventful and unmemorable match, Yorke sprinkled some magic on proceedings after Savo Milošević had won a penalty midway through the second half. Yorke, approaching the ball at speed with the apparent intention of smashing it towards goal, instead paused before delivering a perfect Panenka. Sheffield United goalkeeper Alan Kelly, having already dived to his left, could only watch with mortification as Yorke's gentle chip landed in the centre of his goal. Fifth in the league and an FA Cup fifth round place achieved seemed a more than satisfactory return from the previous three games.

The bubble was burst in the rearranged match at home to Liverpool, which got off on a sentimental footing as Nigel Spink bade Villa Park farewell after a stupendous 19-year career. Once the game itself unfolded, Villa were well beaten 2-0 with the Liverpool front two of Stan Collymore and Robbie Fowler both scoring, a gentle reminder to Brian Little and Villa that the season would not just unfold ceremoniously before them. Little always preached the importance of bouncing back from defeats, and that message had usually been heard, with the side only once having fallen to consecutive losses. That had been back in October when twin reverses against Chelsea and Arsenal had steeled Villa to guard against such occurrences in the future.

There were no such worries against Leeds at Villa Park, where Little's side returned to a flowing and powerful footballing aesthetic in a convincing 3-0 win. The Leeds game saw a different slant on Little's team selection, with

Ugo Ehiogu and Tommy Johnson both missing with minor injuries, but replaced with Steve Staunton and Ian Taylor. The difference of a fully fit, competitive squad was obvious, especially in comparison (with all due respect) to earlier season replacements Riccardo Scimeca or Lee Hendrie.

Staunton and Taylor would demonstrate their industriousness, a characteristic that defined both men across their Villa careers, but it was Dwight Yorke again who stole the limelight. Not for the first time Yorke buried a header from a right-wing Gary Charles cross for his first goal, and 13th of what was proving a highly effective season. A second of the game, and 14th of the campaign, put the game to bed and represented a half century of Villa goals for Yorke. Astonishingly, Villa had only ever lost once when he had scored. While Villa failed to capitalise on their advantage, Yorke's brace further drove home the transformation that Little had overseen in his striker. He was, quite simply, right up there with the best in the Premier League, and while that would prove a problem for Villa in the future, his status as the 'main man' in this team was driving them forward to compete on three fronts, while driving up fans' optimism levels that this season could offer the succour they craved.

Villa's final league outing before their Coca-Cola Cup semi-final first leg with Arsenal was a trip to newly promoted Bolton Wanderers. While publicly Brian Little refused to even discuss the Arsenal clash, his team selection did ever so slightly point to the semi-final, with Paul McGrath rested from the squad completely, a decision afforded the manager by the return to fitness of Steve

Staunton. Tommy Johnson also came back from missing the Leeds game, with the perhaps unfortunate Ian Taylor missing out. Again, it was a reminder that Little now had better, relatively, options in terms of tweaking the side while also ensuring that there was a strong presence on the bench, not that that reminder would have appeased Taylor. In *The Squaddies*, Taylor had been asked what his greatest ambition or wish was, and without missing a beat the midfielder said he'd 'already achieved that by playing for the Villa'. Not being selected must have cut that little bit deeper for the bona fide Villa fan who would have been desperate to influence games at every opportunity. With an air of easy inevitability, two headed Yorke goals saw Villa to a straightforward win, consolidating themselves in fourth place, and an ideal fillip before the pivotal Coca-Cola Cup clash.

Brian Little could not have asked much more of his side. At no point since beating Wolves in the last eight had any attention drifted toward the lure of a glamorous semi-final opportunity. Ten points from a possible 15 was a strong offering, especially given that Villa had played sides around them, namely Manchester United, Spurs and Liverpool, coming through unscathed against all but the latter. Add in progression in the FA Cup and it was a heady mix, fuelled by six Dwight Yorke goals in those six games.

Chapter 27

Cup Campaigns Ignite

IN 1993/94, on their way to winning the Coca-Cola Cup, Aston Villa were involved in possibly the greatest two-legged semi-final the competition had ever seen. The two games against Tranmere Rovers, Villa losing 3-1 away from home in the first before winning the tie on penalties at Villa Park, contained every element of drama and emotion that a football game is capable of. That contest is almost as revered from a nostalgic standpoint as the final itself in that it enabled that Wembley success, when at various points all seemed lost.

Before a ball had been kicked in the 1995/96 iteration, things felt different. The fact it was the second time in three seasons that Villa had reached the last four perhaps lessened the lustre a little, but there was also a sense that Brian Little's reconstructed side was playing with an intent and style that it made it feel like anything was possible, and that went beyond the Coca-Cola Cup. Villa approached their meeting with Tranmere two years previously with a tacit acknowledgement that given their inconsistent form the Coca-Cola Cup by far represented their best chance to secure European football and win that first trophy in over a decade. The 1996 squad didn't have a trophy drought to start with, but equally knew that there were significant gains being made in the Premier League and FA Cup. It's also fair to say that the 1996 run hadn't had the standout moments, until Tommy Johnson scored against Wolves, of previous campaigns. In the image of their manager, Villa had quietly gone about their business with little fuss. The unspoken here is that it somehow felt slightly less important than in 1994, as if less rested on success in the last four from a longer-term perspective. Little saw it slightly differently, writing in hindsight that it was a case of fans 'were already convinced' they would be going to Wembley because of the 1994 experience. Either way you cut it, however, any complacency of thought among the supporters would vanish in an instant once the semi-final arrived.

Villa would face Arsenal in the first leg at Highbury on Wednesday, 14 February. Despite whispered assumptions that the previous league game against Bolton had seen a creative team selection with this game in mind, Brian Little named an unchanged side: Mark Bosnich, Gary Charles, Steve Staunton, Gareth Southgate, Mark Draper, Savo Milošević, Tommy Johnson, Andy Townsend, Alan Wright, Ugo Ehiogu, Dwight Yorke. The substitutes were goalkeeper Michael Oakes, Ian Taylor and Paul McGrath.

As a 14-man squad this was as strong as it got for Little, with Taylor and McGrath both equally as capable of starting as the XI chosen, and thus offering real depth from the replacements. Arsenal, in contrast, were shorn of their erstwhile centre-back pairing Tony Adams and

Steve Bould, and were also missing, with some relief, David Platt. They still possessed a strong and dangerous team, with Dennis Bergkamp revelling in his first season in English football, Ian Wright a constant menace up front and a defence still marshalled with quiet authority by Messrs David Seaman, Lee Dixon and Nigel Winterburn. The stage was set for a monumental clash, in which Villa were categorically seen as the underdogs, in direct contrast to Tranmere two years previously.

The tone was established in the opening minutes as both sides moved forward in a frenzy that belied any anxiety prompted by Wembley being in sight. First, Arsenal winger Glenn Helder sped down the left only to be met with a crunching Ugo Ehiogu sliding tackle. A similarly robust Gareth Southgate challenge then ended a move that had started with a delicious Bergkamp backheel, and the future England manager then played the ball long to give Savo Milošević his turn to run down the flank. Andy Townsend fired a speculative shot in from distance that, seeming to catch Seaman off-guard, swerved menacingly before being palmed away. Townsend's Irish colleague Steve Staunton was further away when he unleashed a similar shot.

All the aggression and energy was from Villa, undermining the pre-match build-up that had centred on the team's record as best defence in the Premier League. England manager Terry Venables was in the ITV studio and had earmarked Tommy Johnson as Villa's dangerman for his ability to drift around the fringes of the game. Johnson justified this attention midway through the first half when he forced Seaman into a smart save after what commentator Brian Moore described as a 'scintillating' Villa move. Arsenal seemed surprised by the cut and thrust Villa were prepared to employ; it was as if they had expected a rearguard action based on protecting a scoreline before the return leg at Villa Park. The home team roused themselves on 28 minutes when, against the run of play, they produced a goal of genuine distinction. Wright dropped slightly deep off Ehiogu to lay back a Paul Merson pass to an awaiting Bergkamp, who from 25 yards sent a low right-footed shot past a helpless Mark Bosnich, who even at his athletically best full stretch could get nowhere near. Worse was to come just five minutes later as Bergkamp found a space between Staunton and Southgate to breach Villa's offside trap before bearing down on Bosnich's goal, nudging the ball between the goalkeeper's legs for a 2-0 lead.

As with two years previously, Villa found themselves in deep trouble in a semi-final first leg and in dire need of a response. At Tranmere it had got worse before it got better, as 2-0 turned to 3-0 and only a late, late Dalian Atkinson goal gave Villa a sliver of hope in the second leg. But this version of Aston Villa, so well drilled by their manager, were not going to be easily sent packing, and Johnson continued to probe down the left flank. One bursting foray led to a corner from Mark Draper which Arsenal struggled to clear with any conviction, the ball pinballing around the penalty box. Somehow it found its way back to Draper who sent a looping header back from whence it came, where Dwight Yorke, waiting at the back post, was able to shoot past Seaman and give Villa renewed hope. ITV summariser Ian St John may have described the goal as a 'comedy of errors' from Arsenal's standpoint but a 2-1 half-time scoreline was the least Villa deserved.

There was no sign of either side relenting in the second period as the game flowed constantly from end to end, but without a genuine clear-cut chance. Draper had a long shot charged down, before Southgate did the same at the other end to quell Bergkamp. Villa continued to probe and press but any time they did get the ball into Arsenal's box Seaman easily gathered it and the threat was gone. The best chance of the second half fell to Ian Wright, who pulled his shot wide when better placed to score, although a raised linesman's flag would have seen it ruled out anyway. Seaman was sprung into action again soon afterwards, parrying a Draper shot wide. Barely two minutes later, Seaman was powerless to prevent Villa drawing level. Johnson fed Milošević down Villa's left, and the Serbian chipped a cross, helped by a semi-fortunate deflection, high into the penalty area, where Yorke hung in the air to meet the ball fractionally ahead of Seaman. Yorke's second of the night to level things up at 2-2 was his 18th of a staggeringly brilliant season, and in the process, despite it only being February, beating his previous best season return for Villa of 17 back in 1991/92. Equally astonishingly this was Yorke's third brace in three consecutive games, meaning the striker was in a blistering run of eight goals in just six games. As the *Birmingham Post*'s headline would read in the morning, 'Yorke leads the Villa charge' was becoming a regular and welcome experience. Things could have got even better for Villa and their star man after Seaman could only block Johnson's effort into Yorke's path only for the goalkeeper to somehow manage to recover to get his legs in the way of what would have been a hat-trick goal. Bosnich, not hugely utilised over the evening, was then called upon to make the save of the match to deny Ray Parlour as an increasingly desperate Arsenal attempted to gain a first-leg advantage.

Some dejected Arsenal faces at the final whistle showed that they would have seen this as an opportunity missed, given they were at home and had been 2-0 to the good. To now head into the away leg all square was a case of diminished returns. Arsenal manager Bruce Rioch, who had mentored Brian Little as an apprentice at Villa, put a brave face on his disappointment, saying he 'would rather go into the next game all square than a goal down' but forced to concede that Seaman had 'had more to do than Bosnich'. In the ITV studio anchorman Bob Wilson and Terry Venables were quick to anoint Villa as favourites for the second leg, and for once Brian Little was less circumspect post-match, clearly buoyed by an outstanding comeback: 'We are leaving here feeling happy to be on level terms after being two goals down. If we can keep it tight in the return leg we should fancy our chances.'

Before facing Arsenal in that return leg, Villa were in FA Cup action at Ipswich, as a double trip to Wembley began to seriously threaten to come into being. Little named another unchanged line-up, but any fears of a lethargic hangover from Highbury were quickly put to rest as Villa left Ipswich in their slipstream. Draper opened the scoring before then turning provider for Yorke's 19th of the season, with Ian Taylor, in for an injured Tommy Johnson, making it three just before the hour. Cruising,

Villa did concede late on, but it was a mere footnote to a serene advance to the last eight as their progress on three fronts began to make others sit up and take notice.

For the pernickety fan there remained just one concern, and that was Savo Milošević. Without a goal since January and the FA Cup defeat of Gravesend, Milošević continued to toil when chances were offered. His build-up play, determination on the periphery and general work rate could not be questioned, but he had been purchased to score goals. Against Ipswich, Savo had at least four presentable goalscoring chances, and while no striker could have expected to bury them all, the fact he drew a blank again was a concern. The reality was that Dwight Yorke's outstanding season had carried the load, but there lingered a seed of fear that at some point Villa might need another outlet. It was clearly an anxiety that jarred with the manager too, who damned his striker with faint praise, saying, 'Overall I could not have too many complaints about his commitment on the pitch and his attitude off it.'

Milošević had actually scored one more goal than Tommy Johnson over the season, but as the second leg with Arsenal loomed large, the latter's potential absence seemed harder to take. Ian Taylor in for Johnson was the solitary change on Wednesday, 21 February in the mission to reach the Coca-Cola Cup Final: Mark Bosnich, Gary Charles, Steve Staunton, Gareth Southgate, Ian Taylor, Mark Draper, Savo Milošević, Andy Townsend, Alan Wright, Ugo Ehiogu, Dwight Yorke. A defensively minded substitutes' bench contained Paul McGrath, Riccardo Scimeca and Michael Oakes.

Arsenal were again without Tony Adams and Steve Bould, although David Platt was back on the bench. Bruce Rioch looked to adapt his side by matching Villa's preferred style, picking Steve Morrow as a third centre-back, hoping that usual full-backs Winterburn and Dixon could get further forward, both as an attacking threat but also as a way of pinning back Villa's own marauding wing-backs Gary Charles and Alan Wright. Ray Parlour also started the second leg in an effort to match the industriousness of Villa's midfield three, and a clear acknowledgement from Rioch that setting about this side would be no easy feat.

In contrast to the Tranmere semi second leg, a packed Villa Park was buoyed by having a slight edge from the 2-2 draw at Highbury, knowing that after extra time away goals would count double. If there wasn't the mountain to climb like against Tranmere, the atmosphere didn't suffer as a result and a quiet confidence appeared to be the dominant emotion pervading the Aston night. Brian Little, reflecting on the occasion from his viewpoint, was more prudent, believing Arsenal remained the favourites although he also admitted, 'I knew that if we worked hard and did things properly we would still have a chance.' Little also recalled the atmosphere as 'tense and nervous', enhanced personally for him in that again he was going toe to toe with someone, in Bruce Rioch, who had been a big inspiration to him as a player and manager.

Once the game kicked off, at a television coverage-enabling time of 8.05pm, it was Arsenal who unsurprisingly made the early running, but although neat passing through midfield was pleasing to the eye there was minimal threat to Mark Bosnich's goal. Villa's strategy seemed to be based on one of containment, and in the early stages often the midfield would drop deep to cover for defenders and maintain a rigid shape. Alongside that degree of conservatism was an obvious secondary plan to break fast and powerfully, with Yorke an ever-willing participant, and one such early progression upfield led to a half-chance for Draper. Moreover, whatever Rioch's tactical plan may have been, it was Villa's wing-backs who were pinning Arsenal back, Charles and Wright pushing on to reduce any width in Arsenal's forward movement at all.

It wasn't until a quarter of an hour in that Arsenal were able to test Bosnich, the Australian stopper reacting well to tip over a Paul Merson header. That didn't prove to be a turning point in the game, however, as Arsenal seemed devoid of a creative vision to try and break down a resolute Villa tactical shape and setup, despite owning the ball. Time and time again Charles, Ehiogu, Southgate, Staunton and Wright cleared unceremoniously, willing to put their bodies on the line to protect the aggregate score. In the 22nd minute Milošević won a free kick on the edge of Arsenal's penalty area and Yorke produced a decent save from David Seaman as Villa grew more into the game. Moments later only a stunning sliding tackle from Andy Linighan prevented Yorke from pulling the trigger inside the box, although the Villa Park faithful, baying for a penalty, were not overly appreciative at the time.

Ian Taylor had started to look a little out of sorts after one-lung-busting foray forward, passing the ball out of play twice in quick succession before being replaced by Paul

McGrath. Taylor, due to a niggling but persistent injury, hadn't got going in the same way as he had dominated the end of 1994/95 and his withdrawal was another personal and collective frustration. It necessitated a move into midfield for Steve Staunton but given the fact Villa could afford to draw 0-0 to win the tie the added experience and nous of Paul McGrath at the back was no downgrade to proceedings. Yorke and Townsend passed up half-chances, but it was to no great amazement that the whistle blew on a goalless first half.

The fourth and final quarter of the tie as a whole started slowly and never really got going as Villa grew more and content in safeguarding their overall advantage and Arsenal continued to flatter to deceive in terms of creating anything remotely resembling a gilt-edged chance. The unfolding of the game was strange as Arsenal would have known that a single goal would put them firmly back in the driving seat. The fact they didn't seize the initiative was to Villa's credit – both the defensive resilience that they were displaying but also the knowledge that if Arsenal did push further forward then Villa's pace on the break through Yorke and Milošević could prove fatal. As former Villa manager Ron Atkinson, who knew all about a Villa Park semi-final commented on ITV, not only was Ian Wright isolated up top for Arsenal but any time the ball did go near him one of Villa's three centre-backs were alert to snuff out the danger. Townsend was proving Villa's most influential player all over the pitch, despite losing a contact lens and then putting its replacement incorrectly into his eye, and his energy pushed his team forward and back as the game ebbed and flowed.

When Arsenal did threaten it was from a more unusual source, that of left-back Nigel Winterburn. A diving header was grabbed by Bosnich before the defender also hit a post as the feeling Villa were not for breaching grew. As the end of 90 minutes drew close a goal for either team would be calamitous for the other, but still they cancelled one another out. With the clock running down it was Villa who had the best chances, substitute Riccardo Scimeca sliding in at the far post before Yorke laid one on a plate for Milošević who, leaning back, blasted high and wide.

With the tie still level at 2-2, and away goals not yet within scope of any calculation, the 39,334 inside Villa Park were subjected to a further 30 minutes of agonising extra time. Milošević was at it again in the first half, getting his feet in a muddle as the ball came to him in the Arsenal penalty box, but even that was more than the away side could muster in the face of an imperious Villa defensive unit. It's difficult to elocute now just how good Villa's centre-backs were on the night but also across the season. As a unit Southgate, Ehiogu and McGrath all offered something different but complemented each other at the same time. In hindsight it really was some achievement that both sides managed to stand firm for the length of time they did, showing the application of the players in not wanting to give an inch, as an epic semi-final second leg descended into a goalless conclusion.

As the final whistle blew on a strenuous and nerve-wracking night, Villa fans entered the playing field with unbridled joy at a second trip to Wembley in the space of three seasons. The end of extra time meant away goals counted and the 0-0 result was enough. The club had warned about any sort of pitch invasion, threatening participants with a bar on potential Wembley tickets, and it seemed likely that a failure to control fans would result in Football Association disciplinary action. The situation was exacerbated when dissatisfied Arsenal supporters also entered the pitch with the intention of creating a melee with home fans, and although any aggressive confrontation was quickly dispersed by police and Villa's own stewarding teams, it left an unsavoury taste in the mouth on a night of celebration.

Brian Little was clearly incredibly proud of his team for the display they put on to keep Arsenal at bay for 120 minutes, saying, 'It was a game that tested us, but the goalless draw turned out to be a terrific result.' There was certainly no apology from the manager about the approach to winning on aggregate via the away goals scored by Yorke at Highbury, and nor should there have been. Villa had drawn on their exceptional defensive ability, built over a stingy league campaign, to do what they needed to do – as ever with Little he had concentrated on what he could control and prepared his team in the most precise way possible. The reward was a record seventh League Cup Final appearance overall for the club, while for Little the opportunity to achieve a remarkable double feat of winning the competition as a player and then as a manager. Wembley here we come, again.

Chapter 28

Not Done Yet

AS WAS the case in 1994, Villa would need to wait to see who they would play at Wembley. The other last-four tie was intriguingly being fought out between Leeds United and Villa's second city rivals Birmingham City, with a 'derby final' being a real possibility, as it had been back in 1963. The first leg at St Andrew's had been a tight affair, with only a late Birmingham own goal giving Leeds a 2-1 winning margin to take back to Elland Road. The second leg went more to form and expectation as Leeds strolled to a 3-0 win with another goal from one of the Premier League's players of the season, Tony Yeboah. A 5-1 aggregate scoreline confirmed Leeds as Villa's opponents and dashed the dream of a Villa–Blues final. It was difficult to predict what kind of test Leeds would put up for Villa, given they were in the midst of a middling Premier League season, and had failed to find any consistency. That lack of reliability was shown through their regular-season games with Villa over 1995/96 – a 2-0 home win and a 3-0 loss at Villa Park. Either way, thoughts of Leeds and Wembley would need to wait for Brian Little and his side, as they were categorically not done on their other fronts – the FA Cup, where they could look forward to a quarter-final, and in the Premier League, where they lay ensconced in a pleasing fourth place.

The initial return to league action came at Selhurst Park against Wimbledon. Amazingly given the exertions of an extra-time semi-final second leg, but less surprisingly given Little's consistency, Villa made only one change, with Riccardo Scimeca coming in for the injured Ian Taylor. The absence of Taylor – and Tommy Johnson – had prompted a foray by Little into the transfer market, returning to his former club Leicester City to purchase forward Julian Joachim for £1.5m, who went straight into the squad at Selhurst Park. Joachim had erupted on to the footballing scene as a young man, scoring Leicester's first Premier League goal and gaining England under-21 honours before a troublesome injury stalled his progress. Rumours were that Villa had been interested and made semi-concrete enquiries from mid-1995 and, having spoken to former team-mate Mark Draper, Joachim made the decision that a move to Villa would be the best thing for him especially given he would be making the jump back to the top flight. It was a good addition for Villa – ultimately Joachim would spend until 2001 at the club – and replicated some of the skill set the side was missing with Johnson's injury but also provided some cover for Dwight Yorke. Ian Taylor once said 'Julian was the quickest thing I've ever seen', which is demonstrative of the qualities Little was bringing in. Interestingly, Joachim's own recollections were emblematic of the culture at Villa that his new manager had engendered. He was joining a team full of belief, confidence and quality, and one that clearly felt more was to come: 'Travelling to games, the lads would laugh and joke about how many goals we would win by. The Villa lads expected to win every single game.' They didn't win Joachim's first game, in which he was a late substitute, as a wild 3-3 draw was secured through a Yorke penalty and a bemusing two Wimbledon own goals.

Things went better for Villa and their new signing next up at home to reigning champions Blackburn Rovers, in a win that would consolidate their fourth-place position. Blackburn had failed to defend their title with any real relish, and along with the Wednesday night kick-off, they contributed to one of the few occasions home attendance had dipped below 30,000 over the season. The 28,008 who were there witnessed Joachim's first goal for the club, heading in a Gary Charles cross from close range. It was also the 4,000th home league goal Villa had scored, not that there was a long wait for the next one, with Gareth Southgate scoring his first league goal to complete a 2-0 win. A sequence of draw-win-loss was completed against third-placed Liverpool, Villa losing 3-0 at Anfield in their worst defeat of the season. As we will see, Liverpool had Villa's number all season, and that wasn't going to change.

Although Little would have been pleased to maintain fourth, the defeat ostensibly meant that catching Liverpool in third was now unlikely. Nevertheless, two good league wins followed against Sheffield Wednesday and Queens Park Rangers, both at Villa Park. In the former, Savo Milošević sent his 13-match goal drought asunder with a brace, alongside an Andy Townsend finish – the midfielder hadn't scored himself for 17 games, although to less consternation than his Serbian team-mate. Savo scored again versus QPR, and Yorke scored another two of an ever-glorious campaign. While fans enjoyed seven goals across the two games, there was also concern about the fact they saw four conceded. Added to the three at Anfield and Selhurst Park, the result meant ten goals given up across four games, a dramatic unravelling of the self-styled best Premier League defence. Injuries had played a part, with Steve Staunton and Paul McGrath both missing games, and Gareth Southgate sometimes being used in midfield to counter the injury to Mark Draper. Against QPR, Southgate himself went off injured as a gruelling season continued to take its toll on Villa's squad.

With league results as a pick-me-up, Villa travelled to Nottingham Forest for the FA Cup quarter-final and the continuing assault on a second trip to Wembley. Villa were down to their bare bones through a mixture of injuries, with Staunton, Southgate and Johnson out, Townsend suspended and Joachim cup-tied, which meant it was going to largely be on the starting XI to find a way to the semi-finals. The big surprise in the line-up was Franz Carr, who made his first start in 13 months as a Villa player. Deployed in the Tommy Johnson role, Carr's selection was mystifying but turned out to be a masterstroke as the former Nottingham Forest winger scored the only goal of the game, streaming past Steve Chettle before thrashing the ball high into Mark Crossley's goal. It showed how teams fighting in multiple competitions and formats can often be reliant on bit-part players to make an impact in the limited times they are called upon. It has become a cliche to talk about football as a squad game, but it was ever so – 1990s squads may have been smaller but the need to utilise what you had doesn't have a better example than Carr's winner. In any evaluation of the season as a whole, it would be the only mention the winger would get but that doesn't diminish the importance, even when compared to those star performers who did it week in and week out. As Villa reached their first FA Cup semi-final for 36 years, Little was effusive afterwards, revelling in the journey his team was on, saying, 'It felt very good afterwards to have achieved [the FA Cup] result, but we don't want the season to end here. We want more. Much more.'

FA Cup last four achieved, there were now only ten calendar days to the Coca-Cola Cup Final at Wembley. But in that period Villa would have to undertake a further two Premier League fixtures, with a stretched squad and the fight to maintain fourth spot intensifying, as Arsenal pushed hard from a place further back. The intervening period ultimately resulted in the sort of mini slump that had not been a factor since October 1995, meaning Villa would go into their Wembley week seemingly in poor form. A trip to Hillsborough to face Sheffield Wednesday was ruined by old boy Guy Whittingham and a 2-0 defeat, before heading back to Villa Park to play Middlesbrough in their last outing before the final. The team Brian Little selected for the last opportunity to prove readiness for Wembley was as depleted a one as Villa fans had seen all season, with a strange brew of suspensions for Ehiogu and Milošević, coupled with genuine injuries and knocks that were imbued with a high level of caution given the Leeds game to come. Alongside the disciplinary-related absentees, Gary Charles, Gareth Southgate, Ian Taylor,

Tommy Johnson and Riccardo Scimeca were all missing, meaning there were full debuts for Lee Hendrie, Paul Browne and Scott Murray and a return for Julian Joachim, who would be cup-tied against Leeds, having missed the FA Cup game for the same reason. A drab 0-0 draw gave the impression that Villa had merely gone through the motions, although Little was annoyed and said, 'We want to finish as high up in the league as possible and it was never our intention to start thinking about Wembley until this fixture was completed.' He went even further, given his usual watchfulness, confirming he 'had got a bit irritable with one or two of the lads who have been injured because I was hoping they would play tonight'. The manager would have been buoyed by the following night's result when Arsenal lost 1-0 at Old Trafford, to leave Villa with a five-point advantage in fourth place, albeit having played a game more. Focus could now shift happily and wholeheartedly to Villa's seventh League Cup Final.

For the lead-in to the final, Villa would stay at the Selsdon Park Hotel in Croydon. It was a venue hand-picked by Little, who remembered visiting there as a young player, and recalled it as a relaxed and secluded location where his players could ease into their preparation for the showdown. The reality of so many games leading up to the final meant that, as John Gregory described it, training was really 'just ticking things over' and constituted the odd seven-a-side, walking, nutrition building and snooker. That is likely some underselling, but it is true that Selsdon didn't have the best footballing facilities per se – Little described them as 'park pitches' and opportunity was also limited by a visiting Stoke City team (they were due to play Charlton Athletic in the First Division) being given priority.

Gregory and Little are both fond of a suggestion that Leeds manager Howard Wilkinson had sent a spy to try and elicit some tactical advantage over Villa, although the person conducting the espionage seemed to have got more than he bargained for. Gregory recalled a particular seven-a-side which was spied upon, consisting of kit man Jim Paul in goal, physio Jim Walker on the wing, and Paul McGrath lolling on the touchline eating apples. Ian Taylor recalled that despite the laissez-faire atmosphere, he still felt incredibly nervous for what was the biggest game of his life, and it's important to remember that for the vast majority of this Villa squad it was their first showpiece game and as a collective they were desperate to rubber-stamp progress with tangible success. Mark Bosnich, Paul McGrath, Steve Staunton and Andy Townsend had all played in the 1994 final, but Ugo Ehiogu and Dwight Yorke had only been travelling squad members. Similarly, Gary Charles had played at Wembley for Forest, but for other core members of Little's squad – Tommy Johnson, Mark Draper, Gareth Southgate, Savo Milošević, Alan Wright and Taylor – this was an exhilarating and novel experience and opportunity. For all the meticulous planning, a long journey to Wembley, through central London from Selsdon, under police motorcycle escort can't have helped settle that nervous energy.

For all the depleted-ness of his last Premier League team selection, Little had an apparently fully fit squad from which to choose for Wembley and the awaiting challenge of Leeds. It was a relief to all connected with the club that

Little could call upon what had been his strongest and most consistent line-up from across the season, and a mirror image of the selection for the opening-day victory against Manchester United: Mark Bosnich, Gary Charles, Alan Wright, Gareth Southgate, Paul McGrath, Ugo Ehiogu, Ian Taylor, Mark Draper, Savo Milošević, Dwight Yorke, Andy Townsend. The substitutes were Steve Staunton, Tommy Johnson and Michael Oakes.

The team selection tells us three important narratives. The first is the fact that fielding the same team that had also started the season's first game is testament to the manager's unerring belief in the system and tactics he was employing, and the best make-up of personnel to deliver that vision. Not that Little was afraid to change the team, it was just that he would only do it if the ends concretely justified the means. The second is the remarkable overhaul that had taken place since the 1994 final. Villa looked and felt different under Little and even those survivors from the highs of the Ron Atkinson era were different beasts in a new era for the club. The third is centred on Little's desire for balance in his side that was, in his words, a 'tribute' to his old manager Ron Saunders. The left-right combination up front of Milošević and Yorke was motivated by Saunders' own use of an either-footed front line, whether it had been Little himself and Andy Gray, or later Peter Withe and Gary Shaw. Little's midfield three of Taylor, Townsend and Draper was also modelled on Villa's most celebrated sides under Saunders – with the leader Andy Townsend as his Dennis Mortimer, the smooth passing and running of Mark Draper a nod to Gordon Cowans and the box-to-box relentlessness of Ian Taylor conjuring recollections of Des Bremner. Little had built a team, if not in his own image exactly, then certainly in an image of historical consciousness of Aston Villa Football Club, and now he had the opportunity to write himself, with further permanence, into that very history.

As an opponent, Leeds exhibited many of the traits that Villa had two years earlier. It was the Yorkshire club's first major final since the 1975 European Cup Final, heightening the expectation of a rare chance to win a trophy, and they also made some niche decisions with youth players to cause some surprise with their line-up. Andy Gray and Mark Ford, like Graham Fenton had for Villa in 1994, started at the expense of more experienced colleagues – for Ray Houghton read Tomas Brolin and Brian Deane. Howard Wilkinson's full team selection was as follows: John Lukic, Gary Kelly, Lucas Radebe, Carlton Palmer, John Pemberton, David Wetherall, Andy Gray, Mark Ford, Tony Yeboah, Gary McAllister, Gary Speed. On the bench were Brian Deane, Tomas Brolin and Nigel Worthington.

Chapter 29

The 1996 Coca-Cola Cup Final

DARLINGTON-BORN REFEREE Robbie Hart led Aston Villa and Leeds United out in front of 77,065 fans at a cold Wembley Stadium on Sunday, 24 March. As ITV commentator Brian Moore described it, this was the 'people's final' with the vast majority of match tickets available to the everyday public, as opposed to the FA Cup Final. Moore was joined on commentary duties by none other than Ron Atkinson, still very much in the public eye two years after his own Aston Villa Wembley moment. The Villa team, adorned in crisp white Reebok sweatshirts, were introduced to the guests of honour (including Virginia Bottomley, then secretary of state for national heritage) by captain Andy Townsend, who had taken on the leadership mantle from his midfield partner Kevin Richardson in the aftermath of the 1994 final. Moore and Atkinson worked their double act effortlessly, poking mischief at Savo Milošević's English skills and praising Ugo Ehiogu, before questioning whether the esteemed invitees might just hurry it along. Atkinson, never one to quit while he was ahead, then went on to question why Bottomley was even there, recalling it made more sense when a 'legend of the game' was involved, Exhibit A being Nat Lofthouse two years earlier. With the national anthem played and sung, Brian Little was pressed for brief comment, only to talk about the 'hassles' the build-up to a game like this entailed before Atkinson numbed the mood even further with a prediction that the viewing public were about to see a 'war of attrition'. Everyone, inside and out of Wembley, was hugely relieved to see the football commence.

Dwight Yorke and Milošević got things under way, and Villa, in claret and blue, quickly won an attacking free kick for a clumsy challenge on the former. It was Yorke, in the unravelling of the free kick, who got in behind the Leeds rearguard but had strayed offside. The opening running was all made by Villa in terms of territory and possession, but they couldn't fashion a particularly strong chance, summed up by a scuffed Milošević effort. At the other end, Little's tried and tested back five ensured Villa's shape was maintained and seemed set to prevent Leeds gaining too much ground. As John Gregory has said since, Villa were 'so comfortable in our own skin' and even in the early exchanges this was evident. For all of Villa's early steadiness of shape, the reality was that the game's first ten minutes left a little to be desired, the battle for midfield supremacy appearing to be central to either team gaining a foothold. Mark Draper, Andy Townsend and Ian Taylor attempted to drift off their markers to create space, while Gary McAllister and Carlton Palmer looked to surge forward with the ball to transition defence to attack quickly for Leeds.

The next ten minutes didn't overly improve the game as a spectacle, with some nice build-up play from both sides (one exquisite flick from Milošević should have been capitalised on by Townsend) and a fleeting chance for Yorke which he venomously hammered against the body of Leeds goalkeeper John Lukic. Lukic's opposite number Mark Bosnich watched an Andy Gray drive flash safely wide, before coming to claim a deep corner, but he would have been glad of his tracksuit bottoms to keep warm.

There were growing seeds, though, of how Villa might be trying to play, with Ian Taylor looking to drag defenders left, freeing up Milošević to drop deeper and pick up the ball. In the 20th minute those ideas came to sparkling fruition with a goal from Milošević, his first in the Coca-Cola Cup campaign. Gary Charles managed to get a foot in on Gary Speed and nick the ball, before Townsend tore into McAllister to do the same. Picking the ball up in the deep position he had started to occupy, Milošević bore down on goal, moving left before sending an extravagant dipping shot into the net. It was a superlative strike and some vindication for the Serb in terms of the criticism he had received, although Taylor also deserved huge credit for the barrelling run he made slightly to Milošević's right, dragging David Wetherall with him, affording the space for the striker to score from 25 yards out. Summarising, Ron Atkinson said it was the least Villa deserved having 'dominated proceedings' and little that immediately followed threatened to alter that. A stony-faced Howard Wilkinson, on the Leeds bench, must have feared the worst even with two-thirds of the game to go. The sense of the game as a whole was starkly different to when Dalian Atkinson opened the scoring in the 1994 final. Both were greeted with euphoric celebration but whereas Atkinson's prompted secondary nervy emotions of 'poking the bear' in terms of Manchester United, Milošević's goal led to a sense of 'we've got this'.

It was all Villa after the goal, with Leeds incapable of conjuring up anything of significance, the dangerous Tony Yeboah looking isolated and frustrated. Villa surged forward with regularity, even Gareth Southgate getting in on the act, and Milošević and Townsend sent innocuous efforts into the hands of Lukic. Although a second goal would seem elusive, Villa's better tempo and energy meant that Leeds just could not respond with any fluency – and on the odd moment when they did beat the midfield press of Townsend et al, they were met by the granite-like Ehiogu and McGrath. Yorke seemed desperate for a goal, not only to top a sensational season but also to banish any sombre memories from 1994 when he hadn't been involved. He knew that, if his position as Villa's main striker and influence was to be cemented, a goalscoring trophy win would just about do it.

With 15 minutes of the first period remaining Yorke drove a shot wide, before McGrath was booked for a tete-a-tete with Yeboah. Milošević, buoyed by his goal, drove into the Leeds box several times and a Townsend free kick was easily gathered by Lukic, but that was about all either side could muster. Even so, Brian Little was visibly winning the tactical battle, his forwards running wide either side of Leeds' three central defenders while Villa's wing-backs were nullifying the same areas for their opponents, and it said it all when as the midfield three passed in triangles for a spell, they were serenaded with oles from the Villa end. As the first half petered out, Milošević broke but couldn't find a galloping Mark Draper, although Villa were by far the happier, 1-0 up and under little threat from a team that were providing little in response.

At half-time, Leeds brought Brian Deane on to add some ballast and physical threat to their front line and immediately Ehiogu realised he was in for a tougher proposition as Deane dragged the big defender out wide. Leeds did look brighter all round, although that was less an epic transformation than a flickering spark brought out of necessity. Deane continued to add to that spark, but Leeds flattered to deceive with Bosnich falling on successive speculative Gray efforts. As Leeds attempted to conjure up an equaliser, space grew in midfield, with only Carlton Palmer exhibiting what could be described as defensive solidity. That soon began to tell, a bursting Yorke break and cross somehow eluding Taylor and Milošević, before Townsend stung Lukic's palms having been given time to manufacture a long-range effort. On 53 minutes, it was Townsend who fed Alan Wright down the left; scampering on to the precise pass, Wright sent a cross deep into the penalty area, aimed towards where Milošević had peeled away at the back post. Savo's movement dragged Lucas Radebe with him, the defender only capable of knocking the ball back into the danger area where an unmarked Taylor was ideally positioned to crash home a left-footed volley. It was a wonderful strike, given extra credence in terms of what it would have meant to former Holte Ender Taylor, and as Brian

Moore said on commentary, it was difficult to see any way back for Leeds. Taylor's goal also confirmed the spirit and camaraderie that Little had built and fostered in his squad, as the manager would later describe: 'Tommy Johnson was desperate to play in the final but found himself on the substitutes' bench. Yet when Ian scored Tommy raced 40 yards down the touchline to be the first to congratulate him, even though Ian had been given the nod ahead of him.'

In the stands, supporters were ebullient as Villa's play became increasingly characterised by a swagger and confidence that they were cruising to victory. A cacophonous rendition of 'Birmingham, are you listening?' was bellowed out as Brian Moore and Ron Atkinson struggled to summon up motivational words for any Leeds fans and the general viewer, settling on a sense of inevitability that a one-sided final was in essence done and dusted. Atkinson feared that the scoreline could become 'humiliating' for Leeds as Draper slammed a swerving half-volley towards Lukic's goal.

The introduction of Tomas Brolin for Lucas Radebe after 66 minutes promoted a positional shift for Leeds, but it all had the air of too little too late (or as Brian Moore said on commentary 'after the horse had bolted') and actually gave Milošević and Yorke more space to break at will. Not that Villa were furiously attacking in search of a third goal, at times wholly content to keep the ball and pass in intricate and pretty patterns before accepting a half-chance. Though no one at the time would have admitted it, the fact that Villa could have one eye on the FA Cup semi-final the following week is emblematic of their dominance and equally a humiliating position to put Leeds in. Gary Charles then curled a long-range shot wide as Villa became encamped in Leeds' half, and to use boxing parlance, keeping their opponent entirely at arm's length.

The emotions watching what was unfolding at Wembley that day could not have been more starkly different than what Villa fans had lived two years earlier. Although they found themselves two goals to the good at similar points in each game, against Manchester United in 1994 they were subjected to a barrage of pressure that needed to be withstood. Initially, they couldn't withstand it, Mark Hughes pulling a goal back for United before Mark Bosnich kept Villa ahead with an otherworldly, match-defining save. Even with Bosnich's heroics there was a sense of dread among the Villa faithful that United would come knocking again, and again. There were categorically no such fears against Leeds – as a final 1996 was the polar opposite to 1994 from a Villa perspective, anxiety around a tantalisingly close victory versus a coasting self-confident procession.

As the game headed to its denouement, Ron Atkinson pointed out that despite not scoring, he would struggle to believe Dwight Yorke had played a better game all season. The striker may well have agreed, but clearly was still striving to score and top off another fabulously freewheeling example of forward play. As the clock ran down, Draper played an incisive through ball to the onrushing Milošević on the right, who galloped towards the goal with (not for the first time) John Pemberton helplessly back-tracking. Unselfishly, Milošević squared for Yorke to hammer the ball high into the net. Villa, 3-0 up and home and hosed, could see out the remaining moments with deserved ease, their supremacy utterly comprehensive.

Chapter 30

One Down

BRIAN LITTLE remembers being 'restrained at the final whistle' having felt his side were 'ready for victory', and while that's not to say the Villa boss was not also ecstatic inside, it says a lot about the levels to which he had raised the team. The aspirations of the 1996 side felt dramatically different to their 1994 peers, despite the fact they had just won exactly the same trophy. For the Villa fandom, was there a slight sense of familiarity breeding contempt? Had a new generation of supporters, starved of any semblance of success, now been cowed by two major trophies in three seasons? There is a kernel of truth in those sentiments although for any football fan, individual seasons and games hold particular resonance and compare favourably or less so, depending on lived experience. For Ron Atkinson, the 1994 success would come to be seen as very much the zenith of his time as Villa manager, but for Brian Little this felt more like a staging post – an important one, but just a staging post nonetheless. There is also the question of the opposition, in that beating Manchester United was perhaps more iconic in hindsight, especially given Villa were clear second favourites – as opposed to comfortably beating a less impressive Leeds side, who they were favoured to prevail over.

For the players, breathless elation might be the best descriptor. Ian Taylor, nabbed immediately on the pitch by ITV's Gary Newbon, described the feeling as 'unbelievable' and was quick to point out that Villa had often played as well as this across the season, and winning was the 'icing on the cake' and that the side 'still had important games to go'. Taylor's comments exemplify the difference that two years had made – if 1994 had felt like a wonderful, cathartic one-off, 1996 felt like a justified beginning of wonderful things to come. The spirit that had been seen during the game was evident again on the pitch with Newbon, as Taylor and Andy Townsend leapt to Savo Milošević's defence, Townsend describing him as an 'easy target' but both glowing as they described that first goal. It was Townsend who was named man of the match among a wide field of candidates in claret and blue, before lifting the trophy with huge pride. Little was as dogmatic as ever, telling Newbon he had been frustrated with the last 15 minutes before softening, confirming it had been a 'great day out'. In fairness to Little he knew more than most what it meant to lose at Wembley having been defeated twice as Leicester manager in play-off finals. It had been a feeling he was determined not to repeat, and as had been the case across his tenure he could reflect on a job well done, celebrate in his own style and move on to the next challenge.

Back in the dressing room, players had no respite from Newbon and were also joined by Rob Bishop, now the de facto guardian of the club's written word, then a local journalist. Bishop recalled the scenes being dominated by a 'tipsy' Dwight Yorke who relentlessly belted out the Frank Sinatra standard, 'New York, New York', which Villa fans had adapted to his name. The players were, in coach John Gregory's words, on the 'crest of a wave', in that the win had provided that rubber stamp of notoriety beyond a simple feeling of 'having had a good season'. Gary Charles went as far as to say to Newbon, 'This will be the first of many, from what will be one of the best teams around.' It's difficult to imagine any of the 1994 squad having the confidence to have said the same thing at a similar moment. Alan Wright told Newbon it was simply 'a great day, a great feeling and a great performance and now we can enjoy the evening', and of course they did.

Doug Ellis hosted a banquet in London for the players, their families and other club connections, describing it as his 'pinnacle in all my days in football'. That's an interesting point of view given he was also chairman two years previously, so this clearly cut different even for Ellis – whether that was the feeling they were building success on success, or some vindication for his sacking of Ron Atkinson and the progress since. Taylor was hazy on the evening's salutations, describing everyone as 'hammered' and vaguely recollecting Tommy Johnson 'in a wig and on a piano'. There was no doubt that there was some letting down of hair, but as Little joked with Newbon at the banquet, 'You might be surprised that a little bit of me is rubbing off on them and they might behave a little better than you expect.' Little was also more reflective with the ITV anchor, describing his children being upstairs eating pizza and telling him that 'everyone had played well'. And indeed, they had – at Wembley as well as across the campaign.

It was a campaign that, as in 1993/94, traversed eight games in total, with only two coming away from Villa Park (both of which were second legs in two-legged ties) and, naturally, the final beneath the twin towers of Wembley. In a bizarre act of symmetry, Villa scored 16 times across the eight games, the same as 1993/94, although they only conceded three, down from seven two years earlier. Fascinatingly, all three goals conceded came in the away legs at Peterborough and Arsenal. Bookended by a thrashing of Peterborough and the convincing win against Leeds, the games in between were settled by small margins, and if not cagey certainly conservative at times, in line with Villa's strong Premier League defensive record. Given Brian Little's preference for consistent team selections, it is not a surprise that eight players started all eight games – Mark Bosnich, Gary Charles, Mark Draper, Ugo Ehiogu, Gareth Southgate, Andy Townsend, Alan Wright and Dwight Yorke – while Savo Milošević missed just one. Paul McGrath started five and came on as a substitute in a sixth, as did Ian Taylor, and Tommy Johnson started four. Those levels of uniformity didn't leave much room for anyone else, with only Steve Staunton (twice) and Riccardo Scimeca (once) starting a game from the wider squad. Gareth Farrelly and, before he had left for Blackburn, Graham Fenton, made one and two substitute appearances respectively.

In line with his contribution across the season as a whole, it was not a shock that Dwight Yorke was the top scorer across the Coca-Cola campaign with six goals. In another twist of fate, that was the same number Dalian Atkinson had scored two years earlier in the same competition, a campaign that Yorke hadn't played a single minute in. Tommy Johnson was the next contributor with two goals, and seven players (Draper, Ehiogu, Milošević, Southgate, Staunton, Taylor and Townsend) scored one each, added to one own goal. Mark Bosnich would have been delighted with his clean sheets, but he had been a secondary figure when compared to the impact he had in 1994. That shows that Villa as a defensive unit had improved exponentially, offering better protection to a goalkeeper who remained capable of the extraordinary. Steve Staunton's role was also diminished from two years previously, remaining unused on the substitutes' bench, although Paul McGrath and Andy Townsend offered a consistent and experienced lineage from the 1994 squad.

Back at the celebratory banquet, Brian Little was asked about the fact that, Coca-Cola Cup secured, his team now had an FA Cup semi-final to contend with against Liverpool at Old Trafford. It speaks to Little's focus and endeavour that he pondered, 'It gets bigger now, a bigger game than ever,' because 'so many people will think we might give in or not care as much', but actually he was desperate to believe that winning at Wembley would actually prompt the club to want it *even more.*

Another League Cup to be celebrated and commended. One target down, but with two more still sharply in focus.

Chapter 31

An FA Cup Semi-Final and Focus on Fourth

VILLA HAD an early opportunity to test Brian Little's hope that his side would not rest on their laurels with the FA Cup semi-final against Liverpool just seven days after the Wembley success against Leeds. As was the case at the time, FA Cup semi-finals were played at a neutral venue as opposed to Wembley, and for Villa v Liverpool, Old Trafford had been chosen, although all parties were disappointed that only 39,072 were in attendance, nearly a quarter of tickets unsold, partly down to an extravagant Football Association pricing strategy. As was now commonplace, Little named an unchanged side, asking the same XI and substitutes who had secured the Coca-Cola Cup to go to the well again.

Liverpool started with darting high energy and Andy Townsend was forced into a sliding attempt to stop a Steve McManaman driving run down the left, although Villa's captain was convinced the winger had dived with no contact actually made. The early encounters felt very much like blood and thunder as Mark Wright and Gareth

Southgate spared no caution when sliding in together on the edge of the penalty box. Southgate came off worse, having a knee strapped up by physio Jim Walker. It was Southgate who lost Robbie Fowler, so often the scourge of Villa, to direct a superb diving header past Mark Bosnich to put Liverpool 1-0 up and prompt the *Irish Independent* to scathingly write that 'Villa would have been better off defending with ten men, because Southgate was not fit physically or mentally to deal with Fowler'.

With Southgate replaced by Steve Staunton, Villa settled and began to exert a modicum of influence in progressing the ball up the field, one such foray leading to Ian Taylor being sandwiched by Liverpool defenders in an action that had Villa baying for a penalty. Referee Paul Durkin quickly dismissed any such claims, a decision that saw a furious Dwight Yorke pursue him back up the other end of the pitch. Savo Milošević, having held the ball up well, then burst forward to send a Wembley-like shot searing towards David James's goal but it veered agonisingly wide. Mark Draper then tried to re-enact the free kick that had first been trialled against Peterborough, with Yorke flicking it up to the midfielder as Townsend had done earlier in the season. Draper's execution was not comparable, and the shot hit Ugo Ehiogu, who couldn't turn the ball home. A series of goalmouth scrambles followed, from which no Villa player could manage to turn the ball home, in part due to the continued efforts of James.

Liverpool were by no means anonymous, especially after half-time, with Jason McAteer and Fowler both having presentable chances although neither forced an intervention from Bosnich. At the other end James was having no similar respite and the future Villa goalkeeper was forced into action again when he somehow saved at point-blank range from Ehiogu after Milošević had headed across goal. Brian Little had famously described the previous week's Coca-Cola Cup Final in terms of 'even the traffic lights were in our favour' to demonstrate how everything had gone Villa's way. Old Trafford felt very different, Villa summoning up a performance but lacking that moment of clarity to get back in the game and equally not experiencing that little bit of luck teams sometimes need. There was a growing sense that Villa's heads were dropping with a tacit acknowledgement that this may not be their day – an uncommon emotion over the season as a whole.

McGrath and then Bosnich's crossbar kept Liverpool out, but those twin forces only delayed the inevitable, with Fowler scoring a superlative half-volley to put Villa two down as the final whistle loomed. A third Liverpool goal, scored by McAteer, put a gloss on the scoreline that was not deserved and gave lie to what had been a strong – if not clinical – Villa performance. Even Liverpool manager Roy Evans described the scoreline as 'misleading', although more instructive was the 8-0 aggregate ascendancy Liverpool held over Villa in three games across 1995/96. Quite simply, Villa hadn't been able to cope with the Reds over the season and especially Fowler, who had scored five goals in the three games.

There was inevitable disappointment that a second Wembley final in a single season had been prevented, the *Birmingham Post* summing up the emotions well with the headline 'Blood and Guts Villa get a raw deal as Fowler wields big stick'. Little was disheartened by the final result and acknowledged that the 'first goal was the difference', also saying, 'We knew we had to get something from somewhere but in fairness we didn't know where to get it from.' A growing sense pervaded post-match that maybe this was just a game too far for Villa in what had been an exceptional season, but one that had necessitated fighting on three fronts deep into March. That exceptionalism wasn't going unnoticed, however, with developments behind the scenes pointing to long-term planning from Doug Ellis, aligned with a belief that Little was creating a long-term project that this season was merely the start of. First there emerged reports, confirmed by Little, that Dwight Yorke would be offered a lucrative new contract that would keep him at Villa beyond 2000. It was a commitment to a player who had established himself fully as the club's main man, but also to his manager, who had finally got the best out of someone who had at times looked destined to operate on the margins. It wouldn't be long until Little, and his assistants John Gregory and Allan Evans, would also be offered new contracts, as with Yorke, on terms that would take them into the new millennium. All of these negotiations pointed to stability and a conscious effort to cement a legacy from what had been a tremendous campaign.

Having played 45 games over the season, amazingly Villa still had six to play – all in the Premier League as they strived to hold on to fourth place. The Coca-Cola Cup win had already secured European football, so the league fixtures were about finishing strongly and maintaining a position they had occupied for large parts of 1995/96. Little was adamant that there should be no drop-off, and his side responded well at the next opportunity, beating Chelsea 2-1 at Stamford Bridge. Having already fallen a goal behind, Bosnich's penalty save boosted Villa collectively to come back, with Milošević and Yorke scoring to secure a valuable and cathartic three points. Between them, Villa's first-choice strike pairing now had 38 goals across all competitions, and while Yorke was always regarded as the weightier contributor, Milošević's 14 in his first season in English football was commendable. Savo had absolutely grown into the campaign, best exemplified with his hold-up play and driving runs that were often selflessly aimed at providing for others – the case in point being Yorke's winner against Chelsea. Little and his coaching team would have been quietly confident that more would be to come from Milošević and the fact he had played every time he was available further underlined that.

Having shone in west London, Milošević had a more sombre afternoon at Villa Park just 48 hours later. Although Villa won routinely, but inspiringly, 3-0 against lowly Southampton, Milošević cut a frustrated figure. After a missed chance the striker had kicked out at the advertising hoardings and then after the game Southampton manager Dave Merrington accused him of punching Tommy Widdrington off the ball. Little preferred to limit his commentary to the fact that frustrations being aired just showed Milošević cared deeply about his own and his team's performances, and that his involvement in the three goals scored by Gary Charles, Ian Taylor and Dwight Yorke was the real story.

In hindsight, that win was as good as it would get for Villa over the remainder of the season, as the squad finally ran out of steam. A 1-0 loss away at Newcastle was no debacle, and as home boss Kevin Keegan pointed out, 'Villa dominated for long periods', but there was a sense of ennui about them, summed up when Yorke limped off with a dead leg. Fortunately, Arsenal could only draw in the north London derby the following day, meaning Villa were safe in fourth, with time running out in terms of anyone catching them. They then secured a valuable point against West Ham, thanks to a Paul McGrath goal, to further tighten their grasp on fourth place but the match was overshadowed by a shocking injury to Gary Charles. Clearly and visibly suffering what would later be confirmed as a severe, career-threatening ankle break and dislocation, Charles was rushed straight into an ambulance with his team-mates visibly shaken by what they had seen. Little was equally dismayed, 'I'm not over-bothered about the result. What happened to Gary knocked the stuffing out of us. I have never seen a dressing room so subdued. We want to finish the season as well as possible, but I am afraid our minds weren't there after the injury. We were gone.'

There were clearly some lingering effects of the injury visible in Villa's final home game of the season, an insipid affair against Manchester City. Beyond Charles, injuries were starting to tell; Southgate, Yorke and Taylor all missed a match that highlighted the transformation Brian Little had overseen since the denouement of 1994/95. Twelve months earlier, Villa had needed to summon a performance in their last home game, against Liverpool, to try and quell the very real relegation threat they were under. Now Manchester City were in that position and found enough energy to scrape a 1-0 win – in contrast Villa couldn't summon up the wherewithal, a lesson in irony given the success of the season as a whole. After the match, Villa paraded the Coca-Cola Cup to effusive praise and celebration from the crowd, a salient reminder of the success that the club had witnessed over that season.

Although Villa had slipped to defeat, Arsenal could only draw against Blackburn, meaning Little's team maintained their position. Arsenal did have a game in hand, but when they drew that in midweek against Liverpool it became clear that it would come down to the final day of the season. An under-strength Villa side, containing Lee Hendrie, Scott Murray and Paul Browne, sunk with little resistance, losing 1-0 at Everton, but the focus was always elsewhere given that Arsenal were three points behind anyway. As Villa were petering out on Merseyside, Arsenal did secure the win they needed against Bolton. However, the 2-1 scoreline wasn't enough to overhaul Villa – miraculously the two sides finished level on 63 points and with an identical goal difference of 17, Villa securing fourth by virtue of the three more goals they had scored. Little conceded that his side had 'ended disappointingly' but ultimately this was a case of job done.

The Everton defeat brought the curtain down on what had been a spectacular season. A League Cup win, accompanied by a fourth-placed Premier League finish and an FA Cup semi-final, domestically was as good as it got. Imagine the rapture if the current Villa side were to replicate that type of season across all three competitions.

Brian Little had crafted a system and team that was forward-thinking and flexible – capable of grinding out a result and eviscerating teams at the same time. The club had overhauled the playing staff to such an extent that the demographic of the personnel was almost unrecognisable, and those decisions had borne fruit in terms of the season that unfolded.

And yet, 1995/96 isn't always remembered as fondly as other successful periods, although hopefully this narrative goes some of the way to altering that perception. Tales for another time, but that may be partly because of how things unfolded in Villa's immediate future and the fact that, spoiler alert, the anticipated success from the foundation of 1995/96 never materialised. No more so is this evident than if we return to those long-term contracts discussed in the wake of the FA Cup semi-final loss and fast forward to 2000. Villa were again at Wembley, this time hoping to win a first FA Cup since 1957, but the twin guiding stars of 1995/96, Brian Little and Dwight Yorke, were long gone. John Gregory remained, but now as manager, as did some of the 1996 Coca-Cola Cup winners including Ugo Ehiogu, Gareth Southgate, Alan Wright and Ian Taylor, but the ultimate defeat signalled the end of most connections to the Brian Little era. From a 1995/96 season that promised so much, little legacy would survive.

Chapter 32

Heritage

IN THE close-season following Champions League qualification in May 2024, Aston Villa undertook their usual smartening up of certain aspects of Villa Park. One of the standout aspects of the cosmetic makeover was a montage added to the North Stand featuring all of Villa's trophies across their storied history. The first of them had been secured in 1886, an FA Cup win setting under way an unprecedented period of success domestically. The latest trophy date on display is 2020/21, when the FA Youth Cup was won, and the one before is 2018/19 when victory in the Championship play-off final secured a return to the top flight.

While it's understandable why those markers are included within the graphics, it is also a salient reminder that the most recent dates for what might be described as a major trophy are the two Coca-Cola Cup wins of 1994 and 1996. It's not just on the North Stand that these achievements are enshrined – as you walk down the side of the Trinity Road Stand, past the players' entrance, images adorn the exterior wall of Villa's achievements, including iconic shots of Dalian Atkinson and the three goalscorers in the 1996 final. At the start of the 2023/24 season an anonymous instigator installed various vinyl type graphics around the approach to Villa Park, and the one that appeared on the gates of Aston Hall and Park was again Atkinson. The new club shop, again refitted in the 2024 close-season, is adorned with nods to the past – including an Ugo Ehiogu signed shirt from 1996 and (slightly more incongruously) a Bryan Small one from 1994. Matchday programmes from both finals are preserved in glass cases, and of course fans can purchase home and away retro shirts from the two campaigns. The 1996 AST shirts are the most modern of the retro reproductions, their association with a trophy locking them into the consciousness of Villa supporters' history.

So what? All of the above comments could also be made about other periods of Villa's history, which are equally acknowledged around Villa Park – you can see a photo of Johnny Dixon lifting the 1957 FA Cup and buy that retro shirt too. The difference is the fact that 1994 and 1996 were the last times Villa won a major trophy, and because of the progression of time for a lot of supporters they represent a staging post of youth that is now at a point where it is being transferred to a new generation. The edge of the Holte End features a semi-permanent celebration of the players who lifted the 1982 European Cup, for ever an integral part of Villa history that I understand and cherish. But I wasn't there – the only two players I saw play were Nigel Spink and Gordon Cowans – and while that fact doesn't diminish the pinnacle of a collective sense of being a Villa fan, I will never be able to talk about it in the same way as 1994 and 1996. My son knows more about Mark Bosnich or Ugo Ehiogu than Tony Morley or Dennis Mortimer because I am able to share a personal experience with him. It's too much to say that the twin Coca-Cola Cup wins act as an albatross but Villa need to be able to have a new generational celebration. There have been fleeting opportunities, the aforementioned 2000 FA Cup Final being one, and a 2015 final in the same competition. The latter campaign's high point had really been the semi-final where Jack Grealish, Fabian Delph and Christian Benteke saw off Liverpool before being humiliated by Arsenal. In the League Cup there was the 2010 final, where Martin O'Neill's splendid Villa team lost out to poor refereeing and a cynically experienced Manchester United, before Dean Smith's newly promoted side lost out to the other side of Manchester in 2020. The play-off final was celebratory but was a means to an end – as Villa fan and broadcaster Dan Bardell has said, 'The play-off final was more a huge sigh of relief than a celebration like winning a trophy.'

The 1994 and 1996 Coca-Cola Cup wins do not just remain important because they were the 'last' but also because of when they were in a broader context. In a much-transformed landscape of English football, monetarily through Sky TV and internationally through global appeal and pull of players, the wins ensured Villa were maintained at the top table, securing European football to keep the club competitive on and off the pitch at a time when there was huge jostling for position. They also – at least superficially – pointed to a movement in the club towards modernity and looking forward whether that be kit suppliers and sponsors, or Serbian strikers and five at the back. The way that Villa's managers changed over this period is intuitive, a movement from manager to coach, brash to urbane and the management shift was in step with a new type of global player who needed managing and guiding. Above the managers, Doug Ellis had famously not been around for the league championship in 1981 and European Cup in 1982 so saw the League Cups as his opportunity to refresh the narrative around the club for a new generation – although as we have seen, he rather preferred the 1996 one in preference to giving Ron Atkinson too much credit for 1994. Even Ellis would not have predicted that, nearly three decades on, Villa would not have captured another major honour.

Recent interviews with the casts of 1994 and 1996 have thrown a light on perceptions around the Coca-Cola Cup wins and what it means for a club like Villa to have last won a major trophy nigh-on 30 years ago. Mark Bosnich, who played in both wins, was asked by The Athletic who was 'better' from a Villa standpoint, him or Emi Martínez. Bosnich was unapologetic, that while Martínez was a superb goalkeeper, until he won a trophy for Villa he would only ever be second best. In a similar vein, 1996 goalscorer Ian Taylor looks back now and describes the 'mixed emotions' of hindsight – that it is 'nice to be part of' the historical narrative, but it is simultaneously 'anti-climactic' given that Villa haven't won anything since. Sage words from those who lived it.

Looking back over the two campaigns is nostalgic but also fortifying in terms of evaluating a personal history within a context of a football club. Dearly departed heroes are remembered and iconic goals re-celebrated, but equally niche away draws are fondly recalled, and peripheral players evaluated. As Swedish writer Frederick Backman has said, 'Never trust people who don't have something in their lives that they love beyond all reason.' For this writer that love is Aston Villa, and it was melded in the crucible of 1993 to 1996.

Up the Villa.

Bibliography

Bishop, R. and Holt, F., *Aston Villa the Complete Record* (Sunderland: TwoCan, 2022)

Daley, T. and Goodyear, S., *The Daley Record* (Boston: Morgan Lawrence, 2023)

Driver-Fisher, J., *Greatest Games Aston Villa* (Durrington: Pitch Publishing, 2015)

Evans, M., *USA 94: The World Cup That Changed the Game* (Chichester: Pitch Publishing, 2022)

Joachim, J., *You Must be Joachim* (Boston: Morgan Lawrence, 2021)

Kaper, J., *Nii Lamptey – The Curse of Pele* (Chichester: Pitch Publishing, 2023)

Little, B. and White, P., *Brian Little – My Aston Villa* (Unknown, 2021)

Shaw, D., *Aston Villa Review 1993* (Warley: Sports Projects Ltd, 1993)

Shaw, D., *Aston Villa Review 1994* (Warley: Sports Projects Ltd, 1994)

Shaw, D., *Aston Villa Review 1995* (Warley: Sports Projects Ltd, 1995)

Shaw, D., *Aston Villa Review 1996* (Warley: Sports Projects Ltd, 1996)

Teale, S. and Carless, R., *Here, There & Everywhere* (Boston: Morgan Lawrence, 2023)

Viven, R., *Second City – Birmingham and the Forging of Modern Britain* (Dublin: Penguin, 2022)

Websites

avfc.co.uk
avfchistory.co.uk
bbc.co.uk
telegraph.co.uk
theguardian.com
thetimes.com

Newspapers and magazines

Birmingham Evening Mail
Birmingham Post
Irish Independent
Sports Argus
These Football Times

Podcasts and YouTube channels

Claret & Blue – An Aston Villa Podcast
My Old Man Said
Villa Boy
Under a Gaslit Lamp
Up The Villa Podcast

VHS

Squaddies
The Pain and the Glory – Aston Villa

Fanzines and programmes

Aston Villa News & Record
Heroes & Villains